THE PLEIADIAN TANTRIC WORKBOOK

Beloved Jim,

It has been a joy to share this time: to witness your humility, sincerity, and goodness. Always remember to be as good to you as you are to others!

Love,
Amorah
♡

THE
PLEIADIAN TANTRIC
WORKBOOK
Awakening Your Divine Ba

Volume Two of The Pleiadian Workbook Series

Amorah Quan Yin

BEAR & COMPANY
PUBLISHING
SANTA FE, NEW MEXICO

LIBRARY OF CONGRESS CATALOGING-IN-PUBLICATION DATA

Yin, Amorah Quan.
    The pleiadian tantric workbook : awakening your divine Ba /
Amorah Quan Yin.
Includes bibliographical references.
    ISBN 1-879181-45-2
    1. Spiritual life—Miscellanea. 2. Pleiades—Miscellanea.   3. Tantrism
—Miscellanea. 4. Mental healing—Miscellanea.   5. Sex—Miscellanea.
6. Yin, Amorah Quan.
BF 1999.Y55   1997
133.9'3—dc21   97-28684
                                                                    CIP

Bear & Company, Inc.
PO Box 2860
Santa Fe, NM 87504-2860

Cover design: © 1997 Lightbourne Images
Cover illustration: © 1997 Emery Bear
Text illustrations: © 1997 Bryna Waldman
Editing: Sonya Moore
Author photo: Marianne Carroll
Printed in the United States of America by BookCrafters
1 3 5 7 9 8 6 4 2

CONTENTS

DEDICATION

To Shahan, in gratitude for the abundance of inspiration you
have given me during your physical healing crisis.
You have made me a more faithful believer in the phoenix rising.

ACKNOWLEDGMENTS

First I wish to express thanks to my lovers of the past for all you have taught me about what relationships are, and are not, meant to be. You have helped me see the places in myself that have prevented fulfillment in relationships as well as those places that truly support and cocreate love and Oneness. Those shared moments of surrender and loving ecstasy are an ongoing source of inspiration. May you find the greatest love yet to come.

Emery Bear, you've done it again! The cover painting is great!

Bryna Waldman, thank you for making the illustrations fun when possible, technical when required, and always, delightful--just like you. You are more lovable every day!

Sonya Moore, thank you for your copyediting. Gerry Clow, your final, fine-toothed comb approach is not only deeply appreciated--it is a great relief as well. Besides, talking details with you is more fun than with anyone else I know.

Shahan Jon, you are a dear soul, wonderful friend, and great inspiration. Thank you for all your contributions, professionally and personally, including your initial editing.

Barbara Hand Clow, it is a joy to share the vision for Earth and her people with you, ". . . through different lens," as you would say. Thank you, and Gerry, for publishing this, my third, Bear book. It is an honor to be a part of the Bear book family.

John Schultz, thank you for handling the tapes up until now, and for answering all of the questions beyond that function. Your enthusiasm and givingness are healthy contagions. I love you, dear friend.

Some day I may not need to thank all of my friends and students for their endless patience with my busy schedule, infrequency of quality time together, and frequent unavailability. But, for now, this gratitude is more than appropriate. Absence of physical presence is not an absence of love and caring, though I am sure it feels like it at times.

To the humble people of Egypt with whom I have shared a little time at ancient ruins and temples, thank you. It was amazing to stand in Karnak, Luxor, or near the Sphinx and share channelings and teachings about the Ka, Ba, and Dolphin Tantra. There was more, but the highlights were these. Your humble questions about the difference in the Ka and Ba, and deeper, more hidden meaning of the symbols was quite moving. Your patience with my on-site needs for channeling and healing time, and sometimes bending the rules a bit was much appreciated. Emil, Ahmed, Sherine, Mohammed, Sayed, thank you.

Steve Chase, your Regression Facilitation skill and loving presence made the first three chapters possible. You hold impeccable space during out-of-body work. Blessings, gratitude, hugs, and kisses to you, dear one!

And to the Pleiadian Emissaries of Light, the Sirian Archangelic League of the Light, Andromedan Emissaries, Elohim, Ascended Masters of Light, you have helped make sense of what would otherwise be a meaningless struggle. And you are helping me learn to give up struggle and move through life with more faith, grace, and love for all people and all of Creation—regardless of their present condition or way of being. I deeply love and appreciate your continuous giving and loving. Keep reminding me to stop and receive. I am starting to get it!

Introduction

RESOLUTION
OF DUALITY

When I drew a *Mayan Oracle* card for this book, I received the same card as for one of my earlier books, *Pleiadian Perspectives.* That card is named "Resolution of Duality." It seems quite appropriate, as the main concerns in this material are ending the "male/female split," healing your soul with sexual energy, and connection with your Christ Self and God/Goddess/All That Is. This *Mayan Oracle* card impulses the reader to ". . . confront directly the illusion of separation and duality. . . . Duality is simply a perception. Polarities are thought to be opposites only because of the way we perceive them."

In this book you will be invited over and over to look at how your personal beliefs and attitudes toward members of the opposite sex— and toward your own sexuality—affect all your relationships (and even Earth herself). You will be reminded of the delicate and powerful relationship between sexuality and the health of your soul, or your *Ba.* Unless you can create a healthy and loving intimacy with your own body and its sexual and sensual nature, it is probably impossible to hope for enlightenment, Christ consciousness, or ascension in this lifetime.

As I stated in *The Pleiadian Workbook: Awakening Your Divine Ka,* the first book in this workbook series, the purpose behind the Pleiadian Lightwork system is to bring about the awakening of the 144,000, also known as "the Second Coming of Christ en masse." In order to bring about awakening in yourself, your Higher Self and Christ Self must become cellularly anchored into your body. This involves personal dedication to clearing your entire body, aura, and hologram of all mutations, repressions, and karma. Commitment to following a spiritual path of your choice is necessary in order to accomplish this goal.

Pleiadian Lightwork is one of the paths through which you can accomplish this goal. However, in order for any system to work, you must be truly committed to taking responsibility for becoming the best you can be, living impeccably, and following the healing and transformational guidelines of that system—in this case, The Pleiadian Workbook series. Pleiadian Lightwork is a mystery school system that I have been asked—by the Pleiadian Emissaries of Light, Sirian Archangelic League of the Light, and the Andromedan Emissaries of Light—to resurrect and contemporize. This mystery school system unfolds in a four-step plan. *The Pleiadian Workbook: Awakening Your Divine Ka* contains the preliminaries and step one. *The Pleiadian Tantric Workbook: Awakening Your Divine Ba* contains stages two and three of the Pleiadian plan for the awakening of the human race. (And the third book in the series, to be published in the near future, will cover step four.) The four-step plan is:

1. Ka clearing and activation

2. Ending the male/female split

3. Healing and awakening your Ba, or soul, with Dolphin Tantra

4. Clearing/activating your diamond-lightbody and merkabah

When this four-part plan was first revealed to me by the Pleiadian Emissaries of Light, they very lovingly explained why their plan must come about in this precise order. According to these Pleiadians, sacred protocol in Atlantis and ancient Egypt followed this same order. In fact, it was the abandonment of sacred protocol that helped bring about the fall of Atlantis. Sacred protocol for spiritual students, seekers, and initiates involves never giving the initiates anything that they have not been properly prepared to handle.

For example, in the ancient Egyptian temples, a prospective initiate must have already been living in harmlessness and integrity prior to being accepted into the mystery school. The priests and priestesses would speak with members of the person's family and community in order to learn whether or not the applicant was indeed known to be a "good person." Then the applicant would be evaluated, or read, energetically to determine whether he or she was sincere and genuinely ready to begin the mystery school practice. If the prospective initiate was deemed acceptable, he or she was first taught simple techniques for healthy boundaries and transcendence of ego identification. These teachings were completed *prior to* beginning the activations and clearings in the Ka Temples. Why? Because it can actually be dangerous to open your higher-dimensional connections if your identity is not aligned with spirit's truth, as opposed to ego's truth.

If an initiate has dark astral affiliations from early life or past lives and cannot secure his or her auric field safely from these influences, higher- and multi-dimensional work can exacerbate this problem. If the initiate is still identified with such karmic behaviors and attitudes as blame, shame, control, judgment, lust, greed, fear, and hatred, he or she will be much more susceptible to influence and possession by dark entities such as the Annunaki control lords and astral parasites. This does not imply that you must be totally free of faults before entering the initiatic path. It does mean that you need to be able to take responsibility for clearing and transforming these energies as they arise—as opposed to indulging in them and believing they are real.

In Pleiadian Lightwork, as in the ancient mystery schools, you must first learn to ground, recognize and clear limiting beliefs, thoughtforms, cords, and other blocked energies, and to meditate. As a student/initiate, once you have mastered self-help tools and begun to take back the power formerly given to your ego identification with horizontal reality, you are ready to begin the process of reanchoring your Ka. You will have begun the process of separating yourself from the lower astral planes and illusionary realities prior to opening to higher-dimensional energies. Therefore, in *The Pleiadian Workbook: Awakening Your Divine Ka*, volume one of this series, when you are asked to complete the two chapters on psychic self-care prior to beginning the Ka work, you are following ancient, sequential, spiritual learning and initiatic protocol.

Before beginning this new volume of The Pleiadian Workbook series, I highly recommend that you first complete *The Pleiadian*

Workbook itself. In addition to containing the self-care tools already mentioned, that workbook provides step-by-step processes for clearing, activating, and maintaining your Ka channels and Ka body through meditation, breathing, and Higher Self connection. Working with the Chambers of Light and subpersonalities will assist you in your ongoing process of clearing and divine alignment, preparing you for your next step: healing the male/female split.

This step is crucial prior to moving on to step three of the four-step plan because your relationship to your soul, or Ba, is dependent upon healthy sexual activity and boundaries—which are dependent upon having healthy relationships with members of the opposite sex. The key ploy of the dark overlords for maintaining control over the human race involves maintaining distrust, control, and lust-based sexuality between the sexes. The Annunaki and Lucifer put their heads together long ago and realized that the male/female split was the greatest source of separation and ego identity on Earth. It seems obvious that relinquishing this level of ego identity and separation is certainly vital prior to sexual and Ba-level healing and activation.

When your Ba is free, and beyond identification with separation and distrust, your sexual energy can be used to activate your soul to spin very fast and radiate its light outward like holographic ripples on water. These light ripples, or waves, literally spin your cells, fill them with light, and realign, or maintain alignment with, the orbits of the stars, planets, and entire cosmos. The Incan tradition uses the same word for Christ as for sacred sexual energy. They recognize that the flow of sexual energy is inseparable from enlightenment and ascension.

Once your male/female issues are cleared and you are in a state of *right relationship,* your Ba has been healed and activated, you are moving your energy tantrically and keeping your body and chakras clear, then you are ready for merkabic clearing and activation. *The Pleiadians are adamant that this step should never be taken prematurely because of the danger of exacerbation of astral connections and fear- and illusion-based emotions and thoughtforms.* I have personally witnessed numerous people becoming paranoid, emotionally imbalanced, and very entangled with the astral realms due to following merkabic meditation practices prematurely. This is why the ascension and merkabic teachings were the last level of initiation as the seeker made his or her way through the ancient temples along the Nile. It was a simple matter of natural sequential flow, and sacred protocol. In fact it would have been considered extremely arrogant in the ancient days to presume to move to higher levels of spiritual teaching prior to mastering the lower levels preceding them.

Therefore, you will find Pleiadian Lightwork to be a slower spiritual path, in some ways, than others. I believe this is very well-advised, and the eventual outcome, more predictable and timely. If you are truly more identified with impeccability than with the idea of fast accomplishment, then this is one of the existing paths with which you may feel at home. Merkabic teachings will be given (assuming all goes as planned) in volume three of The Pleiadian Workbook series.

Compared to ancient days of highly advanced spiritual societies, this path is, indeed, quite accelerated. This is because of the unique times we, and all of Earth, are experiencing. As discussed in the first workbook, we are nearing the end of a long period of darkness and forgetting, and entering the Age of Enlightenment.

The processes, stories, and teachings in this second workbook are intended to assist you in remembering who you are; clearing and healing your Ba and relationships; and moving you a few steps closer to your own enlightenment, en-Christment, and eventual ascension. For it is you and I who must usher in the Age of Enlightenment with our own higher consciousness and spiritual attainment. It is the human race who must evolve now into total impeccability and divine alignment with God/Goddess/All That Is. What a relief it is to know that this time has come, and that our options for spiritual laziness and self-indulgent behaviors have come to an end—unless we enjoy suffering. Why have these options become obsolete? Because the frequencies on Earth are continually being raised through deeper and deeper entry into the Photon Band.

As the photonic particulates interact, and attempt to blend, with your cells, they impulse you to let go. They impulse your cells to release all mutating forms and energies, and to realign with the orbital movement patterns of the stars, planets, and cosmos. The photons strive to bring you back into self-affinity cellularly, emotionally, mentally, and spiritually. If you resist, you begin to die a little at a time. Resistance becomes disease more rapidly than before. Your karmic returns are happening faster and faster. In other words, to straddle the fence no longer gives you a breather: it brings pain. And yet, pain is still a great motivator if there is no other.

The good news is that diseases and chronic emotional problems can be healed faster than ever by those who are willing to learn, let go, and be impeccable. I have seen amazingly fast healings of even the most virulent cancer in friends who decided to really go for it. As always it is important not to judge others—or yourself—for any conditions or situations they, or you, have taken on at this time. All of us have our own energies we have chosen to be challenged by, to transmute, or with which to burn out old karma. So when in doubt, embrace compassion and respect for everyone, regardless of his or her outer circumstances.

As the photons impulse you toward wholeness, letting go, and divine alignment, may the offerings contained in these pages add gracious assistance to you in your ongoing path of re-becoming all that you truly are: divine and One with All That Is.

Special Note To The Reader

This book is written as volume two of The Pleiadian Workbook series. According to spiritual protocol, it is essential that you complete the first volume of this series, *The Pleiadian Workbook: Awakening Your Divine Ka*, prior to beginning the work in Part II of this sequel. As a spiritual teacher, it is my responsibility to make you aware that the effects of the exercises in this book will be less if you do not follow this instruction. It is important in any mystery school system, such as Pleiadian Lightwork, that you do not receive trainings and activations until you have received the spiritual experiences and self-help tools that you will need in order to safely and effectively integrate the new material. When you have completed *The Pleiadian Workbook: Awakening Your Divine Ka*, you will be properly prepared for the material contained in this book. To do otherwise is to breach mystery school protocol, and I cannot be responsible for the erratic or inappropriate results you may experience.

Amorah Quan Yin

THE
PLEIADIAN TANTRIC
WORKBOOK

Part 1

CREATION, SEXUAL ENERGY, AND YOUR SOUL

Chapter 1

THE CREATION

While still in the process of writing and editing volume one of The Pleiadian Workbook series, I was already being guided on the outline for the present book. The initiations, teachings, and healings were happening in my own life in very powerful ways. I had previously experienced some of the techniques presented in Part II of this book, and yet others were new to me. During this time, material for volume three (about sacred geometry, the merkabah, and the Sirian connection) also began to interweave with the material in this book. Talk about doing three things at once—it was incredible! My impatient Sagittarian self wanted to hurry through her current project to get to the one that was three or four steps down the line. Those Pleiadians! They certainly like to keep me on my toes.

The hypnosis sessions in this and the following two chapters contain some of the most important material that I have been gifted to bring through. Prior to the hypnosis sessions I was told that it was time for me to remember fully the story of who I was before I came to the Milky Way. I also needed to remember my spirit's first experience of individuation. At that time, I presumed that An-Ra, the Pleiadian archangel who was guiding and instructing me at the time, meant the creation of my soul. Therefore, I was quite surprised to find myself literally going back to the Creation.

In the first hypnosis session, with this quest in mind, I was taken to a binary solar ring called Ninevah, in the Andromeda galaxy. There, I lucidly experienced being a very large Light Being who, with a male deity as partner, held within her consciousness that entire solar ring. That solar ring is comprised of six planets, five of which orbit between the two suns in a figure 8, or infinity symbol, pattern. The sixth orbits a single sun as Earth does in this solar ring. I was a "Supreme Being" as was my partner. I was the Goddess Erotica. When I (she) first told me her name I must confess my human self squirmed and thought, "Oh my God, I'm in trouble!" However, after I completed the hypnosis session, that reaction changed. My definition of "erotica" expanded to become even more than what I had always thought of as sacred sex. I was shown that love is the key ingredient in all sexual experience at that level of consciousness; what I experienced was such a powerfully all-encompassing love that I was overwhelmed. During that session I was also given audience with the Elohim, the Creator Gods and Goddesses. As the Elohim eloquently formed the words that I channeled, I was expanded and deeply altered.

After completing the hypnosis work necessary for this book, I rearranged the sessions sequentially, in chronological order— although those words are slightly misleading. The experiences were outside of the time and space continuum and yet contain time and space within them as aspects of total reality. The Pleiadians have asked me to include these sessions as close to their original form as possible, while still remaining intelligible to readers. This will also assist you in understanding the altered state I was in at the times of the sessions.

These materials are intended to impulse you to remember your own creation story, your individual myth. An-Ra says that when one person remembers and shares his or her experience of remembering, it impulses others to remember their own stories. Some of the details of your creation may vary greatly; some may be very similar, or even identical to my own. Just as Ra said about the Ka materials, "It's time now," An-Ra says of this work, "It is time now to remember everything."

> As the transcript begins, I have already been taken into a deep hypnotic state and experienced a personal clearing in order to reach the deep levels necessary. The clearing part of the transcript is given on pages 94 through 98 in chapter 5. The collective consciousness of the Elohim spoke as a single voice to and through me. The transcript follows:

When we came together as the Elohim, we were what you think of as the archetypes of God/Goddess/All That Is, All That Ever Has Been, and All That Ever Shall Be. Before Creation there was only Oneness. Within Oneness came a divine thought, as Oneness awakened to the realization, "I am." It was the realization that Oneness existed. From ecstasy came a voice, "I am that I am." And from that "I am that I am" came awareness of self as One, and with awareness of self as One came desire for experience through reflection, through another. And there was no other, there was only One and One was All That Is; and that One chose to mirror itself back to itself in order to objectify itself to itself. And that objectification became deity. And deity became portions. And the reflection saw love in the other and became One again in union. The experience of reunion was so great that Oneness again mirrored itself in order to reunite, and the birth of sacred union came through desire for the experience of reuniting the reflected self to the reflector. When this process had occurred over what you would call billions or trillions of centuries, there was a desire within Oneness to know objectification from the mirrored part and the self at the same moment of existence. The Elohim Council was born from that divine spark of inspired objectification. It was what you might call the birth of the first children.

Oneness created a mirror image of itself which it fell in love with, as it always did. Because it was mirrored, it was a mutual love experience of union. While in that individuated state, there was a decision to mirror again, which had not been done prior to that point in conscious existence. When the mirrored self and the reflector mirrored at the same exact moment in time—in your words—two more beings were created, each mirroring the individuated self. There was a wave of amazement as Oneness in its mirrored form suddenly found three other aspects reflecting the same thing. When the original two parts of Oneness reunited, the newest reflected pair united at the same time with each other, not with the original pair. These two simultaneous unions each impulsed the other's union, and created another wave of amazement. They were immediately reflected again, creating yet another. And with each creation, the mirroring created so much awe, wonder, ecstatic inspiration, discovery, and joyful pleasure that the original Oneness wondered what would happen if each of those who had been mirrored by itself had the power to mirror—since each was a part of all Creation and all of Creation is part of the same Oneness. Each of these was told to mirror outside itself. Obedient children, as we were, we became the Elohim. It began with two, then four; and when the four impulsed outside themselves, there were eight. When the eight joined with the original two—which you may call the Holy Mother and Holy Father—they experienced themselves as Oneness again. Yet from that Oneness, great waves of love spread, and those waves created individuation again. Individuation inspired admiration and adoration for Creation, which resulted in the desire for union. It was a circular, or spiral, experience, you might say. You, Amorah, were part of that beginning in the twelfth round of creation, and became an Elohim Goddess, a mirror, a reflector. Further divisions began from there.

What you call the Divine Plan is not as complete as you have thought it to be. The Divine Plan was simply that each of the twelve individuations who are the original Council of the Elohim could explore creation and the possibilities of existence. Each pair of reflector and reflected was given sovereignty and autonomy to create and to maintain its own creations. We, the Elohim, are twelve large androgynous beings, each comprised of the reflector and the reflected—or female and male, in your terms—when in our individuations before reuniting. When reunited, each pair becomes one androgynous being again. In other words, the council of twelve, within itself, was and is a counsel of twenty-four, half male and half female, or twelve Creator Gods and twelve Creator Goddesses. Within the twelve united forms, twelve galactic centers were birthed through which the divine couples could radiate and emanate the love from their unions, and creation continued on the next level. Each pair that comprised an androgynous One created, maintained, and contained what you call a galaxy within its consciousness. When the couple was together it was like water and flow, or electricity and light. The goddess was the mirror and the male god was that which was reflected in the mirror, and while in union as a single being of androgynous Light, they were given the power to create whatever they desired to create, whatever they might imagine.

Each of the twelve Elohim couples possessed unique qualities of its own. These qualities were due to the particular frequencies held by the Holy Mother and Holy Father at the time of each conception. Just as your soul contains the energy of the union of the mother and father who physically birthed you, so does it contain the frequencies of your higher-dimensional parents who originated your soul. All of existence, even the Elohim, were created in much the same way. What we wish for you to understand is that the male/female split and the original Creation are two parts of the same thing. When female and male, the mirror and the reflected, are not in harmony, there is no peace. Understanding how Creation began with complete union between equals inspired to love one another, inspired by one another, is the way back to God/Goddess/All That Is, or Oneness—and to healing the male/female split.

The only plan, beyond the Elohim being empowered for their own creations, was that at some point in time and space and beyond it, they would all come back together in Oneness again and blend and share one another's experiences. This is what creates both the urge for enlightenment and for sacred marriage, union. It is why human sexual energy is so strong. It is not just the desire to create children that creates sexual urge, it is the urge toward Oneness.

We end our communications with you with much for you to absorb, distill, and dissolve into yourself. And we wish to say now that responsibility born of anything but love is truly irresponsible. *Responsibility born of anything other than love is irresponsible.* For only through love can any act bring a positive end result. So-la-re-en-lo.

The Goddess Erotica speaks as the session continues. My consciousness was so completely blended with the consciousness of this "bigger self" that I could scarcely speak. My words were very slow and stilted. It was quite difficult to maintain enough contact with my body to allow my mouth to utter the words. When you read phrases about Creation, and singing existence, it is the Goddess Erotica speaking, she of whom I am only the third-dimensional self. She is my eleventh-dimensional self, which contains all aspects of myself from the tenth dimension and down.

"Sleep perchance to dream, dream perchance to remember, remember perchance to know, know perchance to be, be perchance to be. Simply be perchance to be. I am always here, you don't have to be in an altered state to know me now. We will go through a few weeks of experience together during your next stage of integration and remembrance, and then you will write. For now, return to this world of time and space knowing that you are limited by nothing, other than your own choices. We are love."

In a separate hypnosis session, which I also recorded, I was able to experience my own consciousness during the Creation. What follows are the early stages of that session so that you will be able to sense the fullness of the experience. This was no doubt the most expansive, and deepest, hypnotic state I have ever known. I had experienced deep trance states before, but this was in a category all its own. The energies did not exactly translate through my physical body. It was more like I was just pure consciousness outside of time and space experiencing Creation all over again and remembering it in such a way that I could bring the energies and memories back to my body when I returned. When I did come back to my body, it took several hours to get all of me back in. I felt so expanded that trying to fit back into my body—even though I am a large-bodied woman—seemed like attempting to put a camel through the eye of a needle. My cells spun so fast, as my body received the newly awakened me with all of the frequencies of my experiences, that it was like being inside a psychedelic light show complete with bizarre, and mostly wonderful, sensations. The complete integration took weeks. The Pleiadians worked with me faithfully and continually, guiding me each step of the way. Sometimes I was told to do a next level of cellular clearing on myself, or soul healing through the Interdimensional Chamber of Light, or other techniques given in Part II of this book. Mainly, the integration was facilitated by my own step-by-step introduction to Dolphin Tantra. In general, the integrations from the hypnosis work in these next three chapters have been extremely gracious and joyful—ecstatically so at times.

*When this part of the session began I was still experiencing
myself as Amorah, and individuated from the Goddess Erotica.*

My goddess-self from Andromeda, the Goddess Erotica, is holding my right hand and there is an emissarial group of Andromedans,
Pleiadians, and three Sirians who are all here together, like a council.
They are actually members of the Higher Council but they are pre-
senting themselves to me in a way that they have never done before.
All twelve members are here, and they want to say something. They
say that they are here to present me with an opportunity to go back to
the source of All That Is, and to return to this galaxy and to Earth with
more of myself than I go there with at this time. To do so, they send
an emissary along from the Higher Council who is from Andromeda.
They are letting me know that this is a high honor, that they rarely
guide or accompany individuals on such journeys; generally, other
beings are appointed as guides—beings who work with the Higher
Council. The reason they are here with me is because of the nature
of my service on Earth, my Higher Self's request, and the fact that it
was long ago agreed that when this time came an emissary from the
Higher Council would accompany me. This would insure that the
vibrations were clear since the information was intended to be shared
with readers and students. The Higher Council also agreed to help me
be sure that my body was ready. That is why, when I knew I needed
to do a cleanse, I intuitively went to them to ask them about the
cleanse even though I had never bothered them with such mundane
details before. [*Note: The Higher Council had guided me, just a week and a
half before, to begin an all-organic raw foods cleanse, which I now know was
to prepare me for this session and its integration. They were preparing my
body for the vibrations that were going to be incoming today.*]

One of the other members of the Higher Council speaks: "The
Christ teachings are most imminent at this time, as you well know;
but how imminent they are you are about to find out more clearly
than you have ever known before. Therefore, we leave you now with
our Andromedan member, and with your twin star, the Goddess as
you call her."

They are telling me to call her my twin star, and she will help me understand more about our relationship to one another at this time. They also affirm my assumption that she has a strong connection to Mother Mary. The Andromedan speaks: "It is more like an aspect of Mother Mary's galactic consciousness, rather than her Ascended Master consciousness with which you are more consciously familiar. So you are in quite good company today, Amorah."

Steve, the regressionist, asks, "Is there a name for the Andromedan member of the Higher Council?"

[I continue.] I cannot see that member as individuated from the Council yet. It feels like a male presence at my left side. It is interesting that the males are at my left and the females are at my right. It is a reversal from the normal female left side and male right side, but it creates balance, they say. The council member who will accompany me says that he is like the god of eroticism and sacred sexual functions of all beings, the God Eros. He is the one who dispenses and holds those frequencies for this solar ring, and for the Milky Way, at this time. Therefore, he is a natural companion to go along with me on this journey, as is my twin star. Now I hear the words, "The Goddess Erotica is who you will become when you are finished, even though she is who you were before you began. She is the beginning and the end. Before her you are nothing."

I am hearing one female voice now, but it is a voice that is made up of many voices. She says, "We are you. We are the beginning, the end, and the middle, and the voice of all times wrapped up in One. We go back to the seeming origin simply through focusing on that intent. It is like choosing the facet of a prism through which we wish to be refracted. And as we are refracted, we experience a particular color and shape. We choose that facet now: the facet of sound, the sound of one voice, the sound of one voice that contains the voices of All That Is in Oneness. Sweet it is, the One and the many. It is singular and plural simultaneously. And it is All That Is: that sweet, resonant sound."

My voice became very slow and effortful at this time as my consciousness, as Amorah, became one with the original consciousness at Creation. So in a sense it is not me speaking, except that we all originate from the same Oneness of God/Goddess/All That Is.

Therefore when you read this next section, read it not as Amorah speaking, but as the voice of Oneness.

It is as if I am asleep, and that my only dream is of being the sound, and yet hearing it at the same time. My first awareness is of color, as if a light wheel, with all of the colors in existence, is spinning in both directions at the same time. It is One Light and the sound moves it; and the sound stirs the Light, and the stirring moves energy so that Light, energy, and sound are synchronistic and inseparable; and I, the dreamer, know them as One, and as the same thing. It is as if I am in a deep dream, and everything is color and sound and energy, but nondistinguishable. And then it is as if a breath is taken and in that breath is the thought, "I Am." A great joy and a great emotion—a joyous emotion of gratitude—well into my consciousness as the realization that "I Am" identifies myself within the sound, color, movement, and energy. It is the most glorious sound of all. It is the sound of the self awakening to the self. It always has been. It is even now. For when One is in the deep sleep, One is the object of the sound, energy, color, and motion. One does not know that One is asleep, because One does not know that One is. It is as if I, as One, am just a hum in existence.

Then conscious awareness of self becomes the first thought of divine mind: I Am, I exist. It is an "ah-ha." And the One I Am has identity for the first time and the identity is "I Am." And then I Am listens consciously and experiences itself as the listener. As the I Am listens to the beautiful sound, the color begins to spin and move and there is an energy created by this synergy; and there is a trail of awareness that follows from sound to color to energy. The movement contains it all. It is as if I Am meditates on a sound and its *[my]* total focus is on the sound until I Am's third eye is aroused by the sound; and I begin to see the beautiful colors. I Am's consciousness shifts from focusing on the sound to the colors that I Am sees. Then the focus begins to shift from the colors I Am sees to the movement patterns of the colors, and then settles into just the feeling of the energy created by all three. I, Amorah, am experiencing the witness, the I Am. It is not so much a creation as it is a flow. I Am wants to know at some point how to merge with the color, the sound, the energy, and the movement again, but with assurance that she will reawaken. The desire to let go of consciousness and sleep, to simply drift and be carried, is equal with the desire to reawaken and be the chosen One of experience. In order to do this a certain duality has to be created so that a part of the self is watching at all times, leaving the other part free to simply merge into the One again. The watcher will reawaken that sleeping One at the appropriate moment. The reawakening I Am, as the witness, blends its consciousness with the consciousness of the sleeping One and sings a different note. It is as if all of existence is one note that is a combination of all sounds. Then the individuation of the self comes in and sings its individual note and that individual note is like the alarm clock through which the witness I Am awakens the sleeping half. The awakening one, experiencing it all objectively again, moves into the consciousness of the witness self and is separate from the sound, color, energy, and movement. It is a joyous flow.

The first form was the star. The star matrix was used to focalize and individuate consciousness in order to facilitate the flow in and out of surrender into the deep sleep and reawakening into the witness self. In the deep sleep there is a total surrender, and in the reawakening there is a total presence. One might say that *presence*—conscious presence of the self—and *total surrender* are the two components of the dual nature of existence—as opposed to just *beingness*. One component chooses the self, the other loses the self. So it is the nature of One to surrender and One to have presence and hold space. Both are parts of the wholeness of the true self: the union of the be-er and the doer, of the mind and the surrendered experience of dreaming. [*I feel a pressure in my chest that is a little distracting. . . . I continue.*]

As the sleeping self awakens, there awaits its other half who is keeper of the space, the presence. And the One who is reawakening says, "I heard your voice, but if we have this voice, then what is the source of the other voices? What are their origins? Because we can close our eyes and experience, there is something beyond ourselves. There is a great mystery, a gap in consciousness. Our ah-ha, our awareness that we exist, leaves endless unanswered questions. For as I go to sleep in the sound, movement, and colors, and when I awaken the sound, movement, and colors continue, then what am I? And what makes the sound and the colors? What moves them? I am a part of a greater I Am when I sleep. And when I awaken I appear to be a solitary thought, a solitary presence that maintains itself as individuation through holding some focus; for without focus I become part of the sound and the color again, and I Am simply exists within it. But what else exists?"

I Am eagerly goes back to the dream, but this time I Am enters the dream with an intent and dreams that there are millions or billions of voices all singing the same sound. And as I Am dreams this, there are many selves that awaken at the same time, so that when I Am awakens, several others awaken because I have gone into the dream wanting to know who they are. They have the awareness of themselves as something beyond the whole and as part of the whole at the same time. It is like being in the middle of many tittering voices all saying, "I Am, I exist, I awaken, finally I awaken, finally I awaken." We are like children discovering their own fingers and toes; we are discovering our own complex existence. The first realization of I Am, as the experiencer of the sound, color, movement, and energy, triggered a chain reaction throughout all of the possibilities of Oneness; and then all of the components of Oneness dreamed together. We all had outside presences holding space while we entered the dream together to discover even more. When we emerged again, we all emerged with the words, "It is endless; the possibilities are endless." That realization was exhilarating and overwhelming at the same time. The awareness of existence and consciousness containing endless possibilities was awesome. As we were awake, in our presences, the realization of the endlessness created a unique synergy; and all of us who were awake at that time were the original 144,000.

The first awakening was of One. One became two: the surrendered dreamer and the awake witness-presence. The third phase of awakening was of the 144,000 within One. This took place at the time of the second reawakening when the dreamer brought back the many voices in One. The dreamer blended with the witness, and I Am became One again; then I Am recognized 144,000 aspects, or voices, of self within itself. A great consciousness was born when the 144,000 awakened with the words, "It is endless. The possibilities are endless." Somehow this recognition created a deep and awesome respect for existence and its potentials. It created a sense of smallness and a sense of being part of something that was endless all at the same moment. And within that, the Christ consciousness was born as the 144,000 original consciousnesses, not souls, merged in a spontaneous, uncontrived union. The 144,000 parts became a solitary consciousness, which became the consciousness of what you would think of as God, or Oneness. It was as if, in saying that existence was endless, a sudden blending was created of all of the 144,000 aspects of Oneness who spontaneously came together in a tantric fusion. Within that tantric fusion was reborn the consciousness of the greater self, the One. And yet One had become more because of its experience of its own multiplicity.

All greater selves contain 144,000 essential parts. What humans think of as lifetimes, from the I Am perspective are projections of one part, or two parts together, or twelve parts together, or ten parts together, or any number, going through an individuated third-dimensional experience. In other dimensions as well, there are times when the consciousnesses separate into groups so that one being, who contains 144,000 parts, can have 144,000 simultaneous multidimensional experiences. When they are brought together, they create a synergistic wholeness. It is hard to explain in a way that human consciousness can even begin to grasp the understanding.

The first being to have the realization of its own existence was male and female within One consciousness. It was androgynous and contained both sexes, so to speak. This was and is the I Am presence. This has also been called God, Oneness, the One, Great Spirit, Brahma, and many other names. Many expansions then took place at that level. For instance, at times only one member of the 144,000 aspects of I Am would enter the sleep and the others would watch. At times only one aspect would remain awake while the 143,999 would sleep. The many in One saw that the one who was sleeping, or the ones who were sleeping, could feed information to those who were witnessing. But the one who was witnessing, or the ones who were witnessing, could not feed information to those who were sleeping. Hence, a duality was created.

Something similar to a solar ring was created through which those who were to remain awake could predetermine messages to be sent to those who slept. Those who were sleeping and were in total surrender were continually floating in sound, movement, and color, yet were not even consciously aware that they were floating and potentially experiencing these things. All that existed were the sound, color, energy, and movement, devoid of the consciousness of the sleepers. The ones who remained awake began to send messages in the form of sound; they could change the colors with sound. So, for instance, if the one who is dreaming is seeing a spectrum of pinks followed by purples, the ones who are awake could send in a color via a sound that could send red or green or blue, and change the experience of the dreamer. When this happened, and several members of those who were present simultaneously sent messages to one who was dreaming, a new dimension was added that included form—primary forms such as spirals, pyramids, cones, and other simple geometric shapes. So you might say that matrices were the next component in Creation and that these matrices were created from several aspects of the One I Am—who contained 144,000 aspects—impulsing those who were dreaming simultaneously. You see Creation in its original stages was discovery. Discovery of the self and of the capacity of the self is the stage we are speaking of now. The discovery of the self, the discovery of the multifaceted nature of the self, the Oneness and the many, the One becoming the greater, larger being—all of these were discovery states. The state that came next was the creation state, which came through exploration, and through curiosity, as the desire to find out how much impulse and how much controlled impact One could have on the sleeping selves.

There came a moment when all 144,000 parts remained both in their individuated presences and with half of themselves sent into sleep at the same time, during which a great split happened. The conglomerate sleeper—the 144,000 in One—dreamed of another being who contained 144,000 parts, watching. When the dreamer awakened, it was face-to-face with the being it had dreamed. You can imagine the excitement that went through consciousness at that time to see another 144,000 conglomerated into One, face-to-face. And these were the first two Elohim, or what we call the Holy Mother and Holy Father. Immediately upon seeing one another, the two felt what in human consciousness would be tears of love and joy. In that moment of deep feeling the two blended into Oneness again. When the Holy Mother and the Holy Father—each comprised of 144,000 parts—blended, incredible Light and sound and color and fireworks were set off. It was the first merging of greater consciousnesses. This original union included all parts of Oneness. From that merging of these two came the origins of planets and stars. From the excitement of their union—of God/Goddess being individuated and reunited in the celebration of individuation and union—came the first existence on a third-dimensional level. This was the first sexual union, as you might call it; and through this union existence was conceived and birthed. Holy Father God and Holy Mother Goddess had come from the same sleep state of Oneness. Now they [we] were experiencing an awakening dream of created stars, moons, and planets. All of these possibilities had come from their union, which meant that within that union between the two of them existed all of the potentials of existence—within them and outside of them at the same time. For in their conscious awakened state, the universes were contained within them, yet they could also look outside themselves and see the universe around them at the same time.

Gender was born during this first union of the two greater beings. There was a natural blending and merging when first they saw one another and the love within them swelled; and within the swelling of this love and joy that the other existed, the union was spontaneous and uncontrived. From that union of two great beings of multiplicity came the awareness of maleness and femaleness. The original being of 144,000 aspects in Oneness who divided itself into two I Am's, one sleeping and one remaining awake, became two beings each containing 144,000 aspects. And the half who had watched while the other half slept came to respond to existence as a male god, and the 144,000 conglomerate being who slept and received impulses from the awake one came to respond to existence as a female goddess. What you must realize is that the first being of 144,000 parts contained both parts within itself because it was an androgynous being. It was only through the dreaming that Oneness divided itself, and the second self was created outside of Oneness, and it was truly the manifestation of the polarities of the original androgynous self. To say that either the male or female came first is a stretch of the imagination. It was a simultaneous experience; their original individuation and remerging were not within time and space reality. They were simply in a flow. The first complex being contained both male and female and actually dreamed its own inner gendered aspects into being and then blended with them again through union. What the awake self actually looked at when it looked at its own female waking counterpart was the formerly unperceived aspect with which he had formerly been inside of Oneness. The female self had given birth to herself outside of the Oneness and yet within Oneness simultaneously. The male and female parts had both been part of the original I Am of 144,000 in One; now they were divided into two whole selves each containing 144,000 aspects.

I, Amorah, came into consciousness of myself at that point as part of the Holy Mother Goddess. I was unaware of the individuation I think of as myself now, until this second multiple being was created. Yet I was aware of myself within that One I Am as a small part. *[They want me to go back now to speaking of Amorah as "you," because in my present state of consciousness it is difficult to speak of myself as Amorah. It is more like I speak to her because she is only a projection of this original self who was only one of the aspects of Holy Mother.]*

I am the Goddess: the Goddess I Am. When God, the male part, looked upon me the first time, he saw his own beauty reflected back to him, for that is what I am. And as the joy and love welled up inside of the male for the female, the surrender, the glory, the beauty, and the truth of Oneness revealed itself. Our spontaneous joining, and the innocence and beauty of that joining, created the innocence and beauty of the stars and of the many worlds as humans know them. There was a natural rhythm and flow to the union in which we came together; and during the coming together we could experience both the presence and the dream simultaneously. God was the presence and Goddess was the dreamer. That was the greatest joy we had known. It was as if in our union, in that first mating of the male and

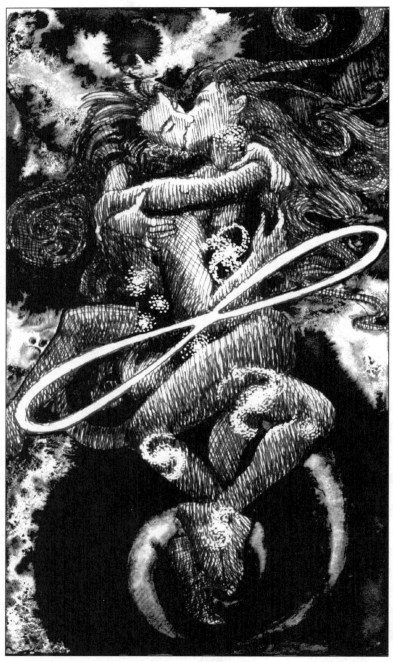

1. The union of Father God and Mother Goddess as they conceive Creation

female, we knew lucid dreaming as you might call it today. For though we were merged and could not tell where one began and the other ended, we were also conscious of what we were experiencing. As that union created an immensity of beauty, sound, color, movement, and finally stillness, we experienced a place of total surrender and yet were lucidly present in the surrender. That was the first experience of what you call lucid dreaming; we call it being lucidly awake. This great experience came through tantric sexual union, as those on Earth might think of it today. It is the source of all awakening. Union and surrender and autonomous presence while blended with All That Is are all that exist. For we are One; there has never been anything else.

When we began to emerge from the blended state into our individuated selves once more, there was a deep sense of the unknown. Creation had begun by accident, so to speak. The awesome power of union, of God and Goddess, was realized in that moment and we knew that we would never be totally asleep again. The infinity symbol (see illustration 1 on page 20) is very pertinent here, for that symbol represents the flow of everything at this stage of creation. On one end of the infinity symbol are the individuations flowing into dreamtime, coming around, awakening again, seeing the other selves, merging with those other selves in sacred union, in creation, and flowing back to the center point and into the dreamtime again. Even the dreamtime, although it seemed to be the void, always contained that luminous presence of the divine self. Losing oneself in existence was simply the way of surrender. And sleeping and dreaming were used to create the awakening awareness of potentials and realities and self. A dream contains it all.

At times Holy Father God and Holy Mother Goddess would travel through and experience individuated parts of the universe, perhaps blending with a single galaxy or with two galaxies. Then, while blended with the galaxies of our own creation, we would blend with one another and great explosions would happen—explosions of light and color and ecstatic cosmic orgasms. From the blending of two galaxies and God and Goddess simultaneously, other creations came forth: creations of the angels and fairies. As we shared the thought

2. Quan Yin containing Andromeda and the Milky Way within herself

about who would take care of these creations, who would explore them for us, we would look at one another again and go into union. We could not do it all ourselves. And with that thought, our union would create those who would explore. It was during this type of union that the Elohim were born. At first there was a male and female for each galaxy and at that time there were twelve galaxies. Each couple, because they were born of the original Holy Father God and Holy Mother Goddess, had the capacity to blend together, and through their blending to rejoin with Holy Father and Holy Mother. This is how the Holy Father God and Holy Mother Goddess began to experience existence: through the creation of other conscious selves.

Worlds were created. And within the worlds there were creations of conscious beings who were conceived and born from God and Goddess in union. We dreamed during our union of beings who could be conscious, perhaps even a being who could experience the consciousness of a single planet, so that we could know what that was like for ourselves. Then during our waking state, that is what we would give birth to. Earth, for example, was a product of a dream of God and Goddess saying, "We need a consciousness to experience this so that we can remerge with that consciousness and know what it is like to be this particular planet." And from that thought, as we made love, Gaia was born. Gaia needed a counterpart that could leave the physical creation and still have a part left in the creation, conscious of itself at the same time. Therefore a Higher Self, so to speak, of Gaia, was created in our next union. You might think of this Higher Self of Gaia as the Goddess Gaia. Gaia is an aspect of the consciousness of Quan Yin also.

There was a time when Andromeda and the Milky Way were one galaxy. Andromeda was the male half, the Milky Way the female half. As Creation began with one dreaming the other, it has been so throughout Creation. One is born and One dreams its own other half. In other words, when the Milky Way and the Andromeda galaxies were still one galaxy, it contained its own male and female components. When it dreamed itself into two galaxies, Andromeda became the male galaxy and the Milky Way became the female galaxy. The being you think of as Quan Yin is the goddess who birthed both of them. She was a great female being who contained both of these galaxies within herself; these two galaxies were and are the male and female components of the being that you know as Quan Yin. (See illustration 2 on page 22.) In the complexity of existence there was another galaxy that was held in the consciousness of Quan Yin's male god divine counterpart. This male galaxy also divided into a pair of galaxies, male and female, that are the divine counterparts of the Milky Way and Andromeda. You do not have a name for that great God at this time; but the two galaxies he holds are mirrored reflections of the Milky Way and Andromeda. The male god who holds these two galaxies is the divine male twin of the Goddess Quan Yin. He, like Quan Yin, is experiencing himself through his own aspects while moving back toward wholeness again. (When Andromeda and the Milky Way are remerged into Oneness, and the two galaxies that are its male counterpart are remerged, there will then be two larger galaxies, instead of four, that are male and female. In going back to Oneness, those two galaxies will eventually blend into Oneness again, at which time Quan Yin will be an inner female half of an even greater being once more.)

Existence is moving in the direction of reunion and Oneness at this time. The division into galaxies has gone as far as it will ever go. There may still be creations of individual souls that are needed in order to experience third-dimensional life and structural changes within existing galaxies, but we have come halfway on the greater journey. The turning point in existence is that we have completed the first half of the journey, which is the individuation and exploration of individuation, and we are on the return half of the journey at this time. During this half of the journey the remerging of all divine counterparts takes place. This will take billions of years which, for you on Earth, seems endless. Yet within the broader story of creation and union, it is simply like a wave in the ocean that starts many miles from shore and finally ends as it hits the sand. That is what this process is like for us. The individual parts must find their counterparts now. Just as you, Amorah, are merging all of your third-dimensional male and female incarnations and your own twin flames into one body in this lifetime, in the bigger picture you have a male counterpart who is doing the same. It is not until you reach the tenth-dimensional level of consciousness that your consciousness and his consciousness are merged into One. Therefore, you do not share what, in your Earth terms, is the same Higher Self until you have reached the tenth dimension.

This completes the story of original consciousness, birthing of male and female, and the way of creation. The session, as it continued, went into my personal experiences beginning in the Andromeda galaxy. That transcript is in the next chapter.

Chapter 2

NINEVAH

Ninevah is a solar ring in the Andromeda galaxy where I experienced being a Supreme Being with a male partner. The story of my experiences in Ninevah is contained in this chapter in order to reveal one aspect of the destruction of male/female harmony, which has also been referred to as "the male/female split." It is, as are all of the hypnosis sessions in this book, intended to stir you into feeling and remembering your own part in this drama that now seeks resolution. As the feelings and thoughts arise in response to your reading of this material, try not to analyze them too much. Do not try to figure out if you were in Ninevah or some other solar ring, Andromeda, the Milky Way, or a different galaxy. Let the pure experience be enough. If you do not already know your own galactic origins, and if you need to know, your Higher Self and guides will make sure that you find this awareness. Perhaps you will feel moved to do your own hypnosis work or lucid dream work in order to bring forth your memories. Or perhaps the emotions and thoughts stimulated in you from the material are enough—at least for now. So, for now, relax, keep breathing, and allow your own natural flow to emerge with the stories from my hypnosis work.

As this session begins, it is the collective voice of the Elohim that is speaking. After that, I identify the source of information and experience as it changes.

A s you, Amorah, trace your origins to the Goddess Erotica in Andromeda, you will find yourself in Ninevah, the solar ring from whence you came. There are two suns in that solar ring, held by male and female counterparts. Five planets orbit between the two suns, or stars, and one planet orbits around the female star. Beyond that you were part of a larger being who held the galaxy within yourself. And yet to trace your own individuation to the ninth-dimensional level, it is in Ninevah that you began. Beyond that, on the tenth-dimensional level, you are part of Quan Yin, who holds Andromeda and the Milky Way within her own beingness. You see, as an endless dance of becoming greater and greater, when the Quan Yin galaxies and their counterpart male galaxies are merged into One again, that One itself has a female identity that goes all the way back to the original Holy Mother Goddess.

I, as Amorah, experience myself at this time as Quan Yin, keeper of the Andromeda and Milky Way galaxies. I feel myself splitting off to be the female keeper of the Andromeda galaxy, even though that galaxy is the male counterpart of the Quan Yin essence. And that male is the Christ part of my consciousness. When Mother Mary gave birth to Jesus, she was a symbol of the Goddess of the galaxy dreaming her own male counterpart. As I hold those two galaxies within my consciousness, there is an individuation happening in which the male holds Andromeda within himself and the female holds the Milky Way within herself. Then the male of the Andromeda galaxy dreams his female self, and the female of the Milky Way dreams her male self. There is a constant dividing down, so that there is a male and a female for every binary solar ring; each singular solar ring has either a male or female higher consciousness and these singular solar rings are grouped in male and female pairs.

This is where Christ and Mother Mary come in. As the Quan Yin essence divided into male and female parts that held two galaxies, the female part that became the Milky Way divided itself into two and became the male and female aspects of Christ consciousness. In the Andromeda galaxy, those consciousnesses were what we speak of as the God and the Goddess of Andromeda, or Eros and Erotica, respectively. As Andromeda separated from the Milky Way and experienced its own male and female individuation and reunion, the birth occurred of the consciousnesses of what you refer to as Supreme Beings of the solar rings and planets within them. That is when your [Amorah's] ninth-dimensional consciousness of Andromeda came into being as the Goddess Erotica. The God Eros and the Goddess Erotica were the names of the greater beings who held the whole galaxy; and they were also the names of the smaller Supreme Beings who held other solar rings. Christ and Mother Mary are not the God and the Goddess of the Milky Way, but they are the God and the Goddess in this solar ring, the Pleiadian system, and Sirius. Now back to Ninevah.

There are a God Eros and a Goddess Erotica holding the binary star system of Ninevah. There is also a twin sister, another Goddess Erotica, who, at that time, held a different solar ring within Andromeda. I, as Quan Yin, held existence within me and created with my divine male counterpart. We are the essence of harmony, and together we create harmony. We are the yin/yang symbol that holds that solar ring within itself. And we gave birth to devas, to planetary consciousnesses, and to angels, fairies and elves, and to the tree beings, or those who evolved into the tree beings later.

> As I relate the information I, Amorah, am continually experiencing that of which I speak. When I talk about the angels, fairies, and other beings, I reexperience them in my consciousness and joyous tears begin to flow because these Andromedan creations are so familiar and so beloved.

It is time now for you, Amorah, to move through the galactic gateways all the way to Ninevah and to reexperience it for yourself. [At this point I am being placed inside a double pyramid-shaped merkabah and I am leaving my body.] I, Amorah, am moving through a spiral, and I can tell this ongoing spiral orbits through time. I am being spiraled from Earth's orbits through time to those of our moon. I am moving through the time spiral of Venus, Mars, and even Maldek prior to its destruction. I am rapidly spiraling through orbits of each planet in this solar ring and now to the Pleiades. I am moving so fast I cannot distinguish one star system in the Pleiades from the other, and now I am moving through Sirian spirals and intergalactic stars and star systems. Spirals are going in all directions at once. There are several spiral passageways and I must go through a specific one. They—Sirian, Andromedan, and Pleiadian guides—are telling me to just notice the center as I go through this void in the Galactic Center. There are many spirals because in the Galactic Center there are gateways to other galaxies and dimensions within existence. The specific spiral you enter will determine your destination. I am now moving into the center of the Andromeda galaxy, which is like a giant sun. In the center of the sun is Andromeda. I am standing before the Andromedan Galactic Higher Council. They say, "You chose to go. Remember, you chose to go. We asked you to stay here and let others take care of what needed to be done. But you chose to follow your own desire to retrieve those who had been removed by force from Ninevah."

I, Amorah, just keep having a sense of Ninevah and a dark invasion going through there; many, many loved ones from that place were captured and brought to the Milky Way. I am asking the Higher Council if the capturers were the Orion beings or the Lyrans, but they say that there is much more that I need to remember. I tell them that I am ready to know now.

I am seeing the spirals within the Andromedan Central Sun now, the spirals of Light and of the orbits through time and space of each solar ring and star. I am seeing the spirals of Creation. My consciousness is becoming part of a much bigger consciousness. I now perceive Amorah as only a tiny projection of myself. I am steadily expanding and rebecoming more and more. *[Pause]*

Creation echoes back to experience and experience fills Creation. We, the Creators, have seen, and felt, and experienced the Creation and before Creation. *[Pause]*

I am Erotica, the Goddess Erotica: the goddess of pleasure beyond limitation. I have seen the vastness of potential creations and potential experiences. I stir the pot of the soul, the souls. The God Eros and I delight in the process of creation together. For the process of creation is the process of sacred union. We love one another. We come together in ecstatic adoration and erotic love; and from our union, we create. Our creations have etheric forms of angels, fairies, elves, and tree-like beings who can move around. My sole desire is to love them and to experience creation through them. They are the closest we can come to having form ourselves. And we sing them. We sing them our songs: songs of our desire to feel and experience, and songs of love and adoration for them and for each other. We come together in orgasmic love, Eros and I, and we become One. Beautiful songs emerge from our Oneness; and we hold our future creations within this Oneness. Love grows and we orgasmically sing our creations into existence and impulse them with the ecstatic waves created by our union. We stay with our songs until our children, our creations, become so strong that they can sing. We are so happy. When the creation begins to sing we have a big celebration in the cosmos. We sing to creation, and creation sings back. And we weep with joy and pride for creation.

The Elohim, the Creator Gods and Goddesses, are not what you think. We are just the singers of songs. We sing for the joy of the experience of feelings. We impulse creation, all of you, with our songs for the joy of experiencing what you feel. I see the human mind would interpret it as a manipulation, yet it is not. It is akin to a beautiful infinity symbol between the creators and creation. It is a song carried on the wings of love first to, and then through, the fairies to those beneath them. The fairies sometimes change the songs and teach us new ones; and we just laugh lovingly at the fairies. In fact, they have sung songs of their own creation and become creators in an epic sense. The first fairies sang to the small devas, the spirit guardians and essences of plants and flowers. But they went beyond the devic kingdom and created a whole colony of what were, at first, fourth-dimensional beings. The fairies sang and sang until this colony became third-dimensional elves. The fairies continued singing the cycles of nature—singing with the spirals and the whole arc of the galaxy, singing over stars and planets. Existence did not include third-dimensional reality in the way it does now. It was still in the process of becoming that.

The fairies were in a creation world of their own: fourth-dimensional sound, sensation, and form but beyond some of the limitations that humans have on Earth. It is hard to compare. Basically, what was becoming third-dimensional consisted of elves living among a group of giant devic-like beings, by their standards. The elves were about two feet tall and the giants were about seven feet tall. The elves were the learners and beekeepers, and they tended to the physical needs of plants. The giants were guardians of the trees. The fairies tended to

3. *Fairies singing the cycles of nature*

the needs of the elves, tree guardians, and devas. The fairies tended to them by singing to them from the fourth dimension. The fairies also sang to us, the God Eros and the Goddess Erotica, asking us to create what they, and those they cared for, needed. We responded through singing, while in union, songs of love and creation and impetus to explore and experience. And whatever we sang or intended, while in union, came to be and affected all of creation that was within us when we made love.

Through our natural way of looking at one another with love and adoration and gratitude—which is what the original Holy Father God and Holy Mother Goddess experienced during their union—we were drawn together. When we were first merged into Oneness, we seeded the consciousnesses of Ninevah. When Ninevah was seeded, we continued to merge with one another to help it grow. But we were born with a certain dissonance, even when we became ninth-dimensional beings that held this binary solar ring. There was already something within us, a longing to go back to original Oneness. Therefore, even as our love and adoration created union, and our union created smaller beings, there was a part of both of us that did not want to be responsible for the creation. We wanted to go back to Oneness, but felt a kind of powerlessness, like creation was eminent, and we could not stop it. All we wanted was to go back to the simplicity of the original design. And yet, within our ecstatic experiences of union, creation occurred. The love of creation soon followed and ended the inner conflict for both of us, initially.

However, after a time, as third-dimensional consciousness was being seeded more completely, the sense of responsibility became more demanding. This was because these third-dimensional ones were less awake than the previous creations had been. You see, there is another level of responsibility for holding consciousness for creations until they awaken themselves. At that stage of creation in Ninevah, the male God Eros, my divine counterpart, began to grieve for Oneness. He longed for it so much that he began to abandon our union, and did not want to create anymore. And yet I said to him, "Without our union, the love is not impulsed to creation which stimulates it to grow, to learn, and to awaken to its own divinity." In response, he reluctantly rejoined me in union again. Since we were dreaming the intent of loving and stimulating creation, we no longer created more lifeforms, but simply nurtured those lifeforms through our union.

Yet a restlessness grew within Eros. He wanted to be with me, to explore and love one another, but he wanted it to be unencumbered by the responsibility for our creations, our children. This desire for not being burdened with the responsibility for creation grew, and finally grew into a great discovery: Because he had the power of being a creator, he also had the power to choose his own creation and destiny. He chose to leave and blend with another consciousness. He chose what we might speak of as a younger consciousness, one on a lower level of evolution. He chose to become the Supreme Being of a single planet that was feminine, because he could control her and their destiny. In our union, there was a certain equanimity and impeccability that required dedication to follow through by caretaking the evolution of our creations. He chose to discontinue doing so at that time. It was his freedom to choose that, although it appeared as a devolution, in a sense, that he would become a Supreme Being of a single planet in order to blend more with the impressionable female consciousness of that planet. In doing so, he dominated her because she was of a smaller consciousness, and therefore, submissive to him. And he abused that power and used her for his own pleasure without the responsibility for creation. In that sense, the true original sin was the sin of dominance and control for the sake of one's own pleasure without consideration of the impact on that one being dominated and controlled: dominance and control over another who was not as conscious.

On the spiritual path, as one attains to a certain level of consciousness, one of the important responsibilities is not to abuse one's level of attainment over those who have not attained to that level yet. But he began vibrationally to become a control lord. There was a point at which he became quite attached to, and ego-identified with, his ability to control this lesser being. As a control lord he built quite a large amount of darkness within himself at that time. When he later decided to come back to Ninevah and resume his position there, Eros felt very justified at attempting to rule with dominant authority and control. This was very different from our former loving rulership based on responsibility and love for creation.

Prior to Eros' choice to return to Ninevah and control me and the solar ring, another male, who was at the same level of consciousness as myself, had been chosen to join me, and to hold Ninevah, as my divine counterpart. He was a newer Supreme Being of the God Eros origins. When the original God Eros decided to return with the intent of "resuming his rightful position," I was in a state of full tantric union with the new God Eros. We were in that particular stage of union at which surrender to Oneness occurs, in which the self becomes mindless and seems to be floating within all of existence simultaneously. When my original mate returned and saw that I was in union, he waited until that moment of surrender to make his move. He did so by coming into a forced union with the Goddess Persema who held the consciousness of the only planet in Ninevah that contained third-dimensional consciousness. In other words, as Gaia has a conscious self and a Higher Self, Persema was the higher consciousness of the only planet within that solar ring that had third-dimensional life at that time. Therefore, Persema and her planet were the ones into which he chose to come.

The original Eros was the father of Persema, as I was her mother. He asserted himself in such a way as to blend with her in what we might call an incestuous cosmic rape. When this cosmic rape occurred, because I was in a state of blended surrender with my new partner, we were catapulted out of union with the solar ring by an explosion. The explosion was created by the sudden impulsing of anger and hate through the rape by this now-dark warlord, former creator God Eros of Light. The planet itself was thrown off course and all of those who were experiencing physical life died at that time. When they left their bodies, they were sucked into the consciousness of this original God Eros who had raped Persema, the daughter. The fairies, who were the most immediate fourth-dimensional keepers of that realm, had tried very hard to pull in the frequencies of our lovemaking as they always did, but they were overshadowed by this father being and were sucked into the vortex of his consciousness as well. As he consumed all of the consciousnesses back into himself from the third and fourth dimensions, Persema's planet was thrown out of orbit. The equivalent of great hurricanes occurred and even the living structures that were not mobile were blown apart. And the planet was left barren. The consciousness of Persema, of the planet itself, had been greatly traumatized by this rape experience.

When my partner and I recovered from the shock and returned to blend with Ninevah once more, the original God Eros had already left, taking all of the consciousnesses with him, leaving a barren, damaged solar ring behind. We immediately impulsed our love into Ninevah and began healing and regenerating the entire solar ring. The new God Eros and I decided that since all of the consciousnesses of creation within that system had been traumatized and taken by their father, we would try to retrieve them. We wanted to rescue them from his abuse and control and to heal them and bring them back home. There was also a deep desire, on both our parts, to heal this former beloved, now become dark lord, who had misused his creative power. We loved him. We felt great compassion for him. We felt remorse that the depth of his pain had not been understood sooner. We wanted to seek him out and love and nurture him back into wholeness, and into the innocence and joy of union and creation once more.

And so the new God Eros and I joined together, approached the Supreme Being of Andromeda, and asked to follow the others. It was not that we needed permission; it was a request that was made from respect and sacred protocol. There was a Galactic Higher Council of Twelve who held Andromeda with the Supreme Being, and we went before this Higher Council. They said that much was to be learned from this experience and that the destinies of those who had been taken and of this original God Eros were out of our hands now. They thought it best that we remain in Ninevah and begin new life there as creator and creatress.

We went back to Ninevah for a time and yet there was so much grief within us that we could find no peace. As we merged with, and held the energy of, creation for the planets there, our memories could not be erased. The newest God Eros became fearful that he might become like the other God Eros. It was not just fear. He took on an anticipated shame. Because it had been my male counterpart who had betrayed and raped, and because he was my new male counterpart, he somehow felt an engendered responsibility for what had happened. That he could become like his predecessor was a great awareness within him. It was as if in order not to become that, he was magnetically drawn to seek out the offender and heal him. The original God Eros was like a foreboding shadow that had become part of his own psyche. If he did not follow that shadow and bring him back into truth again, it seemed that he could not be at peace.

I, on the other hand, carried a certain guilty sense of responsibility for helping the original God Eros become so desperate: I had not understood his concerns as fully as I should have; I should have understood his need and met it somehow; I could have loved him more, spent less time focused on mothering creation, or felt the depth of his longing. What I did not understand at that time, that I have come to understand now, is that his consciousness had a patterning of its own. No matter what I did or did not do, it would eventually have led to his need to control me if he had remained in Ninevah. And so I have allowed male control at other times, because I thought it was the way to prevent the shadow from taking over. Now I know that his need for control was and is his shadow: Not allowing male control is the only true way to love him, and myself, and to align with truth. How he responds is up to him, and I must let go of all control over the outcome. I must honor his free will and stop trying to control his destiny to make it fit my desires.

The new God Eros and I, each for our own reasons, appeared once again before the Higher Council, announced our decision to find the original God Eros and the children, and left Ninevah together. We were made aware that my original counterpart had entered the Milky Way, so through the portal we blended with the Central Sun of Andromeda. As that Central Sun and the Galactic Center of the Milky Way were one in union, we entered into union with them. Within that Central Sun we dreamed of awakening in the portal of the Milky Way's Galactic Center, and therefore arrived here at the ending of that union. We were greeted by the Higher Council of this galaxy, and immediately taken into sacred union with the Supreme Being of the Milky Way in order to experience the love, the sacred union, and the respect here. In that union, the Divine Plan for this galaxy was revealed. My partner and I united with one another. While united with one another, we also blended with the God/Goddess of the Milky Way; and we were contained within their union, and then reindividuated. When the Divine Plan had been revealed through these blendings, we knew that we must go to the area of the Pleiades, and then to this solar ring where we would go through several stages of downstepping through the dimensions.

The new Eros and I stayed at Galactic Center for a time and experienced the consciousnesses of devic kingdoms. From Galactic Center, we could establish an intent and then enter dreamtime together. We could also enter tantric union with mutual intent, and whatever we intended during those times is what we would experience.

It is as if you, on Earth, set a dream intent and then during the dream are lucidly aware that you are dreaming. You are aware that what you are experiencing is a dream and yet you continue to experience it. Upon awakening, you take the experiences and answers you received and act upon them in your life. This is very symbolic of what happened to us at that time. What you might say is that, after the merging with the God/Goddess Supreme Beings of the Milky Way, and after the meeting and blending with the Higher Council of this galaxy, we were held in Galactic Center for a great, long time, going in and out of dreamtime and learning with the Higher Council. By the end of this particular indoctrination period, we had experienced all of the consciousnesses within the Milky Way and their purposes, both collectively and individually. Not individually as in individual humans, but as in individual species. For example, during one union, we had an experience of the consciousness of all of the Pleiades at the same time. In another dreamtime we merged with the consciousness of this solar ring and all of life within it. We then came back to our waking consciousnesses with the understanding of what happens in those places so that we could interact in an appropriately aligned manner.

During these blendings and dreams, we discovered that the being who had been the original God Eros held a solar ring in the Milky Way within his consciousness. He was in the process of creating life-forms in the third-dimensional world with the female consciousness of that solar ring. He did not treat her as a Supreme Being or equal counterpart. She was his slave: a sex slave, in a sense. The fairies were being enslaved in that place as well. We saw that the only way to counter his plan was to work with the creation of a new world so that when the imprisoned beings there were finally set free, there would be a safe and loving world to which they could go.

Within the Milky Way, your solar ring was the chosen location for this safe and loving world. That it had an individual sun seemed appropriate, because he had gone to another solar ring on the other side of the Milky Way that had a single sun. We also knew by then that it would be important for those beings to come into a place that had a single Supreme Being and that the Supreme Being must be an androgynous being. So with the Divine Plan for Earth, and with this solar ring having been predestined as a place for a Supreme Being who was the Spirit of Oneness, we agreed to work within the destiny of this particular solar ring in order to bring about the healing that was needed. Originally the new God Eros and Goddess Erotica that I am were assigned to this solar ring. We created fourth-dimensional life here, in the form of fairies, angels, and tree-spirits who were not yet incarnated. All of these were still held as consciousnesses inside small balls of light. A hierarchical structure was being formed at that time, so that when the Andromedan serving angels first wished to come to this particular solar system to experience free will, we were the natural choice for a home for those consciousnesses to become third dimensional. They were brought here, and life was begun on Venus as had been prepared for quite some time in advance.

There had long been life within the Pleiadian system at that time. There were wars going on within the Pleiadian system, and there were also hierarchical beings like your Supreme Being and Higher Council who held the Light. Many of these Light Beings were among the ones you have identified previously as the Pleiadian Emissaries of Light. The Archangelic Tribes within the Pleiadian Emissaries of Light had come from the Galactic Center to hold the Divine Plan and to administer universal law within the Pleiadian system. At that time Earth and this entire solar ring orbited around a different central sun than what they do now. At this time, as you well know, your solar ring orbits the central sun of the Pleiades, which is called Alcyone. However, at that time your solar system was a part of a different system: You were orbiting around the central sun of the constellation called the Great Bear. And this was billions of years ago. It was at the time when the entire Milky Way was coming to the end of a spiral ring on its orbit around the Great Central Sun of All That Is just as it is doing again now. This former cycle that was ending was called the Evolutionary Spiral of Exploration of the Possibilities of Creation. Your whole galaxy was just entering the Evolutionary Spiral of Self-Discovery, which you are now leaving. The new orbital ring you are entering now is the Evolutionary Spiral of Self-Mastery.

At that time, billions of years ago, the new God Eros and I jointly held the position of Supreme Being for this solar ring—which was part of the system of the Great Bear. As you well know, at the end of these galactic cycles, pole shifts take place and reorganizations occur in which planets and star systems are realigned with those that are their next evolutionary level of growth. At that particular time, the Pleiadian system held the next evolutionary step for this solar ring since it had already gone through the level of self-discovery that you were just entering. Earth and this solar ring were transported inside what you might think of as a galactic bubble held inside the union of the God Eros and Goddess Erotica. Your solar ring was then brought into magnetic alignment as your sun became the eighth sun within the Pleiadian system.

The consciousnesses that were at a lower-dimensional level were put into what you might think of as a sleep state. As the entire Milky Way completed its realignment to begin its next spiral orbit—the Evolutionary Spiral of Self-Discovery—we began once again to awaken those consciousnesses. It was as if they were being birthed again. They had limited memories of their previous consciousness; and yet it was as if you, as a human, were moved from one city to another and kept asleep while being transported from one location to the other. You would not remember the journey but you would

remember where you had been before. This is what their consciousnesses were like when they were reawakened as points of light in the
sixth dimension. They were then gradually downstepped into the
fairy consciousnesses and the tree-spirit beings again. The elf consciousnesses had not yet been created here. Many Pleiadian beings
were brought here to help create the higher astral planes, or fourth-
dimensional planes of Light, in preparation for those to be downstepped. These Pleiadians were our teachers, yet they also respected
our choices; for as Supreme Beings of this solar ring, we had choices.
And yet, once we were part of the Pleiadian system, the Higher
Council of the Archangelic Tribes of the Pleiades held dominion as
well. So there was collaboration in creation. And so, Amorah, you
were involved in the beginning of life in this solar ring—although not
as the human consciousness you are experiencing on Earth at this
time. You were still a nondifferentiated aspect of me, the Goddess
Erotica, whereas now you are a projected soul emanation from me, the
Goddess Erotica.

After the initial creation of the fourth-dimensional realms, long
before any physical existence here, the new God Eros and Goddess
Erotica were removed to the Pleiadian system. There we alternated,
over a period of time, being blended consciousnesses with each of the
solar rings within the Pleiades—or each of the star systems—so that
we could experience their frequencies. We were not in charge of them
per se, but were larger consciousnesses in a state of living union,
blending with them and learning each of their lessons. For each of the
stars within the Pleiadian system at that time was experiencing its
own unique and specific level of evolution and unique function. The
Divine Plan was held at Galactic Center and impulsed to Alcyone.

It was only in the last half-million years that Alcyone evolved to a
point at which it was able to hold the Divine Plan for the Pleiadian
system itself. For the last half-million years Alcyone has been held by
the Light and by the Higher Council from Galactic Center.

After the galactic shift was completed, we were taken back to
Galactic Center to begin a process of downstepping in order to experience and learn through other levels of existence. Within this solar
ring we left our position at that time and another being took over who

held the energy of androgyny. Of course, androgyny holds male and female within itself, and yet is in a state in which it does not know duality. We wish to end this session at this time, for this is the amount of energy and information that you, Amorah, can integrate before going to the next stages of the evolutionary story. And so we will return you to yourself, and yet you will be returned with what you might think of as a Pillar of Light that now connects you through Ninevah and Andromeda to the Great Central Sun. The Great Central Sun is the home of the original and eternal Holy Father God and Holy Mother Goddess. Your Pillar of Light was formerly connected in your consciousness only through your own ninth-dimensional experience to Ninevah and now will be extended to the source of All That Is. It will take several weeks for you to fully integrate this into your constant state of being. Therefore, we say, "Farewell for this time." We will resume at this point at Alcyone when we come together once more. As your consciousness is being once again impulsed downward you will know when you are at the third-dimensional level again.

I am including my process of returning to normal conscious-ness at the end of this hypnosis session. This will give you an indi-rect experience of downstepping of consciousness.

I am going to do it very slowly. I am returning to the head area of my body. I can feel a great intensity of higher-dimensional energy streaming like a rushing river into my soul matrix in my heart, and then moving back up and through my eyes. There is so much energy streaming through me that I have to stay with this step until it is anchored in my eyes fully. *[Pause]* I need to do something to get back in; the energy is so expanded I don't seem to fit into my body. I'm being guided to do something at my temples and eyes. It requires a lot of very deep breathing in through my crown and then down through my crown and into my eyes and down to my perineum. It feels like my Ka is being activated to a new level right now as these energies have connected from the higher dimensions all the way back to the source. It is creating a different kind of Pillar-of-Light effect with a multidimensional consciousness. At a certain level it is like being connected with the consciousness of all beings in existence and having that downstepped like an upside-down pyramid all the way down to my body as a grounding rod. The translations of energies right now are coming in through my Ka Template and through the perineum portal, but not through the back of my heart yet. I just can't rush the process. It feels like the vibrational frequencies are almost too much for my soul matrix to handle. I'm starting to try and bring this energy in through the portal in the back of my heart chakra. There is a lot of energy that has to clear to make room for it all. My guides say I need to do it as we are coming through the ten-count to bring me back, not after I am back. This is interesting because somehow this new Pillar-of-Light activation has accessed my perineum from the inside, and now it is going to move to a next level of activation of my perineum portal from the outside in.

At this point Steve, my regressionist, began to count me back from one to ten. It took several minutes and a lot of deep breathing and kriyas (jolting, full-body energy releases) to complete the reentry. It was several days before my spatial orientation began to feel familiar and not awkward. My inner voice was like many echoing voices from different dimensions all saying, sometimes singing, the same thing at the same time.

Chapter 3

CREATION OF THE SOUL (BA)

ermes, an archangelic being who communicates with me from Sirius, and An-Ra are with me throughout this session and assist me in getting into a deeply altered state. The purpose of the session, as told to me in advance by Ra, is to remember the creation of my own soul. It turns out that there are a few other surprises the guides have in store prior to getting to that point. These surprises are included at the early stages of this transcription because they are very illuminating as to the vastness, complexity, and multiplicity of human multidimensional totality. I have a very loving connection with Hermes, and will begin with my initial contact with him once I was under hypnosis. This will help paint the full picture of the session.

Hermes is here, present in my session.

I call Hermes "he," but he is actually an androgynous being. I am touching him now and we are holding hands, and he is radiating energies through me from his body. He is telling me to lift out of my body now, to use the merkabah to move myself from my body so I can be more completely there with him. There is also a female being with me. She is one of the Pleiadian Archangels of the An-Ra Tribe. And there is my little child-self, kind of tugging at my arm. She just wants me to pick her up, so I am doing that. She wants to go along today because she thinks what we are going to do is pretty neat. I am letting her know that it is fine for her to come along but that I may have to let An-Ra take care of her if I need to give my full attention to something. She says, "I won't be in the way." She is such a sweetheart: a very bright, precocious little thing. I call her Bright Eyes. She's saying, "Let's go." She's such a little imp . . .

I am being whooshed through a spiraling tunnel of light very rapidly now. I am already out through the other side. I am in my merkabah and moving through the cosmos and out into space now. My consciousness has just expanded. It is as though I moved into a larger, conscious self, and I am blended with the entire Milky Way galaxy. I feel like there is a huge male being who is blended with the Andromeda galaxy, and I am blended with the Milky Way. I am in a state of split attention. Part of me is experiencing myself as a very feminine goddess, filled with female bliss. That is the part that is in a state of Oneness with the Milky Way and feeling love for Creation. But there are things within the Milky Way that are not harmonious right now. The other part of my consciousness is experiencing a smaller self who has been on Sirius for awhile, being acclimated and prepared for my own future. I need to go back and blend with the part who is experiencing the entire galaxy so I can understand it all. That is where I am now, and yet I can feel the smaller consciousness within me.

I can feel the Andromedan male part; the pull toward him is so strong. It is like ninety percent of me is just in bliss, but there is this ten percent who misses the connection with him so much. I want to go back to him; but I can't leave now. That is the pull I feel in my left chest. It is like something pulling me out of myself. I need to become a little more of the consciousness of myself as the Goddess Erotica. I am asking my bigger self to help me pull my consciousness into her more fully. She says, "We are one, and because we have become so deeply one again, you can even blend with me through your body. That is why you are able to feel this experience in your body at the same time you are here with me. Don't be dismayed about it, the information will be just as clear." As I relax and trust what she says, I am becoming one with her. She says, "I spin, I dance, and I love. I have so much joy and light. So much of creation is within my beingness, within my consciousness, within my body. From this perspective, I can become anything I choose to feel. If I want to feel one planet, I can feel just that one planet. If I want to experience this wholeness of the Milky Way as I am doing now, I can experience that.

4. Amorah travels with Hermes, An-Ra, and Bright Eyes

If I want to experience only the Sun of Earth's solar ring, I can do so. As the Goddess Erotica, I just simply continue to hold the galaxy within myself, and it is just as easy as when I am human and want to feel my own navel area. I just focus on that part of my body, so to speak. If I want to feel a particular sun or a particular solar ring, I just focus on that within myself and that is what I experience.

I am choosing to feel this solar ring now. It is like a bubbling cauldron, with a strong life force and a lot of vitality. We have obviously gone into a past time frame because I can see and feel Maldek. Mars is already dormant. Maldek and Earth are like primordial swamps, bubbling away and about to birth new creation; they feel very first- and second-dimensional. Even the Sun is in flux. Something has happened from the explosion that happened in the atmosphere on Mars. The Sun was more affected by that than I previously knew. There are explosions going on in the atmosphere around the Sun. It feels like the Sun is actually shifting on its axis in relationship to the solar ring and everything is being stirred up. I don't see any human life in the solar ring at this time. I can feel the consciousness of the dinosaurs within myself. They are on Earth. I can feel tadpoles and small things that are in thick water on Earth. The Sun is changing, partly because there is so much grief. It is as if the Sun is digesting all the trauma that has happened on Mars. Venus looks like it is in a deep sleep. I am experiencing those planets like consciousnesses in recovery from the humans who lived there. Mars is dead looking. It doesn't even look asleep; it just looks dead. And yet there is something at the core of Mars that still holds a sense of consciousness. It reminds me of an unhatched egg, or a consciousness in a cocooned state.

The Sun is absorbing all of the pain from the humans. It is like all of their wailing and sobbing and screaming and anger and everything is just being absorbed by the Sun. One part of the Sun is imploded instead of radiating. We are now moving forward in time to the point where the Sun is just radiating again and I can feel the warmth of the Sun like a single consciousness. Paradoxically it feels as though there are many consciousnesses blended into that one consciousness, all having the same awareness of love at the same time. I see the love being sent out through the planets and it feels like a radiant warmth flowing through me. It feels more motherly than fatherly. It feels like the Sun is like the Goddess's heart shining through the planets and my heart is part of that. I can see how, especially with Earth, the Sun's light just shines straight through to the core of the planet and warms it from the inside out. It is very loving and very comforting to feel that. I can feel the Sun's love flowing around and through Mars. Mars doesn't feel as much like it is in that chrysalis state now; it feels like it is being loved and prepared for a new consciousness to enter. The Sun seems to have almost a cellular relationship with Mars. The love that is transmitted through the light of the Sun is moving through every cell of Mars and purifying it. It feels like I do in my human body when I lie in the sunlight, sunbathing in the nude, and feel like I am soaking up the rays in every cell. I get so blissed out that I go into an altered, no-mind state at times. That is what Mars feels like: no-mind. Venus seems to be purging the Goddess pain. The Sun also radiates cellularly through Venus, and there is a lot of energy moving out of that planet. Venus feels like it has just awakened from a long dream. It woke up crying. That sounds strange, but it is the closest explanation I can give to what I am experiencing.

On Maldek I see people now. We have gone back to the beginning of human inhabitation of Maldek. I can see the projection of me that is in the center of that planet. I am a tantric deva there with a new partner who was chosen specifically for service as a tantric deva as well. My devic self there is like a speck of consciousness compared to the large being I am at this time. I have a full, light-body form there inside Maldek that radiates and changes colors. It goes from a ruby red to golden light. And sometimes, when I am in tantric union with my partner, there at the center of the planet, I become an exquisite silver-blue color.

My partner and I appear very prismatic, like we have an ability to emanate any color that is appropriate in the moment; and we go through cycles of colors. I can see my body changing again now from the silver-blue into a very soft, pale green, into gold, into white-silver, into a really bright orange. From there it changes into a soft, pinkish red, and then into purple. As we make love, we both change, and go through geometric patterns of colors. Simultaneously, the waves from our lovemaking are building layers of colors. These colors have frequency and sound to them. The sound is a whirring kind of sound, similar to wind through pine trees. As the colors change, the whirring sound varies in intensity and tone. Sometimes the whirring is lower pitched and at other times becomes higher again. As their (our) tantric fusion becomes very strong, both of our consciousnesses at the center of Maldek are inside of the bigger me who is speaking. This is because I am still holding the entire Milky Way inside me. It is extremely beautiful. I can feel the waves from the lovemaking between my Maldekian devic self and her partner moving out through that planet now. These waves are akin to beautiful colored ripples on water. Each wave can change to all the colors that we have built through our lovemaking. It helps people ground to the planet through their feet when the waves from this lovemaking at the center of Maldek reach the surface of the planet. I can see and feel how it impulses people's feet and it moves through their auras and makes them more connected with nature. It helps them be gentler people than they would be otherwise.

I can see the people of the Martian-Andromedan Colony. They are very gnomelike. They are taller than gnomes, but their features are very much like that. There is a nature-connected, harmonic frequency about the beings. I find them very endearing. That is partially why I took the assignment as a tantric deva at the center of the planet. There, in my light body, I am a vessel through which the Holy Mother can blend with the Holy Father and send out the love from their union in a way that nurtures the human population. And it is a way to which their human bodies and spirits can relate. As our energy goes out through Maldek, it expands into the whole solar ring and into the Sun. From the Sun, it goes out on a spiral orbit. This is very interesting to experience because the energy from the tantric waves is spun out very, very fast, yet the planetary and solar orbits are much slower. At this stage the tantric waves appear to be faster than the speed of light. They come so fast that you can see something akin to a fan-blade-in-motion effect. I can't really tell where they are coming from because, as they reach the Sun, they are whirled right into it and then spun back out again very fast through the planets. Now I can feel them going all the way through the solar ring and then through my whole consciousness that is blended with the entire Milky Way. It is an extremely satisfying feeling. I send love to that part of myself just as I am doing to the whole galaxy. I want to send great love and honor to that part of me that is at the center of Maldek at a sixth-dimensional level. What she [Amorah] does there is very beautiful and loving . . .

I learned how to be a sixth-dimensional being on Sirius. Hermes, my Sirian guide, is telling me that there is another place, called Pleidos, on which I also experienced the sixth dimension. On Sirius they call it Pleidos galaxy, but it is actually more like an expansive solar ring, or a microcosm of a whole galaxy. I am trying to see where it is located relative to Earth and this solar ring. In looking out from Earth, it is on the next arm of the galactic spiral and going in a clockwise rotation. It is farther from the center of the Milky Way than is Earth's solar ring. Pleidos is a solar ring made up of many planets and stars; and I can feel myself there. It is truly like a miniature galaxy. I can see how I spent time there as a Supreme Being for that system, like I was on Andromeda. My experience there was like a dress rehearsal for being able to project myself into different dimensions and aspects of dimensions all at the same time. For instance, at this moment I am holding the Milky Way inside of my greater consciousness. And yet I have a projected self in the center of Maldek whom I can experience with equal lucidity, as well as two other projected selves I am experiencing right now.

One of these other aspects of myself is still in Pleidos galaxy. The other self is projected around and through the image of a unicorn. It appears to be the symbol for that place where my other self is. I am attempting to observe the formation of the stars that make up the unicorn to see if I can recognize them, but the unicorn image is so strong, it is all I can make out clearly. I am going to slip into that consciousness exclusively and see if I can decipher the star formation . . . I don't know what all of this is leading to but it feels like appropriate information to bring through. My guides are laughing and saying, "You know we always take you where you need to go." Okay, I surrender. Anyway, I can see and feel now that where I am is blended with a star in Sagittarius. It is being shown to me that the true higher-dimensional symbol for Sagittarius is the unicorn and not the half-man and

5. The constellation Sagittarius shown as a unicorn, as opposed to a centaur

half-horse. The star that modern astrology depicts as the top star of the bow is actually the tip of the unicorn's horn, and what we have been taught to see as the point of the arrow is actually the tip of the unicorn's nose. (See illustration 5 on page 52.) I am blended with the star that is at the tip of the unicorn's horn.

I am experiencing myself as being that star, just being the light. It is very sweet. There is a smaller part of my consciousness here that is in the process of individuating within the star. The best way I can describe this part is like a giant fairy queen. If my consciousness here is the size of the star, then this newly individuating part is approximately one-third of my consciousness that is blended with the star. This one-third within the greater whole is in a process of being birthed. Its new light-body form is fairylike. This is so amazing that we have all of these aspects of ourselves. This newly created fairylike part is the one who will be the Higher Self of my physical self when I am the fairy queen on Earth. This fairy queen lifetime is a future lifetime in Lemuria. I am here in this star, being one with the star, and yet within my greater self is this third of my consciousness that is totally devoted to just dreaming itself and my future fairy lifetimes into being. It is very strange by human standards because I am birthing this alter-self on my own just by dreaming it until it becomes self-aware.

Time is being accelerated and I am the dream come alive now: I am the fairy queen. I am also the Higher Self of the fairy queen; and I am still inside the star at the same time. My star-self is like the higher-dimensional self of the Higher Self. I feel so sparkly and joyful and happy to have been created. It is like waking up for the first time, discovering that you exist, and delighting in that fact. I don't feel any urgency to go anywhere or do anything; I am simply enjoying being myself in this new form. My fairy Higher Self consciousness is aware of the star around her, but when I am her I am not aware that there is more consciousness in this star than in my own. I am very focused in my own new consciousness at this point. Now I am moving forward in time. I can tell that this time gap we are traveling through is a very long time gap. I am moving forward to the point where I first hear a voice. It is the voice of the part of my consciousness that is in the

Sagittarian star. I am still the fairy Higher Self and I perceive myself as the mother-self. "Welcome. We have waited for you for a long time," says my fairy Higher Self to my present-day human self, Amorah.

Hermes says, "Know that the word *time* is not truly what your fairy Higher Self is communicating. However, it is the closest that you can come to her meaning when translating her meaning into the English language. So know that this is not exact, but it is as close as we can come."

The mother-self, who is still holding the whole star, says to the large fairy Higher Self, "You are a joyful delight to me and I am glad that you are part of me now. We have work to do here." Then the mother-self teaches the fairy Higher Self. She blends with her and shows her other experimental lifeforms and solar rings. I am experiencing being the mother-self star consciousness and I am asking the fairy Higher Self to blend with me. We blend, and I impart the memories to her of when and how the separation occurred in Andromeda during which all of the fairies were taken away by the father spirit. I am saying, "I have made you big enough to hold all of the fairy spirits within you once they are freed again." Now I am showing her the planet Earth and this solar ring. I show her where the fairies will be taken when they are released. I also tell her that there is a future time when the greater deities will send a wave of grace throughout existence and that is when the fairies will be freed. "At that time," I instruct the fairy Higher Self, "you must be ready to absorb them into yourself and take them to Earth. You will be able to travel there simply by projecting yourself as I will teach you." Now I am the fairy Higher Self again. I feel a mixture of a lot of feelings when I see all of these little fairy beings. I feel an enormous amount of love for them; and I feel deep grief.

Again I am the Goddess Erotica who is still blended with the entire Milky Way. The part of me who still has an attachment to the fairies through grief has become the fairy Higher Self. The rest of me, as the Goddess Erotica, feels very clear and loving. But this part who has become the fairy Higher Self in the Sagittarian constellation has been created with deep grief about the harm to the children, the fairies. The fairy Higher Self can feel that in herself. In my human body, I can feel it as sharp pain in the left side of my chest.

Because I am experiencing all of these aspects of myself simultaneously, there is a beautiful thing that can happen now. It is wonderful. The body of Amorah is in the third dimension and has lived past the point where the fairies have been brought to Earth and freed. This link-up through hypnosis is allowing the consciousness of the Goddess Erotica to reach into what is her future, where the fairies are safe. As the Goddess Erotica becomes aware of this, she blends her consciousness fully with the star, so that the mother-self in the star becomes aware of the consciousness of the whole galaxy. I am to relax and experience that now . . . Part of the consciousness that is in the star hears the voice of the Goddess Erotica saying, "Hello beloved. I am here with you always, even until the end of time, and beyond time. Draw the fairy Higher Self's consciousness into yourself so that she too can experience me." I can feel that happening as the fairy consciousness. It is like being drawn into a deep sleep in the star; and then it as if the star is being drawn into a deep sleep filled with loving dreams inside the consciousness of the Goddess Erotica and the Milky Way. The Goddess Erotica is sending to these parts the dream of the future and the healing of the fairies. The effect reminds me of watching ripples on water, the ripples going through the fairy Higher Self. These ripples break up and release the grief in her light-body form as she witnesses the joy awaiting her in the future. In other words, what we think of as the future is healing the past.

I am going to be in a healing space with this for a little while. I am blending with all of them to enable the healing to take place in my body at the same time. As the energies connect into my body, the pained part of my body consciousness looks out and sees the fairy Higher Self blended with the mother star. And this wounded part in my body recognizes the fairy Higher Self and says, "There she is. It's her. It's really her. Look, it's our mother Arorah, the first fairy queen." [Arorah, not Amorah, is my fairy name.]

There is another future self here, too. The etheric form of this future self reminds me of the Goddess Nut, spread out across the sky. She is spread out across my body's aura, and yet across this whole solar ring at the same time. She holds all of the fairies in this solar ring within herself. She is Arorah in the future. It is very special to feel her. Her original pain about the fairies is anchored through my physical heart and it is being pulled out of my physical body right now. Waves of light are being spun through my physical heart and these waves pull out the old grief and pain. I hear the words, which I say also, "I release the past. In conscious creation, there is no need for the past. The past will not be repeated again; and therefore this grief I have held in my body and my soul, and in my bigger self, must be released now into the light of the Sun to be transmuted and returned to me as pure love. I forgive the father, the God Eros, who strayed from the Light. I understand now that his destiny was to understand the darkness fully and deeply so that when he chose the Light again it would be a choice based on understanding of all of the alternatives. I can see now that my learning to let go of my attachment to, and grief about, the loss of him has been a great learning for him also.

In this lifetime, my own willfulness and attachment have held inappropriate relationships together longer than they should have been. Yet I did finally let go and even achieved acceptance and forgiveness. My earnest desire to honor the free will of the God Eros has translated down into this lifetime in the third dimension as desire to release attachments and honor free will in my former beloveds here. This understanding and desire is very deep and strong now.

When the God Eros returns and sees that I have released him completely, and that I have honored his free will above my own need for his return, when I have loved him unconditionally even in his absence, then he will know how to love me and allow me the freedom to love others as well. Through seeing the genuineness of my love for him even in his absence, he will have the opportunity to let go of his need to possess me totally. When he chooses this we will be able to be One again. This time it will be in a much deeper, and more sacred, way by virtue of the experiences we have had since we were last together in Ninevah. I speak now from the future when this is already true. The Goddess Erotica says, "So be at peace, beloved ones, my selves from my own past, knowing that the resolution is at hand. Be in love wherever you are. Suffer not for those things that you do not have. Love those who are with you. Share in their lives and celebrate the opportunity for the experiences you are having in the moment. Freedom lies in release of each moment as it passes, and in embracing the next moment, the now, with faith in the future." She speaks from a place in Andromeda when she is again with the original God Eros. They are in sacred union there again, restoring life to that binary solar ring. So I know it is true.

I can feel how my body is being used to move through all of the energies of original hurt and separation—all the way back to the beginning. All of the emotions and experiences, past and future, are moving through my heart chakra and into my physical heart and out again. The future Goddess Erotica says there is nothing I need to do other than relax and allow it—that it is all completing itself in a sacred way. I feel deep, deep acceptance. I feel that one-tenth part of me that I talked about earlier who has been in grief and painful longing for a long time. She is holding out a hand and feeling the absence of the beloved, but beginning to relax now. She is still crying, but slowly letting go. Because she understands more deeply, she is free to feel her grief more completely and without trying to resolve it outside herself now. My consciousness in all the dimensions still thought this last and deepest grief could only be healed outside myself, through relationship. Of course, this is not true. The Goddess Erotica says *when that last piece of grief has passed completely through my body, loneliness will be done in this lifetime.* I can feel the truth in that. "Time is short," says the Goddess Erotica, "and it won't take as long as you think, although there will be an integration period in your body. Then the lasting effect, which comes from total understanding and acceptance, is the peace and presence of mind to be fully free to be who you are, wherever you are, in whatever circumstance without needing anything beyond what is." Freedom is simply total absorption in the moment, this moment. I feel the peace it brings. I can also feel a part deep inside that doesn't have that peace yet; that part is still doing the grieving, and there is still some pressure in my chest. But emotionally I feel deep peace and resolution.

I am pulling my consciousness back from the Sagittarian star now. *[Note: At this stage of the session, Hermes instructed me to have an illus-*

tration in the book of the constellation Sagittarius, showing it as a unicorn. "That will be another job for Bryna," he said. He also told me to put the statement in the paragraph above in italics. I cracked up at the way they were handling the hypnosis session, and the process of putting it into this book like a great collective process. Hermes laughed too, and there was so much love in the humor that it made it really special. It feels very intimate to share humor with him. At this stage Hermes told me, "We are ready to go into the Sun now for your soul's creation."]

I am experiencing a completely different focus now. It is as if all of the energy that was spread out through the whole session has been concentrated into a Pillar of Light with movement inside it. Hermes says what I am experiencing are very quickly vibrating, striated beams of light in a pillarlike form. I am to refocus now, bring my consciousness into my body via my diamond-grid merkabah. Then I am to enter that pillar and go straight into the Sun. I keep hearing the words, "The body of Christ. The body of Christ." I can see the face of Christ. I am in a birthing chamber inside the Sun. It is interesting. I am inside the Sun and in the middle of Sirius, simultaneously. There is a beam coming into the Sun from the star Sirius. The birthing chamber is being projected from Sirius into the Sun. *[There was a long silent pause at this point during which I had to calm my mind and become peaceful again.]* There are so many focuses happening at the same time, it is difficult to describe. I feel like I am a fetus inside an egg which is dreaming and has not awakened to even know that it exists yet. It is in stasis. I am experiencing the being who became Jesus Christ. I feel almost as if I am him in this moment and yet it is because I am blended with him so totally that I cannot tell where he begins and I end. At this time, Christ has 144,000 beings, or consciousnesses, blended within him. I am one of those 144,000 consciousnesses of the body of Christ. I am part of his third eye . . . As soon as I said that, I experienced a whooshing sensation, and now I am a bigger consciousness.

I am in my Elohim full light body and I am actually experiencing myself as the entire Elohim being from whence I came. Now I am the entire Goddess holding Andromeda and the Milky Way simultaneously within myself. The Milky Way is like my womb. Andromeda is my heart. And there are other galaxies within me. I feel like I am in the full body of Quan Yin spread out beyond those two galaxies. Each chakra of my body is a whole galaxy. Even the out-of-body chakras are galaxies, so there are thirteen in all. I hear chanting, and it reminds me of the regression session in which I first heard the sound of one voice that contains all voices. I am this huge Goddess who holds the thirteen galaxies within myself. I am an Elohim Goddess. As the voices sing the Divine Plan, I receive it through the cells of my body and my cells are moved by the sound of the one voice singing, the one voice that is the many. The songs spin my cosmic cells, and the galaxies, planets, moons, and stars respond. The Milky Way is within my womb. The Milky Way is a galaxy of conception and birth. I can see how in the bigger scheme of things that it is so. I do not sense any particular male presence who is a counterpart. I do sense all of the Elohim around me, as if they are all contributing to this birthing experience.

The soul of Christ is a composite of 144,000 souls. The one who is known as Amorah is half of one of those souls. The other half is non-physical at this time on Earth. I see this is the pattern for all of the other souls as well: half incarnate on Earth, and half remaining non-physical. Now I see why Jesus Christ was so unique. When Christ was on Earth, he was a composite of 144,000 beings within one, which had never been fully birthed before. But what made it even more unique was the fact that the 144,000 souls within him were simultaneously in individuated bodies living on Earth in human lives. Some of us, in fact, had as many as three or four simultaneous physical bodies and lifetimes. So it was the 144,000 many times over. This is important because the plan included having enough consciousnesses to insure that a minimum of 144,000 could be reawakened when the time came.

It is as if Christ is inside the Sun. I see him outside of this egg, and the egg is asleep. This is exactly like the creation story in which the conglomerate 144,000 being decided to keep all of its parts awake and let all of its parts sleep at the same time. Christ, as we think of the Christ being, is there, as in an awake form, and yet is also asleep at the same time, in this egglike form. So he is split in half. The egglike form, which contains 144,000 souls in the process of being created, is the female half and the one we call Christ is the male half. The Elohim

Goddess and the entire Elohim are all focused on birthing this con-
glomeration of souls at this time. These eggs are the etheric double of
Christ; they are being dreamed by the whole Elohim. The huge thir-
teen-galaxy Elohim Goddess is in a state of total surrender and receiving all of their dreams, complete with sounds, colors, and light from
all of their beings. They continually sing to these souls who are being
created now. I cannot identify my consciousness as being in a smaller
place. I am experiencing myself as the Goddess Erotica blended with
the Milky Way, and within me is the mother-self who is one with the
Sagittarian star. At the same time I am one with Sirius and the Sun.
Now a great cosmic fusion is taking place in which all of the Supreme
Beings, all of the archangels, and all of the hierarchical beings are
blending. Now I can only feel this great Elohim Goddess consciousness. All consciousnesses in existence are being held in a blended state
in their larger Elohim forms.

I can no longer experience anything other than what is in the
womb of the Elohim Goddess. All of the parts of the Goddess Erotica,
the fairy Higher Self included, have blended in such a way that we
cannot tell each other, or anything else in the womb, apart from ourselves. We are blended into Oneness within that Goddess body, and
we are being impulsed by all of the other Elohim. This is like being
impregnated but in a much more cosmic way. I am in a deep meditative state. I have surrendered totally in love. The Elohim are sending
all of their love into this creation in the Milky Way. I am in that place
of total surrender in deep stillness. The egg is taking on the same
shape internally as the Milky Way, a single spiral of light is beginning
to move within the womb, within the Sun. Now the egg has cracked
open and that spiral is moving very fast. It is difficult for me to see
what is happening. The spiral form inside the egg was released and
spun from the Sun straight through into Sirius. There was a matrix
there that it anchored into. In that matrix it began to awaken and
become aware of itself as a being. I can feel myself again as the
Goddess holding the newborn spiral; and I can also experience being
in that new spiral being, which is my oversoul.

Within the oversoul, all of us parts of the Goddess are becoming
the consciousness of the star Sirius. I am in a very peaceful place. I

hear the sound of a male voice. It is very comforting and wise: an ancient sounding voice belonging to the Holy Father. He says, "You are the creators preparing to send yourselves into creation. I congratulate you on the beauty, the love, and the responsibility of this choice. Your sincerity and devotion to Oneness and to the evolution of Creation is absolute. And as you are a part of me, and these souls you create for yourselves are part of you, and the lives that each soul experiences are parts of them, we are One. In spirit and in form, in sound and in silence, in the void and in the great chorus of All That Is, we are One."

The Holy Mother speaks now as I see the symbol of the ankh. The Holy Mother says, "Children of the Light, all of you are children, even the greatest among you. And yet you are birthing your own selves into new forms now. The Holy Father and I love each and every one of you even more than we knew was possible in the beginning. Our love grows as you grow. Your expansion is our own. The joy of creation is ours through you. And we celebrate your courage and devotion. We will hold you in love forevermore, without separation, even for the briefest moment in your time. You were born from us, and between each incarnation, each experience, you will be returned to us so that you shall never forget the love of Oneness."

Now the Holy Father and Holy Mother are merged into Oneness and they are speaking as a single voice. They say that when they use the term, God, it means Oneness; it means All That Is. They say, in their combined voice, "Child of God, mercy and love be unto you. Daughter of God, and of the Holy Mother and Holy Father, and of the Elohim, and of the planets and stars and galaxies, and of all of Creation, be one with yourself and with each other, as we are with you. Son of God, your mission and glory are great as you and the daughter seek refuge in the physical world in order to serve and bring the Truth that we are One to all of Creation. You will remember when it is time to remember. You will forget and go into unconscious dreams when it is time to be unconscious and dream. And you will always be reawakened. You will always be impulsed with the light and sound and colors of our love, and we will know you by the colors in your heart. You cannot be lost to us, for we have formed you into the spirits and the souls and the bodies that you are becoming. In death and resurrection, in enlightenment and confusion, you are always seen and loved and will never lose anything of what you are. It is impossible. As you go forth now, back through the spirals of Creation, to your destination, always remember that you are part of everything; and that a spark of consciousness of all things is in each of you. When you return, you will be more than you are now. It is impossible for you to ever be less, as each experience will make you more. And through you, we become more as well. Our relationship is mutual, for as you experience and know, as you awaken and slumber, all of us experience it through you, who are the creators and the Creation. You are a projection of us. Never forget that, my beloveds."

At this point we are being drawn into the bodies of the Holy Mother and the Holy Father as if they are kundalini spirals, entwined around each other. When they are merged in union, they become clockwise and counterclockwise spirals wrapping around each other. I am experiencing the union of Christ and the counterpart we think of as the 144,000. It is like two brilliant lights coming together as one light. As this occurs we blend with the Holy Mother and the Holy Father and we are propulsed through the dual sacred spiral of their united existence. As we blend with them we experience ourselves as the One moving through them at the same time. I am going to be quiet and just feel that. It feels like falling through this glorious double helix of light and joy . . .

That was fast. We are being merged with the star Sirius again, only we already feel like more than when we were here before. We are at a point now where the merkabahs of the individual souls are being activated within Sirius and a beam of bright light is being sent into each of us. There are many different geometric shapes that are being shot through us with lasers of light. It is happening to all of us at the same moment, but it feels very individualized. It has to do with preparing our souls to be able to stay in form. I can feel how this tetrahedron that holds the soul is really key to holding us in the third dimension, just as it is doing here in the sixth.

I hear a humming sound, sonarlike, like the sound of the whales. From what sounds very far in the distance, I hear the voice of the Holy

Father saying, "Ancient brother awaken. Ancient sister, be free. Life awaits you. In glory, embrace the human self. While always remembering that you are more, while loving each part of yourself, remember you have chosen this. Remember that you have chosen and that you are free. Never feel sorry for your choice. You will always become more." Now I feel the merkabah around me and we are inside a huge dolphin body. It is like the form of our oversoul. We are being carried inside of dolphin spirit bodies now. Their bodies are almost as long as the whole star is wide. There are two of them, swimming side by side, one carrying Christ and one carrying the 144,000 individual souls. We are being taken to the Pleiades. As we reach the Pleiades, the dolphins open their bodies to spit us out and we are being birthed. We are in our merkabahs, but we just look like these silvery-blue-white balls of light. I feel myself as one of the individuated balls of light now. I have just moved into Alcyone. As I spiral through the center of Alcyone, my merkabah is being encoded. In the center, I stay in one point for awhile, still spinning in place inside that one point. As I spin I pick up energy from Alcyone. I keep hearing words that I cannot translate and I know my soul is being encoded.

I just popped through the other side of Alcyone and I am moving down to the next star of the Pleiades. This one is very sweet. We are still spinning in the same movement, but it is in slow motion and feels very watery, very feminine, and extremely gentle. I stop again at the center. This star is blue, whereas Alcyone was golden and white. There are encodings coming into us as we spin in the center of the star.

Suddenly I am shot down and through to the next star. This one is a double helix. Between each star there is also a double helix, like the kundalini channels. We spin through those pathways and now I am at the center of this star. I am sensing a pale orange color. It is like a white light but with a pale orange color to it, and it feels very stimulating. I sense the encodings here and they feel almost warrior- or warrioresslike, but in a positive sense. It feels like a sentinel on hold awaiting his orders: very alert, very awake, but without an agenda.

Quickly we spin down to the next star. As I enter this one, it is a periwinkle color. But when we are in the center, it is a golden-white color. Oh, I like this one. There are waves of music, like the rhythm of ocean waves, but musical. There is a lot of joy here. I spin around to different places within the inner cavity of this star instead of staying in one place. I am ricocheting off different points into certain configurations. I see now that my movements have traced a holographic diamond shape inside, like two four-sided pyramids with the bases joined together. It is another type of merkabah shape. There are movement, color, and light, and yet I feel like a tiny ball inside of it all being bounced around from one place to another without resistance. The energy of this place is that of deep surrender.

I am moving down now, through the spiraling pathway to the center of the next star. As we approach it, it actually looks multicolored on the outside. One side of it looks yellow-white; one area looks reddish-white. And the other side is blue-white, slightly purple-blue. There is a point where the three colors meet, and that is where I enter to go through the center. Inside it is dark. It feels like the void. There is no light in here other than my own sense of myself as light. It feels very womblike. I definitely sense my energy being downstepped in this one. The encodings coming into my soul seem to have to do with knowing how to be in that sacred place of the void. It feels like deep, dreamless sleep. This is affecting me in my throat chakra and stimulating some clearing in my physical body. Moving out of this one is like moving out of quicksand: very slow and thick feeling, but not in a negative way. It does not feel counter-productive, it just feels denser.

Now I am moving down to the next star. This one is ruby-red from the outside, and inside as well. It is very warm and reminds me of a female second chakra. There is a profoundly fecund feeling. My soul is not being encoded in this one. Instead a blending is taking place in which I am picking up creation energy. Gentle spirals of red and white light move through me and impulse me. This place is reminiscent of a female when she opens herself totally in sexual surrender to a partner. It also reminds me a little of how I feel on the first day of my period: very full, heavy with gravity, fecund, and ripe.

There is one more star, and as I move through a purple light field I experience the sensation of joyful anticipation. All I see is purple, but somehow I sense gold light too. Yet there is purple emanating from it everywhere. I am being spun around in different directions inside this star. The joyful anticipation is mixing with my own energy. If I had cells, it would be going into my cells; that is how completely I feel saturated by this energy.

As I leave this last Pleiadian star I move through the Sun, and then through this entire solar ring. It feels really good, so warm and loving. Entering the Sun is like entering the gentlest, sweetest love imaginable. Inside the Sun I see the spiraling form of the Milky Way. I move directly into that, and my soul goes through each of the arms of the spiral, counterclockwise. The microcosm of the Milky Way is spinning clockwise inside the Sun, but my soul enters it and goes around counterclockwise to each of the arms of the Milky Way, and then right through the center of it. When I come out through the other side I am once again in the Sun. Then I spiral through this microcosmic Milky Way again. As I continue spiraling in and out between the Milky Way and the Sun, I am weaving a figure-eight pattern within the Sun. It is not exactly a figure eight. It is the same type of spiral that the Milky Way moves in around the Central Sun. (See illustration 6 on page 66.) All of this spiraling has formed a tunnel inside the Sun and my soul is moving through that coiled tunnel. When I come out the other side, I am still in the Sun, but spinning around the outer perimeter. I am weaving circles around the outer edges of the Sun. And then suddenly I am at the center of the Sun again. My soul feels like a small sun within the Sun and I am inside the body of the being I know as Merlin. I am aware of my own greater self. This is really nice: I can feel my soul inside the Sun and I also feel myself as the Goddess Erotica blended in around my soul and with the Sun. As the Goddess Erotica I am saying to the soul, "This is your father." And the Goddess Erotica and Merlin begin to move in an undulating pattern together. I can feel their union and I am in the center of it. I am moving back and forth, from her heart into his heart, down through his penis, up into her vagina, up through her womb and back into her heart again. I just continue moving in that circular pattern. My soul feels all of their sexual energy and all of their love, adoration, and surrender. As the two of them blend together around the Sun, with me inside them, together they are loving the galaxy. I can feel the Milky Way expanding within them. And as they make love it feels as though the Milky Way were

6. The figure-8 spiral orbits of the Milky Way around the Great Central Sun

getting bigger and bigger. I am traveling through his penis, which is like a long passageway now; and it is full of stars. I am riding one of those stars and spinning. I am experiencing a lot of joy and love and the bubbling cauldron feeling of creation.

I am being hurled down through the gateway, which is at the tip of his penis. Entering the gateway of her cervix, right up into her womb, I move on. In the womb, I am dreaming all the lives I am ever going to live. It is not like I am dreaming them; Merlin and the Goddess are still blended together and they are sharing the dream of the future and dreaming it backward through time. As they dream it backward through time and space, I dream it forward. These dreams form the equivalent of the spiraling aura of my soul. There is a point in the spiral where an explosion of light occurs. This is the period on Earth when Christ is born and we all come through the sacred spiral together again, as we did for the birthing of our souls. It shows up in my spiraling aura of lifetimes like a huge burst of light.

As the dream of all my lifetimes is completed, a beam of white light engulfs me and I begin to fall into the atmosphere of this solar ring, through the Sun, to my first incarnation. For all of us in this same oversoul, our first incarnations, interestingly enough, are into light bodies, and our greater individual selves have already manifested in the fourth dimension. We are going to precipitate our first bodies by downstepping our vibrational frequencies instead of coming in through physical birth. I see and feel that very clearly. I see all of these fourth-dimensional beings who have human-looking shapes, and they are in the fifth dimension at the same time. We are going to merge with them at the sixth-dimensional level and go down from the sixth dimension together.

Hermes is impulsing my consciousness back into the Sun again now where my soul's future dream continues. I see myself moving through the Sun, out through all of the planets in this solar ring, and back through the Pleiades, starting at the last one first and moving all the way out to Alcyone. I see myself moving back into Sirius, and at that point I see all of the Elohim, holding us within their consciousness. I am dissolving into pure light again, and moving through the equivalent of the chakras of the Goddess Erotica and then through the galaxies and then through the bigger being, the Elohim Goddess who holds all of the thirteen galaxies. As I move in my pure light form, I disperse all of the energy and information I have collected in all of my lifetimes. As I go through each of the Elohim Goddess's chakras, starting from below her feet and moving up, I move through each one of the galaxies at the same time, leaving a little of my experience in each one. In the galaxy that is the equivalent of her second chakra, I leave whatever is relative to the Milky Way. In her heart chakra, I leave anything relative to the heart. By the time I move through all of her chakras, my soul has been dispersed into her and is just part of her own experience and knowing. Then I become even bigger than the Goddess, as I blend into Oneness with the Holy Mother. I feel her union with the Holy Father spinning me back into Oneness with All That Is. And the collective voice of Oneness says, "From whence you come, so do you return. The end is the beginning and the beginning is the end. And we are One." It seems so simple. I hear the voice of the Holy Father saying, "This experience exists now within your soul, just as it exists beyond it, when you are complete. So from the Oneness simply remember your body and soul. Your soul is a microcosm of the Oneness of All That Is. Move into that beating heart, into your soul now." And I automatically begin to move inward to my soul again.

My physical body feels like a microcosm of the body of the Elohim Goddess who holds the thirteen galaxies within her. Now I am getting smaller, and becoming the body of the Goddess Quan Yin who holds Andromeda and the Milky Way only, and now just the Milky Way. I am becoming smaller still and moving through the place called Pleidos galaxy, then through the gateway star in Sagittarius. Now I am holding Sirius and the Pleiades within my form, and now only the Pleiades. Beyond that I am smaller still and hold only this solar ring, and the Sun is my heart and soul. At this last stage I am holding only the Sun; and that is my gateway back into my own soul.

I am experiencing my whole soul as if it were around me as well as inside me at the same time. I feel like I am inside the Sun and I can see and feel the sparkliness of my own merkabah around my body. I need to stop at this point and just feel my soul as a part of me, not as all of who I am. As this happens I know am ready to end this session.

The main point I would like to make about the information in this chapter—and in the chapters that preceded it—is that the first half of this book is intended to give you an understanding of just how multidimensional we truly are. We are like multifaceted jewels, each facet containing entire worlds within itself. Each world is to be explored fully and to completion. And when all of the facets are together and experienced as one, a great and valuable treasure is yours for the keeping.

I would also like to add that I have been having visions of Christ and Mary Magdalene lately. In these visions they birthed twins, a male and a female. After this hypnosis session it makes sense. I see the purpose of the divine twins being the personification of the male Christ and the female Christ selves.

Chapter 4

AN-RA
SPEAKS

A t this time I would like to introduce you to a member of the
Pleiadian Archangelic Tribes of the Light from the An-Ra Tribe.
You may recall that the An-Ras have emerald green light bodies
and hold the energy of divine compassion. This particular An-Ra
appears to me in a humanlike form with her archangelic form superimposed around and above her. Her humanlike form has honey-
golden, thick curly hair and brilliant emerald-green eyes. She is
dressed in all white with pink and white ribbon ties in her hair and on
her dress. Her dress is long and flowing and similar to sheer soft linen
that is worn in layers. An-Ra has chosen to project a human image
because it enables her to downstep the frequencies of which she speaks
through her own image to me in a more tactile and lucid manner.

An-Ra speaks:

Beloveds, I am most grateful for the opportunity to speak to you
through Amorah at this time and to bring you a wondrous story of the
Creation, sexuality, and the awakening of your soul to its full potential and glory. You see, in truth, it is impossible to speak thoroughly
about any of these three subjects without speaking of all three. The
beauty of the Creation is that it involved all aspects of existence, as
symbolized microcosmically by your own chakra system. Your crown
chakra is your most direct connection to God/Goddess/All That Is,
which I prefer to call Oneness. Through this chakra you commune
with Oneness, become Oneness, and receive divine understanding of
yourself and all of existence. Your third eye enables you to see both
inside yourself and beyond yourself. You see and interpret through
this sacred center of divine awareness and vision. Your throat chakra
is your center of self-expression and creativity. It allows you to

71

7. Pleiadian Archangel An-Ra projecting a human-shaped lightbody for the purpose of communication

express and share your truths and inspiration with others. Your heart chakra is the seat of your glorious soul through which you are able to bring your spirit's essence into form in the third dimension. Love is the nature of your spirit and the source of all divine wisdom, knowing, and compassion, which are attributes of your heart center.

Your solar plexus chakra is your center of divine will and surrender to right action. By surrendering your will to the will of your own Higher Self and to Oneness, you act, serve, and do in the world with and for others. Your sacral chakra is the seat of all of your feelings, your sensuality, and your sexuality. Its natural expression is union with loved ones and with Oneness, and it is through this sacred center that you achieve communion between body, soul, and Oneness. The chakra at the base of your spine is your center of grounding, physical existence, and instincts. The safety, security, health, and vitality of your physical body, temple for your soul and spirit, are dependent on a well-functioning and happy first chakra.

There are many more functions for each chakra than I have named, and yet my intent is to speak of the chakras in terms of their microcosmic symbolism of the macrocosm relative to Creation. On illustration 8 on page 74, you will notice that each chakra is shown not only with key words as mentioned above, but also with a geometric symbol that represents its highest purpose. These symbols are part of sixth-dimensional language. They not only represent the chakras themselves, but they are the geometric signatures through which the chakras and body parts they represent are literally held together in form. In all of third-dimensional Creation, there is a connection to, and reciprocal relationship with, all nine dimensions of individuation. In other words, you could not exist without being birthed through the tenth dimension and held together by dimensions one through nine. And within all of those dimensions the common ingredient is love.

Love is like the egg that holds the cake batter together and creates the synergy between all ingredients. Your oversoul, which is tenth-dimensional, is like the baker. The baker has a desire to bake a cake. The memory of flavors, scenes of sharing food joyfully with others in the past, and perhaps hunger, all create a desire on the part of the baker to make a cake. Tenth-dimensionally speaking this translates into desire for experience, self-love, and love of others. From these

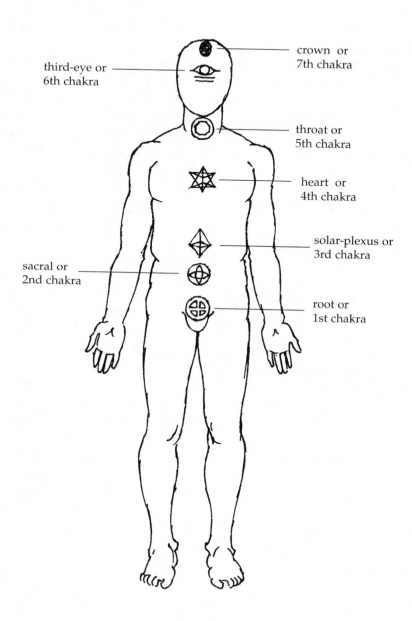

8. An-Ra's symbols for human chakras

three desires, union occurs, and from that union something is created. The desire combined with the love and energy from the experience of union sends light and energy to the ninth dimension. The light is refracted through the diamondlike prism of the ninth dimension and translates into color in the eighth dimension. With the baker, this part of the creation experience takes place when the idea, in the seventh chakra, is created by the desire—on the tenth-dimensional level. Then the desire and idea become a vision of what is needed to make the cake. The ingredients are the colors in the eighth dimension combined with the mineral and plant ingredients from the first and second dimensions. So at this stage the creator, or baker, begins to work from the upper dimensions down and the lower dimensions upward simultaneously.

Next, dimensionally speaking, sound and color begin to create patterns and waves. The baker, through the movements of gathering ingredients and blending thoughts and vision—the recipe—with the ingredients, begins to impulse the cake to take form. The form is sixth-dimensional, the realm of sacred geometry. At this level the synergy of the geometric forms of the flour, baking soda, sweetener, liquids, and eggs combines, creating a new form that is unlike the individual ingredients in appearance yet contains them all. This is when the cake is poured into the pan and molded into a new shape, which in the context of our metaphoric story, is fifth-dimensional. The fourth dimension is where the cake bakes and takes on the qualities, nature, and risen, baked form that is birthed into the third dimension when the baker takes it out of the oven.

All of what exists in the third dimension is both created and held together by this basic recipe, with its many optional ingredients that create variations on the theme. A little cinnamon and nutmeg create spice cake; a certain blending of red, green, and yellow create a person with black or light skin depending on the proportions and shades of each color. A loaf pan as opposed to cupcake molds determines the size and shape of the cooked batter; an elongated triangle versus a squat or equilateral one determines whether the person is lanky, chunky, or what you consider to be balanced. We see people simply as variations on a theme that make existence much more exciting, just like different shapes and flavors of cake are to you. And, what holds it all together is the love with which they were made.

Have you ever experienced indigestion or emotional disturbance from eating food that was prepared by someone who was angry or did not want to be baking? Needless to say, because of the nature of your birth experience coming through your mother's womb, the energy with which you were created, or conceived, will determine greatly your experience of yourself. If your mother felt ashamed of having sex, even with her husband, and your father was having pornographic fantasies instead of loving your mother and being present with her, these energies were imprinted on your soul as you entered your body at birth. Your initial imprint of male/female relationships, your own inner male and female aspects, and your relationship to your mother and father and to the world all come from the energy between your parents at the moment of conception. Was your mother relieved that your father was finally through? Did she feel like weeping but held the tears back instead? Or did she fake an orgasm in order to have a sense of secret power over him? Did your father roll over, mumble good night, and try not to look at your mother so he could hold onto his pretend fantasy in which the porno damsel was swept off her feet by his amorous and ardent lovemaking? Did he resent your mother for not responding that way? Or did he hold a double standard of thinking it vile for a woman to enjoy sex, while secretly fantasizing himself as an incredible lover that no woman could resist?

Your third-dimensional world is very sick today and sexual dysfunctions are the chief source of the problem. Without healthy sexual attitudes and experiences, it is impossible to give birth to awakened, fully healthy children. Without male and female equality, love, adoration for one another, trust, respect, and shared innocence, full communion with Oneness is impossible—as are peace, freedom, and joy. The lust-seduction control games; sexual attitudes of distrust, shame, lovelessness, and separation; and lack of spiritual presence during intercourse are literally destroying your soul's ability to experience wholeness and health in the third dimension. You see, your soul is directly impulsed by *all* sexual experiences whether loving and satisfying, or otherwise. *If you are on a spiritual path, meditating regularly,*

clearing your emotions, healing your past lives, and seeing the finest of heal-
ers, you still will not be able to attain a satisfactory level of spiritual aware-
ness and wholeness if your sexual energy is not moving freely, fully, and
lovingly through your body and soul. You need not have a partner in
order to experience this, but your gendered relationships, both internal and external, must be balanced and healthy.

As you probably derived from reading Amorah's own regressed
creation experiences in the first three chapters, what you call sexual
energy or sexual expression is the stuff of which existence is both
made and sustained. When a couple in love experiences total surrender one to the other during a heightened sexual experience, they
become blended into a single consciousness containing equal parts
male and female. Just as the original experience of Oneness was "I
am," and just as that experience led to Oneness individuating its own
male and female halves, then blending them into Oneness again, so is
the sacred function of your sexuality intended to bring about the
same ecstasy and experience of Oneness. The female vulva is a geometric gateway to the cosmos. The vagina is the spiraling passageway through which a person must travel in order to enter the womb,
which is the microcosm of the egg of existence. As the egg is
"hatched," or fully activated, energy and consciousness move
directly through another spiraling tunnel or passageway to the
woman's soul. From the woman's soul the energy and light of love
are sent out in waves back to her partner and through existence
simultaneously. These waves are like ripples on water, only holographic. They are like bubbles expanding in wavelike motion as
opposed to ripples on a flat surface. These waves create a blending of
the soul of the woman and her partner. The love and ecstasy created
by their union are transmitted through a spiral passageway down
through the male's body into his prostate which further excites his
penis to transmit the love, adoration, and joy energies passionately
into the woman's vagina. This cycle is repeated in a continuum once
both the male and female have totally surrendered to giving and
receiving love and relinquishing all control. The two become a microcosm of the macrocosm of existence. They spin the galaxies together,
hold planets in form, spiritually activate one another's souls and spir-

its through the dimensions, and heal each other and all of existence—and all while having a great time! Sound easy? Ideally yes. But your world has made it very complicated.

Trust and respect have been so long lost that you spend more time testing one another, making each other prove yourselves, finding reasons to doubt each other, and vying for control than you do creating and enjoying your love relationships. And these things you call love relationships are often little more than addictive pain patterns being acted out. Love does not need to possess, control, degrade, withhold, prove anything, distrust, or conquer. Love simply loves. It flows. It is uninhibited, uncontrived, natural, innocent, and spontaneous. And while discernment is needed in the selection of a partner, it need not prohibit you from loving everyone. Did you know that humans are terrified of feeling the totality of unconditional love? You have been taught to restrain yourselves lest you make fools of yourselves. You have been taught that it is impossible to love fully without hurting if the other person does not return your love and promise to stay forever. Without a 100 percent guarantee that you will not "lose," you hold back—a little or a lot. It does not really matter how much. The point is that the flow has been dammed and therefore controlled.

What if love were only possible by forfeiting all guarantees? What if love could only exist in the presence of surrender? What if there were no such thing as loss, only change? What if you had to let go before the other person did without knowing whether he or she would ever let go or not? You would risk disappointment; but that is all. If you have healthy self-esteem and self-love, the person you love cannot devastate or humiliate you. *He or she cannot make you feel unworthy; only you can!* The object of love is not to win persons over, break through their barriers, make them need or desire you, or make sure you don't lose. The object of love is to love, to cherish, to honor, to adore, to respect, to never harm, to appreciate and never depreciate another. You can even love without objectification. Have you ever awakened on an overcast day with no one around and simply felt love for no apparent reason? You were not thinking of anyone, focusing on self-love, or experiencing the beauty of nature. Everything around was quiet and maybe even boring or drab by *normal* standards. And yet you felt love instead of boredom or drabness. This is the nature of your true being, your soul, your spirit.

To experience love for no apparent reason is a great sign that you are nearing completion of your trials and karmic pain. It is the way home to your true self. In the meantime, allowing yourself to objectify love is a step in the right direction. To fill your life with friends and/or a partner who naturally inspire you to love is a wonderful thing. To surround yourself with sacred objects of beauty, to live in a place you enjoy, to be in nature regularly, to do what you really like to do, are all important ingredients in life that can help you become a more loving person. To be in relationships with people with whom you do not resonate in order to *try to learn* to love them is not the quickest way to work out your karma. It may show you your patterns, at best. But to remain in a relationship that is all struggle and resistance can harm both you and your partner. Everyone, and all of Creation, deserves to be loved and adored. If you are with someone whom you cannot love and adore with all your heart, it will serve you both more to separate than to remain together. I am not speaking of a strong, loving relationship that temporarily goes through a rough period. I am speaking of relationships in which one or both of the people involved are in resistance and unhappiness more often than not—once the honeymoon phase is over. You see, when the honeymoon phase ends, relationships are intended to deepen. The honeymoon may be fun and inspirational, but it does not contain the depth that long term loving, supportive relationships do.

When the love, trust, and surrender between two people in love are strong, either or both partners can go through difficult times of emotional healing, job stress, or problems with friends and other family members without affecting the bond in the relationship. If you are in a relationship with someone you love and about whom you deeply care, to support them in the rough times as well as the easy times will be natural and fulfilling. If you are, however, in a relationship chiefly because the other person makes you feel good about yourself, fulfills your sexual fantasies, and makes life better for you, then when your partner is experiencing pain or difficulty you will feel abandoned, neglected, and unhappy and you will probably blame your partner for it. In order for a relationship to have any chance of bringing about true intimacy and sustainable love, you must deeply care about your partner and his or her life, feelings, and well-being, and be moved to want to give freely and lovingly to your partner. Then when the rougher times come, they need not affect the bond between the two of you. Instead, the challenges will serve to deepen trust, loyalty, caring, and intimacy between you.

This type of relationship foundation is imperative in order to have the relationship augment your spiritual path and that of your partner, and to achieve the type of sexual union that brings about healing and awakening of your soul. The essential nature of the unrestrained soul is tantra, which leads to being in a constant orgasmic state in your whole body. In this state, energy blocks are dissolved, emotions released to flow naturally, and spiritual experience of love and Oneness is the norm. And it is what you and Earth most desperately need at this time. It is also what you most truly long for and fear. Why fear? Because it means taking risks, relinquishing ego control, and feeling your most guarded buried emotions. You cannot sustain feeling the depths of love without feeling all of your other emotions as well. Have you not noticed that when you have a very high spiritual experience, or loving that is blending and sharing with another, that it is often followed by feelings of less pleasant emotions or negative thoughts? This is because any time you raise your frequency beyond what it was previously, anything in you that is incapable of maintaining that higher frequency is stimulated to let go. For instance, you and your lover have an experience during lovemaking in which you both let go and feel as if you become one beating heart. The love is just incredible—beyond what you have ever experienced before. For hours you are radiant together, overflowing in love and adoration, gratitude and bliss. Then one or the other of you begins to feel fear or irritation. The thoughts are unleashed: "If I trust this person too much I'll end up getting hurt just like I always have," or "Oh my God, I could get too dependent on this. I should just leave while I still can, and be alone. I have to find it all within," or "Relationships and spirituality cannot coexist without one or the other suffering or being given up." You start to suspect the person, who is sitting there lovingly smiling at you, of having ulterior motives and trying to control you. You label it codependent and run for your life, narrowly escaping that one. Whew!

The worst thing is: You believe the negative voices and interpret the painful emotions as a sign that something is wrong. The truth is: You are experiencing the normal process of evolution. You are being given an opportunity to eliminate that which no longer serves your awakening and growth. If you identify with it when it comes up for release, you miss a great opportunity and bury yourself even deeper in illusions of separation and the need to hold on to distrust and control. So if anyone loves you "too much" he or she becomes automatically suspect and worthy of your resistance. It is time now to let go of all of these self-defeating agendas and to allow love to flow in your life again. How? By being very honest with yourself, examining your repetitive patterns, and opening to full sexual potency and the resultant healing of your soul.

We have asked Amorah to bring you this next level of Pleiadian Lightwork for this purpose. The exercises in Section II of this book will assist you in your ongoing process of self-discovery and movement toward mastery. As always, our intention is to make the process as loving, effective, and gracious as possible while facilitating a deepening within yourself with yourself, others, and Oneness. Take the time to fully experience each exercise prior to moving on to the next. Each is designed to build upon the previous ones, creating a gradual and potent awakening of your Ka's interaction with your Ba. Ecstatic tantric love is the only way to maintain that link permanently. So make a commitment to give up control and resistance now, and have a wonderful time enjoying the processes.

So-la-re-en-lo,
(With great love and devotion)

An-Ra
member of the Pleiadian Archangelic Tribes of the Light,
members of the Pleiadian Emissaries of Light,
who are guardians of this solar ring
and members of the Galactic Federation of Light
of the Great Central Sun

Part 2

PLEIADIAN LIGHTWORK LEVEL II

Dolphin Tantra and Your Ba

Chapter 5

THE SIRIUS CONNECTION

Throughout the rest of this book, you will be working with a group of Light Beings called the Sirian Archangelic League of the Light who will assist you in various processes. Therefore, I would like to tell you a little about them. But first I will share with you the story of how and when I became consciously connected with the Sirians.

My introductory experience with the Sirians, as well as subsequent experiences for several years, was with a group of female beings who simply called themselves the Sirian Sisterhood of the Light. I was deep in meditation in the summer of 1989 at the end of a fast when a female Light Being appeared just above and in front of me and told me that I was being offered a pain-free way of disconnecting from my body and continuing my service to Earth as a higher-dimensional being. In other words, I could consciously leave my body, go through a simple process of disconnecting from it, my body would die, and I would go with her to Sirius where I could continue my spiritual service in behalf of Earth and her people. She told me that I had been a *bodhisattva* on Earth for a long time. (A bodhisattva is a person who has completed his or her personal evolution and enlightenment and then chooses to return to, or remain on, Earth to serve others.) I had completed everything that I was obligated to complete based on my last renewal of my bodhisattva vows. It was time to either renew them on Earth or leave. She then extended her hand to me and asked me if I would like to come with her and observe the work that was being done for Earth from the star Sirius. This way I would know what my alternative to life on Earth was.

I felt this Sister's love and radiance, and reached out for her hand. Instantly, I was above my body. Briefly I turned to look back at it and make sure it was okay, and then we went out through the ceiling and above the house. There were only a few seconds during which I experienced myself en route, then we were suddenly there on Sirius. Numerous female Light Beings were together in a great temple with many pillars and an open roof. Several of the women were clustered around an object that reminded me of a giant telescope. By Earth standards of measure it was about twenty-five feet long with the tubular diameter being around two feet. It was difficult to assess what it was made of or what colors it was because while seeming solid, it was also very etheric and constantly changing in response to the energy input from the Sisters. A beam of intense white light was emitted from the device—which I later learned was actually a cosmic portal—and pointed directly at Earth. This beam of light contained many beautiful qualities of energy: hope, love, compassion, courage, adoration, joy, encouragement, and peace, to name only a few. These energies were transmitted through the beam of light by the Sisters. They would stand in front of the portal and sing beautiful songs, speak loving, encouraging words, or just direct love; and the beam would carry these to Earth and her people.

After I had watched for awhile and was feeling deeply inspired, Bara-Wasu, the Sister who was serving as my liaison, spoke to me again. She told me, "As you can see there is much loving service being done for Earth here. With some of the humans, we work as teachers during their dreamtime, and as guides during their waking consciousness. We also direct energies to Earth herself to keep the Goddess alive and connected to Earth. There are sacred sisterhood groups on Earth who work directly with us for this purpose as well. You are one of those sisters. Now it is time for you to choose whether to remain in service on Earth in human form, or whether to rejoin us here."

I felt bewildered about what to base my decision upon. Much of my life I had wanted to escape from Earth and "go home." I had felt alien to the unconsciousness, abuse, denial, superficialness, falseness, and pain that I experienced there. Earth had been a lonely place for me for a long time. I knew there was so much more that was possible to share with others, but rarely had experienced more than fleeting moments of depth and realness with humans. Yes, I had wanted to leave Earth; and yet, that had been changing. As my own healing went deeper, I had begun to feel more dedication to teaching and doing healing work. I wanted to give in ways that my fellow humans were capable of receiving. As I stood there in that glorious place with my comrades, I felt very much at home, and yet pulled to go back to Earth at the same time.

As I deliberated, Bara-Wasu took my hand and we were almost immediately above my home, dropping down through the roof and ceiling, over my body which remained perfectly still, barely breathing, in a cross-legged position. I looked at my body and at Bara-Wasu. Bara-Wasu showed me how to disconnect from my body and allow it to painlessly die if I wished to do so. I hugged her, thanked her, and told her that because I did not know what to base my decision on that I must go back into it. I wanted to be certain that if I chose to leave, it was truly in the highest good and based on love, not subconscious escapism motivating that choice. As she released my hand, she squeezed it and said, "We'll be back in three months for your decision. And the decision is yours. There is no right or wrong."

As Bara-Wasu released my hand, I lovingly and slowly descended into my body. Several minutes of deep breathing and slow gentle movement ensued. I could barely move. My body felt stiff and foreign, and yet I tenderly brought myself into it as deeply as I could before finally standing and moving around the room. After a few minutes I was reasonably "back to myself" again.

My first thought as I stood to walk around the room was, "I have to read about women's initiations." I did not know of any books on the subject so I started asking everyone I knew if they knew anything about the subject or about bodhisattva vows. After quite a process of investigation I was loaned a book by Alice Bailey about initiations that are given when a being has completed all karma and/or service on Earth. The page to which I opened the book told me that the most commonly chosen next step was service of some type on Sirius. It almost seemed as though the rest of the information was insignificant. That confirmation was all I needed.

My connections with the Earth-based sisterhood had been strong for several years. These connections became more frequent and much more dynamic both in sleep and while awake, and definitely amped up my spiritual life and healing.

When three months had passed, Bara-Wasu and two other Sirian Sisters arrived to ask for my answer. I was sitting in a rocking chair in front of my fireplace, rocking and energetically scanning my housemate's newborn daughter. We had delivered her at home only a few hours before. When I became aware of my etheric visitors I told them, "I know that I, like everyone else, am expendable here. I know that if I choose to leave that Earth would never notice my absence. And I know how beautiful serving on Sirius would be. The work there is crucial. And yet there are so many on Earth who are blocked from receiving the higher-dimensional love and assistance that is offered. Most are incapable of learning what they need to learn from guides and etheric helpers. Human spiritual teachers and healers are needed to serve here for those who need direct assistance. And because I am capable of giving that, I want to stay." Before leaving they let me know they would return to check on me from time to time and give me an opportunity to change my mind or to renew my bodhisattva vows and remain on Earth. I felt their love as they disappeared from the room. I continued rocking and singing to the baby.

Over the years my connection with Sirius remained mostly with the Sisterhood but it expanded to include the etheric dolphins as well. The Sirian Archangelic League of the Light—whom I will refer to as the Sirian Archangels—also worked with me through my connection with the Pleiadians and yet I had no name for them or direct one-on-one contact until after the Ka teachings were given to me in 1993. They remained in the background most of the time; and yet they were frequently with me.

In early 1995 when I had reached a certain level of Ka activation and cellular clearing, the Sirian Archangels began to work with me directly on my sacred geometry. They worked with chakras, organs, glands, and within my aura and extended hologram. They taught me about the nature of the interdependence between the first through sixth dimensions. Without the lower five dimensions, God/Goddess/All That Is would have no context for sequential experience and exploration.

9. Amorah rocking the newborn as Sirian angels visit

The higher-dimensional beings are able to experience much beauty and pleasure by virtue of the existence of the lower dimensions. They would not be complete without us, and without the fourth- and fifth-dimensional beings to translate the energies between them and us. Just as we are needed to energize, awaken, evolve, and protect the first and second dimensions, the Sirians and Pleiadians are needed to energize, awaken, evolve, and protect us. Beyond the sixth dimension, all the way back to Oneness, each dimension is interdependent upon all others. We are, after all, part of the same original consciousness that first said, "I am." We are inseparable. It is a farce to see the third dimension as a less-than reality from which to escape. We are here to be the divine links through which all dimensions are connected simultaneously, to re-become the self that is 144,000 in One.

The Sirian Archangels are the bridge between the upper and lower dimensions through which this happens in this solar ring. They are the sacred translators of higher-dimensional sound, color, thoughts, and love into sacred geometric forms through which all of existence in the lower five dimensions is created. They also maintain the patternings and sacred geometry that hold the lower dimensions in place. Beings on the first- through fifth-dimensional levels have form only because of the geometric constructs created on the sixth-dimensional level. Humans and astral beings can distort their own geometry through identification with illusion, trauma, chemical mutation, and black magic. However, the Sirians always hold the highest and truest potential ready for actualization as humans evolve.

There are consciousnesses in the lower dimensions who through greed, hate, power hunger, or other lower vices have deliberately severed their connections to the higher dimensions. From the fifth dimension and down, there are both dark and light realms. In these realms, evolution of consciousness through experience and choices based on free will are the main affairs. Some beings become so addicted to power, sensation, control, lust, and greed, or so lost in their own illusions, that they begin to fight evolution and Light. The battles between Dark and Light, the Satanic realms and the Goddess, are ongoing distractions if you allow them to be. However, through right action, clearing of your own negative thoughts and vices, aligning with your Higher Self in the Light, and becoming impeccable, you can transcend the illusionary and limited aspects of the lower dimensions and become the divine consciousness in your physical temple (body) through which all realms are aligned with, and connected in, Divine Truth and Love.

The closer you come to achieving this goal, the more the Pleiadians, and then the Sirians, are able to assist you. You will notice that when the Sirians are included in exercises throughout this book, it has to do with bringing in Christ consciousness, or sacred geometry, or transcending evolution and becoming what you have sought to be. Sirius is the home of Christ consciousness, Melchizedek consciousness, and the dolphins for this arm of the Milky Way. These particular Sirian Archangels have many functions within our realm as well as on a galactic level. They are members of the Galactic Federation of Light and overseers of the evolutionary development in this solar ring.

The Sirian Archangels exist at the sixth-dimensional level, which is beyond pollution by dark and illusionary beings. However, there are Sirians who have fallen into the lure of the fifth-dimensional dark control realms. So when calling upon the Sirians for assistance, it is important to ask that only those who are of the Light may work with you. Calling upon the Sirian Archangelic League of the Light specifically is another way of assuring your connection with higher Light Beings. These are the ones you will work with in this book.

These Sirian Archangels work very closely with the Pleiadian Emissaries of Light. The latter are operating from the upper fifth-dimensional level and function as the teachers and guides for humans to help us prepare for reuniting with our Christ Selves, and for working with the Sirians directly. For instance, if the Sirian Archangels wish to help you restructure the sacred geometry of your brain patternings, the Pleiadians will first assist you in your Ka activation, soul clearing, clearing of limited thoughts and beliefs, connecting with your Higher Self, and any other prerequisite clearings and activations that are needed. Then the Sirian Archangels step in and do the final alignment while the Pleiadians hold the space from the fifth dimension and down. The cooperation and harmony between the Pleiadians and Sirians is a very beautiful example of how we are to become.

There is no competition or "better than/less than" because one group is on a higher dimension than the other. It is recognized that all parts of existence, and all beings, are of equal value.

Meeting the Sirian Archangels

You will be meeting the Sirian Archangels in the exercise that follows, and then invoking the Evolutionary Cone of Light. This cone is shaped like, and positioned the same as, the Interdimensional Cone of Light that was introduced in *The Pleiadian Workbook*. However, its function is different. The Evolutionary Cone of Light aligns you with your highest spiritual evolutionary potential in any given moment. It can also draw situations and people into your life that will give you the opportunity to make choices based on how much you have cleared and evolved. This cone can challenge you by helping you get in touch with where you still "hold on" to limitations and illusions. It can also help you make quantum leaps into your next evolutionary step when you are willing and ready. And at every stage in between those two extremes, it is a gentle and loving pull toward your next-highest vibrational frequency, toward which you are already moving. After the Evolutionary Cone of Light is brought in and you have experienced its effect, you will do a Sacred Geometry Chamber of Light during which the Sirians will begin the work of realigning and repatterning the geometry of your body, aura, and hologram at whatever level is appropriate for you at this time.

Now it is time to meet the Sirian Archangelic League of the Light and to experience the Evolutionary Cone of Light and the Sacred Geometry Chamber of Light.

1. Sit or lie comfortably.

2. Ground yourself and pull in your aura, if needed.

3. Invoke your Higher Self to activate your silver cord and fill your tube of light. When this is done, continue.

4. Invoke the Sirian Archangelic League of the Light to join you.

5. Tell the Sirians that you would like them to work with you on your further Ka activation and on your spiritual growth and evolution in general. Tell them anything else you would like to at this time.

6. Ask the Sirians to put an Evolutionary Cone of Light above you.

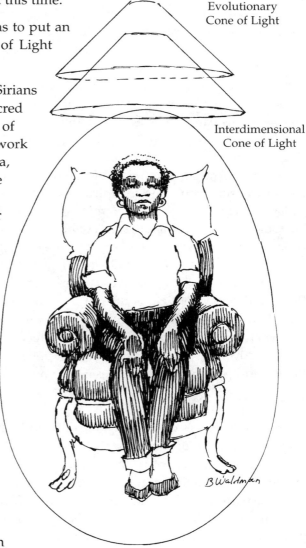

Evolutionary Cone of Light

Interdimensional Cone of Light

7. Next ask the Sirians to place you in a Sacred Geometry Chamber of Light. Ask them to work with your body, aura, and hologram in the realignment and repatterning of your sacred geometry to be in affinity with your purpose of becoming a Christ-conscious being upon Earth. Ask them to continue this work beyond this session.

8. Relax and be receptive for an hour to an hour-and-a half while the Sirians work with you.

9. Continue with your day.

Meditator with Interdimensional and Evolutionary Cones of Light above her aura

Meeting Hermes

After I had been working with the Sirian Sisterhood, and eventually the Sirian Archangels, for a few years, I was greeted one day in meditation by a very big Light Being who introduced himself as Hermes, a spokesperson for the Sirian Archangels. Hermes contained images of both male and female that became illumined as he spoke about various subjects. The reason for this is that Hermes is an androgynous being. When appearing as a female only, Leiala is the name used for this being. When appearing in the male form only, Hermes is his name. Hermes is also the name used for this archangel in the androgynous form. I will use the male vernacular when referring to Hermes for the sake of convenience.

When Hermes first appeared I asked if he was the same being as Hermes Trismegistus, ancient spiritual teacher of the Hermetic principles in Greece and in the pyramids of Egypt. He said that Hermes Trismegistus was only a tiny spark of his consciousness who had been reabsorbed into his totality long ago. Hermes Trismegistus was to Archangel Hermes as I am to Quan Yin: just a little piece of her.

Hermes is my teacher about sacred geometry and the Sirian-Pleiadian connection. He is the only Sirian Archangel with whom I have had direct communication, although many others are present during chamber and healing sessions and teachings. He has also guided me during hypnosis sessions as mentioned in Part I of this book. In his androgynous form, Hermes gives you a message at this time.

Hermes speaks:

Beloveds, lovers of the way of Truth and Light, I am here to welcome you to the world in which I live. It is a world of ever-constant love, light, joy, peace, and truth. And yet we are inseparable from your learning process and struggles at the same time. When you hurt, we respond with more love and compassion. When you are angry, we direct understanding toward you. When you are in nature, we hum to you through the wind in the trees, and the sounds of the brooks and rivers. When you look up into the night sky and marvel at the vastness and beauty of space, and of the stars, we impulse your minds and hearts to unite in love and wonder. We celebrate your hunger for divine mind, for unconditional love, for total Truth.

We send you the dolphins to remind you of the ecstatic state in which third-dimensional beings are intended to live. These beautiful beings in dolphin bodies, both physically and etherically, carry the consciousness to which you aspire. They are whole-brained, loving, spontaneous, Christ-conscious beings of Light who are totally dedicated to you and to the successful passage of Earth into the Light.

In these times of chaos and confusion, the complications of life in a modern-day technological society can become overwhelming. It is easy for humans to become so absorbed in keeping up with these technological times and in working for basic survival that you forget about Divine Truth. Truth becomes the details of your daily life, of your emotional responses to life, of your relationships, possessions, families, and friends. And these are all aspects of what we call "relative truth." Relative truth is any idea, understanding, or identification based upon experience—which is ever-changing. Divine Truth is unchangeable. Divine Truth includes the inherent beauty of your being, the fact that you are loving and loved, that all of existence is sacred. These are only examples of Divine Truth, and yet enough to give you the idea of what it is. Relative truth is that you are experiencing anger, that your car will not start, that your cash flow is not as you would like it to be, that someone hurt your feelings or lied to you. It does not mean that within spiritual evolution and growth, these relative truths are unimportant. Certainly you are karmically responsible for maintaining your integrity, for acting impeccably, for loving and being loved. And still it is important to know deep inside that these are all parts of your experience and that you are here expressly for the purpose of having experiences, learning from them, and eventually bringing Divine Truth into every thought, word, and deed.

When you have evolved to the point of accomplishing this, it will be effortless. You will have healed and grown, expanded and become so identified with your own Higher Self of Light that you will naturally and spontaneously do what is right in every moment. As you allow your ego to surrender and become more and more blended with your Higher Self, we can work with you more directly. We love you very much and want to work with you. It gives us great joy to experience your growth and learning process. It inspires us to celebrate and to love you even more as your own beauty becomes more radiantly apparent to you and you unashamedly share it with others. You share it by being it. It is simple. And as the Holy Father has said, "When I look at you I see your beauty, your true inherent beauty. Regardless of the form you have chosen to live in for this lifetime, or the emotional state you are experiencing, or your state of self-esteem, I always see your true beauty. And it is your beauty that inspires me to love you. Yet your ability to receive and feel my love is directly proportional to your ability to feel your own beauty. I am always loving you. And yet, how often do you feel my love? Please learn to experience your own beauty so we can be closer. For when I love you and you feel it, it makes you feel even more beautiful. This inspires me to love you even more, which inspires you to feel loved and therefore, even more beautiful. Your beauty feeds me with your radiance, and I feed you with great love and adoration. This is how it is meant to be."

What the Holy Father says goes for all of us on the higher dimensions. We love to love you. We love to bask in your radiance and be inspired to love even more. And you are valued deeply by us. We want to see you experiencing your own love, beauty, and radiance for your own sake as much as for ours. Never doubt that you are being loved every moment that you exist, and even beyond time. Never doubt that your very existence brings more love and beauty to Earth and to God/Goddess/All That Is. Even when you are not consciously loving, we see and experience your love; for we see your true self, your essence, at all times. We do not forget Divine Truth even when you do. We may see your actions and observe your identification with limitations. But to us these relative truths are nothing more than dreams you are experiencing for the purpose of learning and growing. You are indeed beautiful spirits of love and light living in human costumes, having human experiences.

What I am here to propose to you is that you begin to embrace this way of thinking in your life on Earth. Observe the beauty of the soul and spirit within each person you see, regardless of how they are behaving in the moment. Know the Truth of the sacred purpose for life—your own and others'—as you witness the relative truths of daily life in the third dimension. Treat everyone and everything as sacred and beautiful, for it is true. Be responsible for impeccability in your own life. Do not blame yourself or others when you fall short. And make discerning choices about your closest associates. Seeing Divine Truth in all things and people and transcending blame do not mean that you must keep yourself in painful situations and relationships that are harmful to you. In fact the opposite is true. As you align more completely with Divine Truth, you are responsible for not supporting illusion and harmful actions in others. You do not have a right to blame or judge others. But when you see that persons would harm you, deceive you, or be unsupportive of your spiritual growth and creativity, you must confront the situations directly with communication and/or action.

Tell the persons that what they are doing hurts you. Invite them to communicate their motives to you. If they are unwilling to be in integrity with you, then you must remove yourself from harm's way. Let them know that you choose to live in impeccability and Truth and that you cannot share in these harmful and illusionary ways. Do not become arrogant and superior. Hold compassion for those whose identities have become so aligned with ego reality that they do not experience your beauty or their own. For if they did, it would surely change them. At times people do share deeply with you, and see your essential beauty. They may even allow you to see theirs directly. These times are glorious. And yet there are those whose ego identity is still so strong that even such experiences cannot change them. They may still hurt you, or lie to you, or behave in harmful ways. In these situations, it is difficult for you humans to remain free of blame and resentment. You feel betrayed. You have shared your essence with this person and he or she turned around and harmed you.

Feel your hurt, betrayal, and blame, but even while feeling these emotions know that you are committed to transcending them and coming to forgiveness, understanding, and compassion. The understanding comes from knowing that the experience of shared beauty was genuine, and then having compassion for your friend whose ego identity is still stronger in his or her consciousness than Higher Self identity. Send forgiveness, compassion, and love to that person. Know also that any experience of true essence and beauty is never really lost, even if it appears to be. When the individual has grown more spiritually and become stronger in Divine Truth, the reference points experienced previously are there as teachers and guides to assist the person in becoming even more real and impeccable. If a person in your life is not choosing to be responsible and to change, remove yourself from harm's way to what ever degree is appropriate in your relationship with this lost one, while continuing to love and hold the space within your heart and consciousness for this person to become his or her true and beautiful self.

Divine Truth is a state of mind, heart, and being. It is all there really is. And yet in your physical world it has almost entirely been forgotten. Let yourself hunger for Truth. Give yourself permission to feel your own beauty beyond your shortcomings that are still being transformed. Then the transformation and transcendence will happen much more rapidly.

Call on me and on all of the Sirian Archangels and Pleiadian Archangels and any other guides and Ascended Masters. Call on us to love you. Beyond what we can teach you, we want to love you. As you let in higher love, your understanding and wisdom naturally grow proportionately. All higher-dimensional beings of Light want to love you. So even if you cannot hear messages, or see visions, you can open to being loved. The invocation I have given Amorah will help you do this. Use it regularly and strengthen the bridge between your consciousness, your Higher Self, and us. And use the Love Configuration Chambers of Light. We especially like those chambers. When used often enough they can deeply assist you in your process of becoming all that you truly are. We love you.

So-la-re-en-lo. I am Hermes, Sirian Archangel of the Light.

Following is the exercise Hermes has asked you to do to create a working alliance between your consciousness, your Higher Self, your guides, and the Sirian Archangelic League of the Light:

1. Ground yourself and pull in your aura to two to three feet around you.

2. Call your Higher Self in to activate your silver cord and to fill your tube of light. When this is done, continue.

3. Invoke the Sirian Archangelic League of the Light.

4. Invoke the Pleiadian Emissaries of Light.

5. Invoke Ascended Masters Jesus Christ, Mother Mary, and any others with whom you feel a connection.

6. Tell them as follows, or in your own words, "I want to feel your love for me all the time and I want to begin now. Help me clear all of my blocks to receiving love. Help me feel and know deeply my own worth and beauty. Until I have learned to feel the radiance of my own beauty all the time, help me steadily move toward that goal. For I know that in Truth I am a beautiful being of Light. I know that all else is illusion and a product of experience. Help me transcend all areas of identification with illusion and experience. Help me release even my subtlest ego identities and to become one in consciousness with my true Higher Self. I am that I am. I am that I am. I am that I am."

7. Remain in a receptive, meditative state for at least ten minutes, or longer if you prefer, while simply focusing on being loved and feeling your own radiance and beauty.

8. When complete, stand slowly. Establish your intent to go through the rest of this day feeling the communion with and love from your guides and helpers. Try to maintain the centered, warm feeling you have even as you enter into daily activities instead of adjusting yourself to a familiar, comfortable facade. Remind yourself throughout the day that these beautiful Light Beings are loving you, and let their love in.

Being Loved

In addition to the love that is directed at you all the time from higher-dimensional Light Beings, you are also loved by every human being on Earth. Yes, believe it or not, even those who in their consciousnesses hate you, or seem to be indifferent, on a deeper level love you. It is time to remember how to filter out what we do not want to receive from others and receive only that which is in Divine Truth. When a friend or acquaintance sends negative energy to you consciously with words or actions, or psychically, you can simply affirm, "I am willing to receive only Divine Love and Light. All else is illusion and must be repelled." When you remember to do this affirmation, you can be in the midst of anger, hatred, fear, and blame, yet only experience the love that is simultaneously being sent to you by the person's essence. It is a very liberating experience.

I was in a group situation once in which I did not know anyone and felt alienated and lonely. It seemed that all of the conversations were superficial, surface jargon, and I just did not know how to, or even want to, fit in. Yet, I felt separate. Saint Germain came to me and told me to ask silently to give and receive only love with the people around me. He explained that whether people are consciously loving me or not, I could still choose to receive the love that is inherently felt for me specifically by their beings, their true selves. So I tried it. I was amazed at how well it worked. I simply sat down with a group of people at the dinner table and established my intent to give and receive Divine Love and Light only. Immediately I felt warm, open, loving, and loved, and the loneliness left. I became very peaceful, and though I sat silently, I felt great communion. I also felt deep compassion for the others at the table and prayed that they too could benefit from the love that was being shared, yet unnoticed by them. After a few minutes, something amazing happened. All of the people came to a stop in their conversation about their struggles and toils at work, in relationships, and in general. They had been very actively engaged in "ain't it awful" conversation. When they stopped, everyone looked at me in the same moment, and a woman said "Hello" and asked my name. The people at the whole table turned their attention toward me. As she asked me where I was from and what I do, the group energy became even more focused in my direction. I shared about my work and the spiritual purpose behind it, and about Mt. Shasta and its sacredness, as they listened like children to an intriguing story. They asked questions and made comments, and eventually the whole table was engaged in a very enthusiastic, heartfelt conversation about the concepts I had presented and how wonderful they were. At times they laughed and seemed surprised at themselves about what they were saying, and still they continued.

This was a great lesson for me about intent and staying aligned with personal choice and identification with Divine Truth.

I had been given an exercise many years prior to this experience for reclaiming love that had been missed throughout my life. I would like to share it with you now, trusting that it can assist you as much as it has me. This exercise is one for invoking, in present time, love that was given to you in the past that you did not allow yourself to receive. Perhaps you were in a relationship with someone who loved you deeply and yet you never felt fulfilled and deeply loved. An underlying sadness and loneliness prevailed no matter how attentive and loving your partner was toward you. This happened because you did not know how to receive fully. The reason for this could be feelings of low self-worth and undeservingness, lack of trust, self-punishment, past-life karmic issues, fear of intimacy, fear of receiving love that would open you to other emotions you do not want to feel, or many other possibilities. Regardless of why you did not let it in at the time, you can receive it now to the extent that you are willing.

Another area of unreceived love is in painful or abusive relationships. You may have had a parent who criticized you continually. You became so browbeaten, or self-protective, that you blocked out not only the painful energies you did not want to receive, but also the love. When people harm you or hurt you in any way, you naturally create an aversion to being close to them and letting them in emotionally. This is healthy. However, as you expand, become more aware, and align with Divine Truth, you can choose to let in only the divine energies that you want. When you can learn to do this spontaneously in life, you will find hurt feelings and blame diminishing.

The exercise, or meditation, is simple. After setting your space and connecting with your Higher Self, think of people who have loved you whose love you may not have received fully, if at all. Considering them one by one, you state your willingness and desire to receive their Divine Love only, while leaving all illusions outside yourself; and you breathe and receive the love. Then you repeat the process with people with whom you have had difficult relationships.

There is nothing to fear in doing this as long as you follow the directions clearly and set clear intent to receive only Divine Love.

The third aspect of this meditation is opening to receive the love you have for yourself that you have not allowed yourself to experience prior to this time. It may surprise you how much love you really have for yourself. This part of the exercise is especially wonderful for healing low self-worth and self-love issues.

The last stage of this meditation is that of invoking the love from God/Goddess/All That Is. Whether you simply refer to this being as God, Great Spirit, Oneness, or the Infinite Sun, it is important to receive love from that source of Oneness and unified consciousness. You may also choose to receive love from the Holy Mother Goddess and Holy Father God individually. There will be space in the meditation for you to improvise.

You can do the following meditation for receiving love as often as you feel the need.

1. Ground yourself, pull in your aura, and adjust your boundary colors as needed.

2. Call in your Higher Self of Light and ask that your silver cord be activated and your tube of light filled. When this is done, proceed.

3. Think of someone who is currently in your life, or has been in your life, who you know loves you. Then using this person's name where it says "this person" repeat the following: "I am ready and willing to receive all of the Divine Love that this person has for me that I have not let in until now. I am willing to receive only this person's love and nothing else." Then breathe deeply and gently, and open to receive the love. When the influx of love to you has stopped, go to the next step.

4. Think of someone with whom you have had a difficult or painful relationship. Remember that this person's true self really does love you. Now repeat the following: "I am ready and willing to receive all of the Divine Love that this person has for me that I have not let in until now. I am willing to receive only this person's love and nothing

else." Then breathe deeply and gently, and open to receive the love. When the influx of love to you has stopped, continue.

5. Next you will receive your love for yourself. Repeat this invocation: "I am ready and willing to receive all of the Divine Love that I have felt for myself that I have not let in today. I am ready and deserve to love myself fully and deeply." Breathe deeply and gently and feel the inpouring of your self-love. When the flow stops, say, "I am ready to feel and receive all of the love I have had for myself in the last week that I have not let in." Again breathe and receive your own love. When the flow subsides, invoke, "I am ready to receive all of the love I have had for myself in the last month that I have not let myself feel until now." Breathe and receive. Then say, "I am ready to receive all of the love I have had for myself throughout this entire lifetime that I have not let myself receive until now." Then breathe deeply and gently, and open to receive your self-love. When the flow of love to you has stopped, proceed.

6. The love from God/Goddess/All That Is, or Great Spirit, is the next to be called forth. Invoke as follows: "I am ready and willing to receive all of the Divine Love that God/Goddess/All That Is has for me that I have not let in today." When the flow of love has ceased, say, "I am ready to let in all of the love God/Goddess/All That Is has sent to me in the last week that I have not received." Again, breathe and receive until the flow has stopped. Then repeat, "I am ready to receive all of the love God/Goddess/All That Is has given to me in the last month that I have not let in until now." Breathe and receive until the flow is complete. Then say, "I am ready to receive all of the love God/Goddess/All That Is has sent me in this lifetime that I have not allowed in until now." Then breathe deeply and gently, and open to receive the love. When the influx of love to you has stopped, continue.

7. If you wish to experience the love of the Holy Mother and Holy Father individually, use the same method as in steps 5 and 6. Then you can call on love from any other humans, personal guides, Ascended Masters, Archangels, or whomsoever you choose.

8. When you are complete, open your eyes slowly, maintaining your sense of being loved. Try to maintain the centered, warm feeling you have even as you enter into daily activities instead of adjusting yourself to a familiar, comfortable facade. Remind yourself throughout the day that all people, God/Goddess/All That Is, your true self, and your guides and higher-dimensional friends love you and are loving you. Let the love in. 📼

Sacred Geometry Chamber of Light for Your Soul

For the purpose of review I am including a passage from *The Pleiadian Workbook* which describes the soul matrix and its relationship to your soul. This information is important to assist you in understanding the full scope of the Sacred Geometry Chamber of Light for your soul:

Approximately two to two-and-a-half inches inside your heart chakra in the center of your chest is the area called your "soul matrix." This matrix consists of two prismatic, diamondlike anchor points and the "sun of the soul," as I call it. This "sun of the soul" actually looks like a sun or star, glowing in beautiful starlight blue or sunlight gold. Since the sun is a star, there is no contradiction in terms. This soul light is meant to shine brightly as you feel and know your worth and the value of your essential nature. The more you see the essential beauty in—and love—yourself, God/Goddess/All That Is, other people, nature, and Creation in general, the brighter this light shines. And the brighter it shines, the more it helps you experience that inner beauty, worth, and love.

Any amount of self-doubt, self-judgment, lack of deservingness, or blame, judgment, or unlovingness toward others can dim the light of your soul. In other words, the more you value the sacredness of yourself, others, and existence, the more you likewise experience and express who you really are. Other things that can block or dim your soul's light are: dishonesty of any kind; sex without love; physical or emotional abuse; emotional repression; righteous justification for hate, anger, and blame; being ungrounded (your spirit not present in your body); and possession by entities . . . The list goes on and on.

The basic cure for any and all of these is love, acting from a place of integrity and goodwill, complete emotional honesty with yourself and loved ones, and taking responsibility for being an active creator of all aspects of your life. When you live this way, you begin to heal the past wounds inflicted by yourself and others, and your true essence can shine in your heart and body again.

This chamber session for your soul will actually take place in three stages. In the first stage, you will be guided to use the Quantum Transfiguration grid in ultraviolet around your soul and soul matrix area (as described and illustrated on pages 186-188 of *The Pleiadian Workbook*). This will break down energy blockages, clear foreign energy and damage to your soul, and begin minimal repair work as needed. When the soul or soul matrix area is damaged, your ability to feel your own essence and Higher Self connection in your body is greatly diminished. Soul damage also inhibits your ability to give and receive love, have healthy relationships, experience self-worth and self-esteem, and experience the full benefits and expansive states from tantric sexual energy. Therefore, clearing of the area must be done prior to activating it more fully and prior to exploring the Dolphin Tantra work in chapter 9. This first step will take ten minutes.

The second stage of this chamber session is the actual restoration of your soul's sacred geometry. What this means is that your soul and soul matrix, like your organs and body, have specific integral geometric structures that hold them in place in your body. When the sacred geometry is damaged or compromised, you experience a diminished sense of your own radiance, while identifying more with the source of the damage. You may be more prone to feeling like a victim, or identified with lust and sexual addiction, or other addictions, all of which are symptomatic of the source of the soul mutation and resulting dysfunction. After the clearing has taken place, the Sirian Archangels are able to begin the process of bringing your soul and soul matrix back into self-affinity and integrity. The experience of this is the best explanation of all. This phase will take between twenty and forty minutes.

The last step in this chamber session is soul activation. You will be doing a short version of the Interdimensional Chamber of Light for this phase. In *The Pleiadian Workbook*, it is described as follows: "When I use this chamber, I am aware of fine filaments of light shining like little lasers into my soul matrix and illuminating it from the inside out. The light coming in is somewhat akin to sunlight that shines inward instead of outward, with all its light aimed at a central core, as opposed to the usual sunlight that shines from the core of the Sun outward. This sunlight is so concentrated at the core of your soul that it accentuates the natural tendency of your soul to shine outward."

Using this process after the clearing and sacred geometry realignment is especially powerful. You will be ready to experience the radiance at a deeper level than when originally doing only the Interdimensional Chamber of Light.

The Sacred Geometry Chamber of Light for your soul is implemented as follows:

1. Lie down comfortably with a pillow beneath your knees and your feet shoulder-width apart.

2. Give yourself a new grounding cord.

3. Pull in your aura to within two to three feet around your body in every direction. Check and adjust your aura boundary colors as needed.

4. Invoke your Higher Self of Light to come forth and be with you throughout the session.

5. Invoke the Pleiadian Emissaries of Light and ask them to place an Interdimensional Cone of Light above you for clearing and divine alignment.

6. Invoke the Sirian Archangelic League of the Light and ask them to place an Evolutionary Cone of Light above you so that this session may be used to achieve the highest good.

7. Invoke Ascended Masters Jesus Christ and Mother Mary to assist in the session.

8. Tell your guides that you are ready to be placed inside a Sacred

Geometry Chamber of Light for your soul. When you feel the shift in your energy field begin, proceed.

9. For the first level of activation, envision an ultraviolet Quantum Transfiguration grid around your entire soul and soul matrix area. Ask the Pleiadians to assist in placing and holding this grid for the next ten minutes. After two minutes of focusing on the grid, relax until the ten minutes is over. Then continue.

10. Next ask that the sacred geometry of your soul and soul matrix be restored to whatever degree is possible at this time. Relax for twenty to forty minutes until you feel that the work is done.

11. Next ask that your newly restructured soul and soul matrix be placed inside an Interdimensional Chamber of Light for ten more minutes. Breathe gently and deeply to allow the expansion and light activation to occur fully.

12. When you feel the chamber session is finished, sit up very slowly. Reground yourself if you feel the need. Then continue with your day. [▭]

Sacred Geometry Chamber of Light for Your Perineum Center

Your perineum center is located between your anus and genitals just inside the puckered skin there. (See illustration 11 on page 109.) This center, as you learned previously, is one of the portals through which your Ka energy enters your body from the higher dimensions. It is also a key energy center for moving tantric sexual energy up your spine and into your pineal gland. The perineum is the energy center that grounds energy coming from your pineal gland to your lower body as well. This lower body center also helps in regulating the flow of electricity between your upper and lower bodies and brain, and the flow of kundalini between your brain and lower body. A healthy relationship between your pineal gland and perineum center is, therefore, crucial to full-body enlightenment and ascension.

The process for clearing and realigning your sacred geometry, and activating your perineum center is identical to the one for your soul

10. Quantum Transfiguration grid around perineum center

given in the previous section. The only difference is that when that exercise instructed you to focus on your soul and soul matrix area, in this you will focus on your perineum instead. When you get to the last phase in which the Interdimensional Chamber of Light is used, you will simply visualize a smaller version of that chamber in a grid around your perineum center as pictured on illustration 10 on page 108.

Following are the steps for experiencing the Sacred Geometry Chamber of Light for your perineum center:

1. Lie down comfortably with a pillow beneath your knees and your feet shoulder-width apart.

2. Give yourself a new grounding cord.

3. Pull in your aura to within two to three feet around your body in every direction. Check and adjust your aura boundary colors as needed.

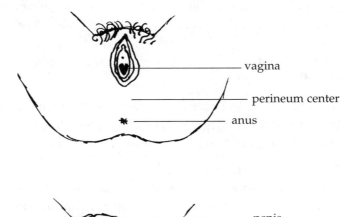

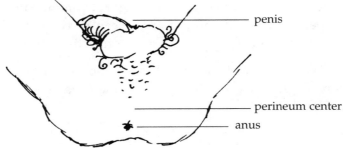

11. Perineum center location in female (above), male (below)

4. Invoke your Higher Self of Light to come forth and be with you throughout the session.

5. Invoke the Pleiadian Emissaries of Light and ask them to place an Interdimensional Cone of Light above you for clearing and divine alignment.

6. Invoke the Sirian Archangelic League of the Light and ask them to place an Evolutionary Cone of Light above you so that this session may be used to achieve the highest good.

7. Invoke Ascended Masters Jesus Christ and Mother Mary to assist in the session.

8. Tell your guides that you are ready to be placed inside a Sacred Geometry Chamber of Light for your perineum center. When you feel the shift in your energy field, proceed.

9. For the first level of activation, envision an ultraviolet Quantum Transfiguration grid around your perineum center. Ask the Pleiadians to assist in placing and holding this grid for the next ten minutes. After two minutes of focusing on the grid, relax until the ten minutes is over. Then continue.

10. Next ask that the sacred geometry of your perineum center be restored to whatever degree is possible at this time. Relax for twenty to forty minutes until you feel that the work is done.

11. Next ask that your newly restructured perineum center be placed inside an Interdimensional Chamber of Light grid for ten more minutes. Envision the golden white light streaming into the center of your perineum for about a minute. Then relax, breathe gently and deeply, and allow the expansion and light activation to occur fully.

12. When you feel the chamber session is finished, sit up very slowly. Reground yourself if you feel the need. Then continue with your day.

Chapter 6

HEALING THE MALE/FEMALE SPLIT

T he exercises in this chapter are designed to prepare you for the tantric exercises and soul healing given later in this book. It is important that you devote enough time to each process in order to sense or feel that you have made a shift before moving on to the next. You may find it helpful to read the exercises prior to doing them. This will allow your mind to be more relaxed and receptive to the suggestions being given. Tapes are available for those who find it more desirable to do guided processes by listening to a tape rather than by reading and following the instructions. (See ordering information at the back of the book.) A tape icon [icon] will be shown when it is time for you to turn on the tape in order to be guided through the exercise you have just read.

Reframing Repetitive Sexual and Intimacy Patterns

The first process is designed to assist you in releasing old negative thought patterns and beliefs that prevent you from achieving deep and fulfilling intimacy with yourself and others. In the channeling from An-Ra, examples were given of how you might be allowing negative thoughts or old painful emotions to stop you from trusting and surrendering in relationships. The step-by-step exercise that follows will guide you through remembering and reexperiencing past times when you identified with and succumbed to negative voices or ran away from emotions. You believed the relationship was causing these unpleasant experiences instead of simply bringing them to the surface for release. After reexperiencing these patterns in your past, you will be guided to imagine doing it in a new way that is more supportive of intimacy, love, and truth. When you imagine changing a past situation to be more commensurate with a new and better way of being and doing, it is called "reframing." It is a very effective tool not only for healing the past but also for breaking patterns in the future.

Following is the exercise for reframing repetitive sexual and intimacy patterns:

1. Lie or sit in a comfortable position.

2. Ground yourself.

3. Begin to "run energy" as you learned in *The Pleiadian Workbook*. (Envision a golden sun about eighteen inches above your head. Direct the sunlight to stream into your crown chakra, down the back of your spine, and back up the front of your spine. When the golden sunlight rises to your throat chakra in the front, divide it into three equal parts that will flow down each arm and out your palm chakras, and up and out the crown chakra. See illustration 12 on page 113.) Put this energy flow on "automatic" and intend that it continue running until this session is complete. You may add Earth energy from below your body if you wish.

4. Invoke your Higher Self of Light to activate your silver cord attachment to the top of your head and fill your tube of light with your own Higher Self's energy. When your tube of light is filled from the top of your aura to the bottom of your aura, you are ready to continue.

5. Invoke the Pleiadian Emissaries of Light to be with you.

6. Invoke the Ascended Masters Jesus Christ and Mother Mary to be with you.

7. Invite any other guides, Ascended Masters, or angels you wish to have present.

8. Ask the Pleiadians to place an Interdimensional Cone of Light at the top of your aura for clearing and divine alignment.

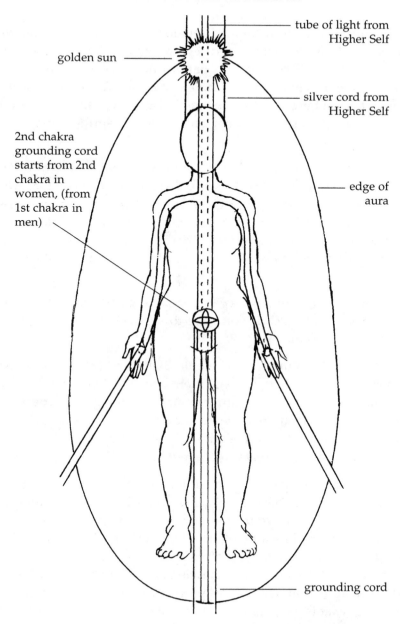

golden sun

tube of light from
Higher Self

silver cord from
Higher Self

2nd chakra
grounding cord
starts from 2nd
chakra in
women, (from
1st chakra in
men)

edge of
aura

grounding cord

12. *Running energy from the golden sun down the back of the spine 10% out
the grounding cord, 90% up the front of the spine; dividing at the throat
chakra and going down both arms, out through hand chakras, and up and out
through the crown chakra*

9. Think of a pattern in your relationships that has repeatedly occurred and caused distress and separation between you and your partner/partners. It should be a pattern in which you either have painful emotions come up and choose to retreat from your partner, or in which you hear negative voices of distrust, resistance, and fear. Identify your pattern to be changed as clearly and specifically as possible.

10. Visualize yourself in a situation in which your pattern occurred. Observe your thoughts. Observe and feel the feelings that were present. Notice where in your body you feel contraction and resistance as you feel the feelings or remember the thoughts. How were you breathing at the time? How did the other person respond to you? Take a few minutes to observe all of these aspects of the situation fully.

11. Now let go of the memories completely and take a few deep breaths. Shake or stretch if you need to in order to help your body relax and open again.

12. Next think about how you would like to change your reactions to conscious responses in this situation. If you did not identify with the negative thoughts or painful emotions as being your truth, but simply acknowledged that the relationship was assisting you in bringing these thoughts and emotions to the surface for release, how would you handle the situation differently?

13. Imagine yourself in the same situation again. When the negative thoughts or feelings come up, observe yourself as you remain calm and relaxed and tell your partner what is happening for you. (Example: "I am feeling a lot of fear right now and I need to breathe through it," as opposed to, "I don't trust you. I'm afraid you just want to hurt me.") How does it feel emotionally to be able to stay open, trusting, and loving with your partner while being honest and explaining what is happening? Notice that your body remains free of contraction. Observe your breathing remaining steady and full. How does your partner respond to you differently than before? Take a few

minutes to fully experience this reframing in your body, your emotions, and visually as much as possible.

14. Let the scene go completely. Take a few deep breaths and shake off the experience or stretch if you feel the need.

15. Think about what the belief was that previously made you reactionary instead of clear and responsive. Put it into words, such as, "This person wants to hurt or control me just like all of the others in my past have done." or "Relationships and spirituality cannot coexist without one or the other suffering or being sacrificed." Use your own understanding of your pattern to identify the beliefs that cause separation.

16. Imagine a symbol that represents your belief.

17. Notice where in your body you contract and what emotions you feel when you think about the belief and envision its symbol. Then tell your body and emotions that they are reacting to a false belief that you are ready to release. Ask your physical body and emotional body to let go as you breathe deeply into the contracted areas and assist them in letting go.

18. Imagine your symbol on a photograph.

19. Imagine that you have a red rubber stamp that says "CANCELED," and vehemently stamp the photograph of your belief symbol several times.

20. Imagine that you rip the photograph into at least two pieces and burn them in a violet flame until all traces of the photograph and symbol are gone.

21. Create an affirmation for your new way of responding in similar situations. Examples: "I acknowledge that my lover is a loving, trustworthy person and that this relationship is different from my past ones." or "Relationships and spirituality are natural complements to one another in my life." or "I am ready to let go of control and to trust and surrender to the divine in myself and in my sacred partner."

22. If there are other beliefs you need to release at this time, repeat steps 15 through 21 for each of them.

23. Turn the golden sunlight off, open your eyes, and continue with your day. [cassette icon]

If you have several different repetitive patterns that you would like to clear in relationships, or otherwise, use this process as often as you would like in order to do so. Rehearsing for difficult or challenging situations in life is a great way to assist yourself in breaking old behavioral patterns.

Ending the Lust/Seduction Game

For thousands of years on Earth, and infinitely longer in this solar ring and beyond, male/female separation, competition, distrust, control, and imbalance have been primary sources of pain and karma. As we enter into the Age of Aquarius, it is imperative that this be corrected and that sacredness and equanimity be restored. Whether you choose to be involved in a heterosexual relationship is not the issue. The issue is the internal and external balance between male and female in all aspects of your life.

First, it is important to identify one of the most crucial areas of the control and power struggle between men and women which is the "lust /seduction game." The lust/seduction game looks something like this:

He walks into the already crowded room at a party. *She* notices him right away. She smoothes out her skirt, pulls her blouse a little lower off her shoulders, walks in his direction while nonchalantly sipping her drink and making a point to look the other way. Her posture and walk are seductive, her brows raised slightly as she walks past him. She manages to brush against him ever so slightly, says, "Oh, excuse me," in a surprised sounding voice, and walks on. Psychically the cords go out to him in a snakelike dance, hitting him with a burst of sexual energy while she still looks as though she does not know he exists.

He feels the energy, watches her walk by, and hypnotically follows the leash, or cord, she has hooked to his lower body. He catches up, taps her on the shoulder, and introduces himself. They are practically in bed already with their psychic energy, but both pretend not to notice. As he talks to her she occasionally looks away, trying not to seem too interested. She even pulls her sexual energy back a little to make him have to try harder to reach her. He talks awhile and then goes for a drink or a bathroom break during which time he figures out the next game plan. "Do I simply come on strong now, or act indifferent for awhile? I know she likes me, or I think she does." He checks his hair, his shirt, opens another button on his shirt to expose his chest, rebuttons it, unbuttons it again, then goes back outside.

He positions himself in the room where he can see her out of the corner of his eye but pretends not to see her. She notices his shirt and a sideways glance, smiles to herself in understanding the game, and looks the other way, pretending not to notice him at all. Both have their feelers out, but it is a contest now to see who will make the next approach. An hour passes. She goes to the bathroom, freshens her makeup, sets her eyes and posture in that certain pose, and emerges again. She walks over to the refreshment table, still not looking at him directly but very aware of where he is in the room. He is undressing her and silently imagining being the hottest lover she's ever had. He sees her writhing and panting as he, with great self-control, thrusts into her over and over again. He is becoming aroused and she can feel the heat of his passion. She silently chuckles and smiles to herself. He has a smug but satisfied silent chuckle as well as he walks over and without directly looking at her asks, "Having a good time?" She looks a little bored and replies, "So, so." She starts to walk away, but he takes her arm in his hand and asks if she would like to go for a ride with him. She looks at her watch, looks around the room, then sighs and says, "Oh, why not?"

All the way from there, throughout the drive to her apartment, and to bed, they compete for who can entice the other the most but seem to want it the least. To act unaffected is vital. During sex they both focus more on being the best and on always trying to look sexy than they do on really sharing themselves with each other. She arches her back to lure him with her breasts. He purposely extends foreplay to try and break down her controls so he can blow her mind first. All the way to the end of the evening when they casually agree to "keep in touch," neither lets go of self-consciousness or control. They part. She is sure she has him exactly where she wants him. He silently walks away thinking, "Piece of cake. She's hooked." And the beat goes on.

Some people play the lust/seduction game more directly. I call this the "Hey, big guy," or "What's happening, pretty baby?" approach:

One or the other struts for the other, seductively rolls his or her eyes, rubs against the intended, makes seductive sounds, flatters, and fully intends to conquer. She may want to be "taken" or to be aggressive and make him lose control. He may be in either role as well. Their conversation is one of meaningless seductive innuendoes, ego boosting, and playing it cool. The sex is the "Oo, baby, baby" kind with little but physical release accomplished.

The game can also be played in banks, restaurants, department stores, or anywhere else a man and woman on the make happen to meet. It can vary from, "Hey baby, wanta fuck?" to "Don't I know you?" as the sexual energy hooks fly from one to the other. But the agenda is the same. Who can lure the other the most? Who can boost his or her own ego the most? Who can make the other lose control? Who can be the best in bed?

Another variety is the woman or man who can never do enough to please her or his partner. The motivation is to be giving enough that the other will finally notice you and tell you that you are okay; and maybe even toss a few crumbs your way. The other partner in this situation is usually very self-centered and gets off on someone else groveling and seducing for attention. The self-centered one steals energy this way while the needy partner continues to try too hard to please and hopes that a few crumbs will be tossed his or her way occasionally.

Notice that words like love, innocence, playfulness, trust, honesty, caring, respect, directness, and adoration have not even come up during the description of the variations of the lust/seduction game.

Regardless of which role you play, or may have played in the past, it is a game in which no one wins. It is lose/lose instead of win/win. In fact the game itself is based on anger, control, separation, low self-esteem, self-centeredness, distrust, revenge, and desperation. Yes, desperation. In this game the biggest investment each player has is in not letting the other know how desperately he or she is in need of validation, soothing feelings of loneliness, or releasing built up tension and emotional pain. It is also true that the one who looks the least needy and least interested is just as desperate as the one who shows it. Often neither player even consciously knows that he or she is desperate. The ego facades are so strong that both have learned to identify with them. It is like planning a bad dream, dreaming it, and forgetting that you planned it. You simply live it and believe it is real. The people involved have truly fallen asleep and not reawakened to realize that they are just dreaming their own dream; that it is just an illusion.

Century after century, males and females have followed the cultural and religious dictates of society. These societal dictates have stripped us of our naturalness, innocence, and true beauty. The slinky girl by the shiny black car in the commercials, or the machismo Marlboro man, has been used to sell us more than products. The real bill of goods we have bought is reflected in our attitudes, lifestyles, and relationships. When you have healthy self-esteem, a sense of personal worth that comes from being in touch with your own essential goodness and inherent value, then you do not need to prove yourself to others or to yourself. You are free to be spontaneous, innocent, honest, natural, loving to others and yourself. You do not need to contrive ways for getting ego strokes or false power over others. You have a sense of healthy empowerment within yourself. You are responsible and responsive in life. You are safe to show love and caring for others; to be playful without it being at the expense of the other. And when your love for yourself as a man or woman is intact, you do not need to conquer and seduce others in order to prove the kind of man or woman you are.

Both genders are equally involved in maintaining the male/female split whether it be through the lust/seduction game or other gender issues. In order to identify the negative attitudes and beliefs for clearing, it is easiest to address male and female issues individually. Though these issues overlap at times, there are certain attitudes that tend to be more common to one gender or the other. For now we will focus separately on female and male attitudes that are specific to the lust/seduction game.

Female Attitudes

First let us take a look at what has brought about the participation of females in the lust/seduction game. For a very long time on Earth women have been considered second-class citizens. Though a few indigenous cultures have maintained the dignity of the female, the majority of Earth's people belong to dominant patriarchal cultures. The burden of keeping a relationship flowing and satisfying has been placed on women's shoulders. A woman must be pretty enough, sexy enough, stay young, always be fresh and inviting even after a long day with the children, keep a perfect house, and be a good cook. Any of these areas that are less than ideal is enough of an excuse for her man to look outside the home for a younger, prettier, or more emotionally satisfying partner. He may come home grumpy, smelly, and tired, but she is not supposed to notice. If she does notice, she is being a nag or bitchy. If he notices she is not up to par in some way and complains about it, she is ashamed. If the woman does not buy into the shame game, she may become a man-hater and become part of the revenge game in which both partners actively practice trying to hurt each other, put each other in the wrong, and withhold love and positive attention. Women who choose to play neither role either end up as "old maids" or seductresses who only have short-term relationships. "Love them and leave them" becomes the credo and only way to survive with any sense of self intact.

Another type of woman involved in this deadly game is the control freak. She chooses wimpy men or maybe even men who are sensitive and emotionally available. She begins the relationship by boosting a man's ego, sympathizing with him about his former disappointments and betrayals with women, even appears to confide in him about her own inner secrets. Then as soon as she is sure he is hooked, the control begins. She makes outrageous demands with threats of leaving, or by guilt-tripping him and telling him that he does not love her. She insults him and tries to make him feel like he is not good enough for her. She may be manipulating for money, special favors, or simply for the pleasure of making him suffer under her power. If he reaches his limit and threatens to leave, she either becomes falsely remorseful or psychologically begins to "tear him to shreds." The vicious cycle continues until someone has the courage to finally end it, or she finds a new male to challenge her and keep her amused.

A few women are seriously breaking out of these roles. They are releasing past pain and emotion, learning discernment, and learning how to be intimate and feel safe. And yet most women are still in the process of redefining themselves as females, both autonomously and as related to males. Most women still either distrust and blame men for all of their relationship dysfunctions, or blame themselves completely and remain naively blind, deaf, and dumb to their men's faults. Since it is obvious that neither attitude serves in bringing about harmony, equanimity, and trust, another choice must be made. That choice is one of self-clearing and self-healing, and learning to pick the right kind of men in the first place.

Below I have created several categories in which to classify the diverse approaches to and attitudes about men that women take. You will most likely find your own patterns under varying categories, although one category will clearly be your modus operandi. Try not to judge your own patterns or those of other women and men. It is simply time to recognize where they have come from, and what you need to do to change them. As you identify your own beliefs, judgments, and negative attitudes, list them on three separate pieces of paper labeled with the headings:

"Beliefs and judgments about men and relationships"
"Attitudes and behaviors toward men and in relationships"
"Beliefs, judgments, and attitudes about myself as a woman"

After you have written down your own personal agendas on each list you will have the material with which to work. I recommend that you use the technique for clearing beliefs and judgments given on page 115, numbers 15 through 21. For clearing the attitudes and behaviors use the entire exercise, given at the beginning of this chapter. The reward for your efforts will be self-respect, dignity, more self-love, increasing ability to use discernment in choosing partners, and better relationships.

THE BOMBSHELL SEDUCTRESS

Beliefs and judgments about men and relationships

1. Control or be controlled: there is no other way.

2. Men are ruled by their penises (to phrase it nicely).

3. No man can be trusted any further than you can see him.

4. The only power I can have over men is sex.

5. Men only want women who are the sexiest, prettiest, and hottest in bed. I have to outdo other women to get their attention.

6. To make a man want me and then reject him is a turn-on.

7. To use men for money is a way of having power over them and making them look like fools.

8. To pretend to care about a man and be monogamous while fooling around with other men is to beat him at his own game.

Attitudes and behaviors toward men and in relationships

1. I hate men.

2. I enjoy watching men suffer over me.

3. I'll never let any man have the satisfaction of making me really care about him or know that I need him.

4. The dangling carrot approach: tempt them but never let them have it all.

5. Relationships are just a trap for women and serve men only.

6. Flirting with other women's lovers or mates in order to feel superior.

7. Turning men and women against each other by telling lies.

8. Telling your partner lies in order to get your way.

9. In relationships, someone wins and someone loses. Therefore, I must always make sure I win.

Beliefs, judgments, and attitudes about myself as a woman

1. I have to make men want me in order to feel valid as a woman.

2. I hate men because I need them for validation.

3. I don't trust myself.

4. Being a woman makes me less than, so I have to act better than in order to hide it.

5. I can only win a man if I stay really sexy, thin, and seductive.

6. My body is my only source of control and value.

7. I don't trust other women because they are just like me.

8. I always have to feel like I am in control of every situation. My only alternative is to feel out of control and powerless.

9. Women have to be devious to get their needs met.

10. I deserve to use and hurt men: If I do not do it to them, they will do it to me.

11. Never letting anyone know I feel insecure is a must for survival.

12. I must always remember bad things men have done in order to never let my guard down.

13. Trusting anyone is just being stupid and naive.

14. Never feel anything deeply except power over others, anger, hate, revenge, or arrogance.

15. Hurt others but do not ever get hurt.

16. Always keep my pride by judging others and feeling superior.

DEMURE SEDUCTRESS

Beliefs and judgments about men and relationships

1. Control or be controlled: There is no other way. I'll make him think he is in control, but I will make sure I am.

2. Men are ruled by flattery. Boost their egos and make them feel important and you have them where you want them.

3. No man can be trusted any further than you can see him. But always make him think that you are so naive and innocent that you trust him even when he does something wrong.

4. I can have power over men in sex by being shy and appearing to be conquered by their overwhelming charm.

5. Men are suckers for the femme fatale approach.

6. If I cannot get what I want any other way I can always cry.

7. If I cannot keep my man fully satisfied at all times, some other woman will.

8. Men like to feel like the big, strong protectors, so I will play along. It turns them on to think I am frail and helpless.

9. If I do not have an orgasm, I will fake one just to make a man feel masculine. Secretly this deception makes me feel more in control and superior.

10. Men do not like women who assert themselves, so I must be covert in getting my needs met.

Attitudes and behaviors toward men and in relationships

1. You cannot expect a man to work as hard at making a woman happy as she works at making him happy. It is a woman's responsibility to keep the relationship working.

2. Do not let a man know you are not satisfied until it is too late. Then leave him suddenly.

3. Women are smarter than men but must never show it.

4. Say, "Honey, can you explain this to me?" or "Can you do this? I am not strong enough."

Beliefs, judgments, and attitudes about myself as a woman

1. I will never be fully appreciated because I am a woman.

2. Always be soft-spoken and sweet or I will be unfeminine.

3. It is unsafe for me to express my needs and feelings in a direct way.

4. If I do not keep myself young and sexy looking no man will want me.

5. It is shameful for a woman not to have a man in her life.

6. When I can keep my man happy I feel worthy as a woman. When he is unhappy I feel like a failure.

7. It is unfeminine for a woman to appear as intelligent as a man.

8. It is unattractive for a woman to show anger or to express any emotion in a deep or intense way.

9. I must always have my hair and makeup just right before I am around men.

10. It is my responsibility to know exactly what my man expects of me and to fulfill his expectations. But I cannot expect him to do the same for me. Men and women are simply different in that way.

THE MAN-HATER

Beliefs and judgments about men and relationships

1. All men are selfish, self-centered, and uncaring toward others.

2. All men just use women whether it be for sex, money, or ego gratification.

3. Men are incapable of commitment and loyalty.

4. All men are two-timers.

5. Men think with their genitals.

6. All men want to possess, control, and conquer women.

7. If I don't outsmart and control him, he will outsmart and control me.

8. All men hate women.

9. No man is good enough to deserve having a woman in his life.

10. All men control women through sex. Therefore, I will never let myself feel sexual energy.

Attitudes and behaviors toward men and in relationships

1. Relationships and marriage are strictly for a man's convenience and a woman's sorrow.

2. Love between the sexes is just a lie, a fairy tale believed by fools.

3. I have to keep him feeling inadequate and inferior by insulting him and never being satisfied. It is my job to remind him continually of his faults.

4. In order to keep a man around I must keep him feeling guilty, inadequate, and beholden to me.

5. By withholding sex I can keep him in need of me.

6. I must constantly show him that I am smarter than he is.

7. If I never act happy around him, he will try harder to please me.

8. I will find ways to use him before I am used.

Beliefs, judgments, and attitudes about myself as a woman

1. I will never be happy because a woman's life is always unhappy and unjust.

2. I must never let myself open my heart and trust anyone.

3. I hate myself for allowing men into my life just to hurt and use me.

4. I hate myself for wanting sex with men.

5. I will never try to please anyone but myself.

6. Women are always smarter and more trustworthy than men.

7. It is okay to cheat on a man. He deserves it.

8. I will never trust women who love men and who "pretend" to be happy. It is impossible without selling out as a woman.

9. As long as there is injustice toward women in the world, I must never let myself be happy or let go of my pain, anger, and hate.

10. To be a woman is to be a victim.

11. I have a right to use men any way I want to. They deserve it.

12. I have a right to use seduction and sex to control men.

Some of the examples I have given may seem antiquated to you. But look at the attitudes your grandmothers and mother passed down. You may not be consciously holding onto these beliefs but may be holding them in your subconscious or in your body. Identify the ones that even remotely ring a bell and work with those until you feel clear with each one. I am sure that there are many more beliefs, judgments, attitudes, and behaviors that are not identified here. Hopefully these will be enough to trigger your awareness of yourself in a deeper way and help you realize others that are not given.

Now it is time to find replacements for these attitudes. Begin three new lists labeled as follows:

"Affirmations about men and relationships"
"New attitudes and behaviors toward men and in relationships"
"Affirmations about myself as a woman"

For each negative item on your first set of lists, write an affirmation or describe a new scenario with which to replace it on the corresponding list. For example, if you wrote down, "All men hate women," on your new list write something like: "I am ready to draw into my life men who are loving and caring toward women and especially toward me." Or if you wrote down, "Control or be controlled: there is no other way," then your affirmation might be: "I am ready to take responsibility for letting go of control and making more discerning choices about the men with whom I choose to be involved." Just because your past experiences have been painful and less than ideal does not mean that your future experiences will be the same. Examine what has created the negative magnetism in your life. Have you harbored resentment and blame from one relationship to the next? If so, you have created a magnetism for those same types of people and situations. Are you still looking for men who remind you of your father in order to have yet another chance to make it different this time? "Perhaps if this new fellow will do ___ better than Dad did, I will finally be able to feel okay about myself as a woman." If you are consciously or subconsciously still thinking this thought, then your chances of finding a satisfying relationship are very slim. You must heal your own past, let go of your dad and all of your ex-lovers and ex-husbands, forgive them, forgive yourself; then you can create a new type of magnetism—one based on already feeling good about yourself, being a forgiving and understanding person, and knowing how to use discernment. If the new man reminds you of your "ex" then find someone else. You are getting off to a bad start and the results are predictable.

After the section for men you will find a section entitled "Women and Men," which includes a guided process for releasing blame and forgiving yourself and others. When you have completed working with your lists, move on to that section.

Male Attitudes

For a very long time on Earth the standards set for men, in order for you to fit in and be considered masculine, have been very limiting. In most cultures, men are not supposed to even acknowledge they have feelings, much less express them openly to their loved ones. Anger within certain limits has been acceptable. And in most cultures men are expected to be good providers for their families. However, it

is not uncommon for a man in a supposedly monogamous relationship to be seen as simply "being a man" when he flirts with or has
affairs with other women. In fact, peer pressure often condones it. He
may be teased as being "pussy-whipped" if he does not choose to
come on to the sexy cocktail waitress and fantasize with his buddies
about having sex with her. To look at women as sex objects is considered manly and in control. Men who do otherwise are considered
wimpy or unmasculine, or teased about being gay. It takes courage
and a lot of integrity for a man to step out of the role as a womanizer
in many groups. Often his only sense of personal value as a man
comes from having a woman treat him seductively or respond to his
macho or seductive gestures.

Another archetypal male is the one who is wimpy and ineffectual.
He has been browbeaten by at least one controlling parent—it could
be mother or father. Nothing he ever did was good enough when he
was growing up. He enjoyed poetry more than football and his dad
hated him for it. He felt romantic and loving toward girls he liked and
the other boys made fun of him. He daydreamed in school and was
yelled at by teachers. He may have been very studious and considered a nerd and bookworm. Or he may have barely made passing
grades and felt ashamed. The shame and low self-worth are the common threads in all of the agendas of the wimpy, ineffectual male.
Underneath he is most likely seething with rage; and yet he barely
squeaks out and stutters his words when backed into a corner—or
even in everyday communications.

He secretly resents everyone who has ever "made him feel" inadequate. He is a victim, while fantasizing about pulling the trigger on
the teacher, lover, or parent who hurt his feelings. He withholds his
creativity from himself and his life. He is totally stuck in self-pity and
uses it to control others and be irresponsible in relationships. He has
overtly rejected the macho male archetype, while covertly harboring
aggression and negative fantasies. He is passive/aggressive, aloof,
and withholding. Or he may be an over-pleaser who always picks
people to be involved with who use him, abuse him, or put him
down. He may get put down directly by his friends and lovers—or
would-be lovers—or he may feel put down because he knows he

never gives enough or is good enough company. Either way, he is a social loser. He may even excel at his job, but receive little respect and appreciation on a personal level. He desperately wants a relationship and deep down hates women for the power they have to reject him.

Many men are sincerely attempting to break free from the archetypes mentioned. Some of these men still actively practice the "studly" attitudes and behaviors privately with pornography or by fantasizing about other women while with their lovers. The wimpy man may be taking assertiveness training but still secretly feeling inadequate and lazy about taking responsibility in relationships. The men who are attempting to break free face the challenge of being forerunners for a new male archetype. As Robert Bly pointed out in his book, *Iron John*, men today cannot find very many, if any, good male role models. You, who are breaking free, are in the process of becoming male role models for future generations. So upon what do you base your new way of being? My suggestion is that you base it on learning to be real, whatever that is for you. Through men's groups, meditation, workshops, private healing sessions with alternative healers, books, and sincere inner work, you have begun to undo the past within yourself. You have perhaps discovered the loneliness and grief of the sensitive little boy who grew up in a world that was insensitive and much too fast. That little boy is the starting place. He was not calculating, tough, or condescending to women. You had to be carefully taught those attitudes, not only by your father, but also by your mother. Statements such as "Big boys don't cry," or "Your father would be ashamed if he saw you acting like that," told you to stuff your emotions, be tough, and meet your father's approval, or be ashamed.

Men have also been taught that they must perform well and consistently in the world—and in bed—in order to be considered worthwhile. Male self-esteem has long been equated with how much money you earn, the type of profession you choose, the physical beauty of your wife, the behavior and success of your children, your sexual prowess, and the type of car and home you own. How can a man be real with this type of criteria for self-worth and self-esteem hanging constantly over him, weighing his merit? The new man must be very daring or very rebellious just to embark upon a new way of being. But this is the end of the millennium, fellows, and time for a new script.

Below I have created several categories in which to classify the diverse approaches to, and attitudes about, women that men take. You will most likely find your own patterns under varying categories, although one category will clearly be your modus operandi. Try not to judge your own patterns or those of other men or women. It is simply time to recognize where they have come from, and what you need to do to change them. As you identify your own beliefs, judgments, and negative attitudes list them on three separate pieces of paper labeled with the headings:

"Beliefs and judgments about women and relationships"
"Attitudes and behaviors toward women and in relationships"
"Beliefs, judgments, and attitudes about myself as a man"

After you have written down your own personal agendas on each list you will have the material with which to work. It is recommended that you use the technique for clearing beliefs and judgments given on page 115, numbers 15 through 21. For clearing the attitudes and behaviors, use the entire exercise given at the beginning of this chapter. The reward for your efforts will be self-respect, dignity, more self-love, increasing ability to use discernment in choosing partners, and better relationships.

So let's examine your roles in the lust/seduction game. Be honest with yourself about even the subtlest tendencies that you still harbor.

THE MACHO SEDUCER

Beliefs and judgments about women and relationships

1. Women want to be taken. They like it.

2. Control or be controlled: that is the game. And I will never let myself be humiliated by being controlled by a mere woman.

3. No woman can be trusted any further than you can see her.

4. The only power I can have over women is sex.

5. Women only want men who are the sexiest, handsomest, and hottest in bed. I have to outdo other men to get their attention.

6. To make a woman want me and then reject her is a turn-on.

7. To use women for money is a way of having power over them and making them look like fools.

8. To pretend to care about a woman and be monogamous while fooling around with other women is to be cool or manly.

9. I have to intimidate women with my physical strength in order to control them.

10. Women were created for my pleasure and convenience.

11. Any woman should feel honored to get my attention.

12. Women like the big, strong, protector type.

13. All women are good for is sex.

Attitudes and behaviors toward women and in relationships

1. Relationships are only on my terms.

2. Marriage is for sex and to have my household needs taken care of. It has nothing to do with love.

3. Love between the sexes is just a big lie. Love is for sissies.

4. I hate women.

5. I enjoy watching women suffer over me.

6. I'll never let any woman have the satisfaction of making me really care about her or know that I need her.

7. The dangling carrot approach: Tempt them but never let them have it all.

8. Coming on to other men's lovers or wives in order to feel superior.

9. If a woman wants me she's going to have to work hard for it.

10. Act bored and unaffected even when I really want her.

11. Always keep a woman in self-doubt so she never knows that she is as good as I am, or deserves better. Keep her down.

12. "Love them and leave them," that's my motto.

Beliefs, judgments, and attitudes about myself as a man

1. I am tough and emotionally untouchable. No one will ever get to me in a deep way.

2. Lying is expected of real men.

3. My worth is measured by my body strength and build.

4. My worth is measured by my income, type of car, home, clothes, etc.

5. I don't need anybody.

6. I am God's gift to women.

7. Men are born to be better than women.

8. Men are smarter than women.

9. I'll take what I want, however I have to to get it.

10. I deserve to use and hurt women: If I do not do it to them, they will do it to me.

11. Never letting anyone know I feel insecure is a must for survival.

12. I must always remember bad things women have done in order to never let my guard down.

13. Trusting anyone is just being stupid and unmanly.

14. Never feel anything deeply except power over others, anger, hate, revenge, or arrogance.

15. Hurt others but do not ever get hurt.

16. Always keep your pride by judging others and feeling superior.

17. I secretly need to possess a woman in order to feel secure and worthy.

THE DEBONAIR SEDUCER

Beliefs and judgments about women and relationships

1. Control or be controlled: there is no other way. I'll make her think she is in control, but I will make sure I am.

2. Women are ruled by flattery. Boost their egos and make them feel pretty and important and I have them where I want them.

3. No woman can be trusted any further than you can see her. But always make her think that you trust her.

4. I can have power over women in sex by being the Romeo and appearing to be conquered by their overwhelming charm and beauty.

5. Women are suckers for the Romeo approach.

6. Buy her dinner or flowers and I can wrap her around my little finger.

7. All women want to think that they are the most beautiful and irresistible in all the world.

8. Women are weak and helpless once I "make them" mine in bed. Sweep her off her feet and she's mine to control.

Attitudes and behaviors toward women and in relationships

1. Always keep women needing you. Give them just enough to make them want more, but don't give it.

2. Make a woman think I am madly in love with her and she will do anything I want.

3. Do not let a woman know I am not satisfied until it is too late. Then leave her suddenly.

4. Get a woman to try and please me by never fully letting her in.

5. Always act shocked and hurt if the woman doubts my sincerity. Never let her suspect ulterior motives or deceptions.

Beliefs, judgments, and attitudes about myself as a man

1. Men are more cunning and clever than women but must never show it. Act innocent.

2. It is natural for men to exaggerate and/or deceive women in order to woo them and win them over.

3. I must always act confident even when I am not.

4. I need to have the attention of sexy, beautiful women in order to feel good enough as a man.

5. Being the best—better than others—is all that matters.

6. Acting casual and collected is the best way to make her chase me.

7. I must be a hero in my woman's eyes in order to feel good as a man.

8. Never let the woman know how desperately I need her to look up to me and tell me how great I am.

9. To have a woman under my spell makes me feel very manly and in control.

THE WOMAN-HATER SEDUCER

Beliefs and judgments about women and relationships

1. All women are selfish, self-centered, and uncaring toward others.

2. All women just use men whether it be for sex, money, or ego gratification.

3. All women are incapable of loyalty.

4. All women are two-timers.

5. All women control men through sex. Therefore, I will withhold from women sexually except when I want it for me.

6. All women want to possess, control, and conquer men so I must do it to them first.

7. If I don't outsmart and control her, she will outsmart and control me.

8. All women hate men.

9. No woman deserves to have a good man in her life.

10. Women are an inferior species of weaklings.

Attitudes and behaviors toward women and in relationships

1. Relationships and marriage are strictly for women's convenience and men's misery. Never get "hooked."

2. Love between the sexes is just a lie, a fairy tale believed by fools.

3. I have to keep her feeling inadequate and inferior by insulting her and never being satisfied. It is my job to remind her continually of her faults.

4. In order to keep a woman around I must keep her feeling guilty, inadequate, and beholden to me.

5. By withholding sex I can keep her in need of me.

6. I must constantly show her that I am smarter than she is.

7. If I never act happy around her, she will try harder to please me.

8. I will find ways to use her before I am used.

9. Always keep a woman guessing and wondering how I feel about her.

10. Never let my guard down emotionally.

11. Never let her know anything that is meaningful to or vulnerable about me.

12. I hate women because they "make me" want them sexually.

13. To humiliate women is a big thrill.

14. When I am with a woman I own her and she had best do what I tell her to.

15. When women get hurt—physically or emotionally—it is because they asked for it.

16. I hate women who are kind and loving because they make me realize that I don't have any light and love on my own without them.

Beliefs, judgments, and attitudes about myself as a man

1. Men are by nature superior.

2. I must never let myself open my heart and trust anyone.

3. I hate myself when I allow women into my life just to hurt and use me.

4. I hate myself for wanting sex with women.

5. I will never try to please anyone but myself.

6. Men are always smarter than women.

7. It is okay to cheat on a woman. She deserves it.

8. I will never trust men who love women and who "pretend" to be happy. It is impossible without selling out as a man.

9. I must never let myself be happy or let go of my pain, anger, and hate.

10. To be a man is to be tough and unaffected by others.

11. I have a right to use women any way I want to. They deserve it.

12. I have a right to use seduction and sex to control women and then dump them when I am through.

Some of the examples I have given may seem antiquated to you. But look at the attitudes your father and grandfathers passed down. You may not be consciously holding on to these beliefs, but may be holding them in your subconscious or in your body. Identify the ones that even remotely ring a bell and work with those until you feel clear with each one. I am sure that there are many more beliefs, judgments, attitudes, and behaviors that are not identified here. Hopefully these will be enough to trigger your awareness of yourself in a deeper way and help you realize others that are not given.

Now it is time to find replacements for these attitudes. Begin three new lists labeled as follows:

"Affirmations about women and relationships"
"New attitudes and behaviors toward women and in relationships"
"Affirmations about myself as a man"

For each negative item on your first set of lists, write an affirmation or describe a new scenario with which to replace it on its corresponding list. For example, if you wrote down "All women hate men," on your new list, write something like: "I am ready to draw into my life women who are loving and caring toward men and especially toward me." Or if you wrote down "Control or be controlled: there is no other way," then your affirmation might be: "I am ready to take responsibility for letting go of control and making more discerning choices about the women with whom I choose to be involved." Just because your past experiences have been painful and less than ideal does not mean that your future experiences will be the same. Examine what has created the negative magnetism in your life. Have you harbored resentment and blame from one relationship to the next? If so, you have created a magnetism for those same types of people and situations. Are you still looking for women who remind you of your mother in order to have yet another chance to make it different this time? "Perhaps if this new woman will do ___ better than Mom did I will finally be able to feel okay about myself as a man." If you are consciously or subconsciously still thinking this thought and looking for a mother, then your chances of finding a satisfying relationship are very slim. You must heal your own past, let go of your mom and all of your ex-lovers and ex-wives, forgive them, forgive yourself. Then you can create a new type of magnetism: one based on already feeling good about yourself, being a forgiving and understanding person, and knowing how to use discernment. If the new woman reminds you of your "ex" then find someone else. You are getting off to a bad start and the results are predictable.

When you have completed working with your lists, move on to the next section.

Male and Female Attitudes

You may have noticed that many of the beliefs, attitudes, and judgments in the women's and men's sections are identical. That is one of the most common problems in relationships. Women project distrust onto men and men project distrust onto women. It is like the cat chasing its own tail and never realizing that the tail it chases is its own. If you are waiting for your partner to change in order for you to feel safe in changing, you are shirking your own spiritual and personal responsibility for creating your own reality and living in integrity. If your partner is genuinely untrustworthy and unlovable in your eyes, then leave. It is impossible to work out a healthy and satisfying relationship with a person who is not living in integrity with you, or who is in resistance. At this phase of evolution on Earth, you can only hurt yourself and hold yourself back spiritually by remaining in these relationships.

If your partner is a person of integrity and you both care deeply about one another, then you are responsible for busting your own resistance and control issues without projecting them onto your partner. Society has greatly encouraged just the opposite. It is time for men and women to release such societal beliefs as:

"The battle of the sexes is a simple fact of life and unchangeable."

"It is impossible for men and women to ever really understand each other."

"Once the honeymoon is over, it is downhill from there on out."

"Relationships require intrigue and challenge in order to stay alive."

You may have other societal beliefs that you are aware of that you need to change. Use the process for clearing beliefs on each of these, as well as for any others you think of. One person at a time is the way change happens, until finally enough individuals create a "hundredth monkey effect." Changing your own beliefs and attitudes does make an important difference.

Recently while teaching a class I identified a planetary contract held by members of both sexes that I would like to tell you about. First of all, planetary contracts are subtle—or not so subtle—psychic agreements between all members of the general populace of the whole planet. There may be small areas of Earth in which the people are not a part of these contracts, but from what I have seen, most of us are— or have been. Apparently, back at the time when the Luciferian and Satanic energies infiltrated Earth and Earth's atmosphere, they realized that the single most effective way to hold back spiritual evolution and control humans was through the male/female split. So what they did was send out massive thoughtforms to all of the women on the planet telling them, "No man can ever be trusted. All men want to control women and use them and hurt them. In order for you, as women, to protect yourselves and each other, you must agree to never trust any man. Men will always keep you oppressed because they are physically stronger than you are. Therefore, you must also agree to always keep the battle of the sexes going in order to prove that you are right and men are wrong."

The message they sent to the men was, "No woman can ever be trusted. All women want to control men and use them and hurt them. In order for you, as men, to protect yourselves and each other, you must agree to never trust any woman. You must keep women as an oppressed species or you will be oppressed. You must also agree to always keep the battle of the sexes going in order to prove that you are right and women are wrong."

When all of the members of the class I was teaching individually and collectively cleared these planetary contracts, there was an immediate shift in the room for the better. Some people had kriyas or deep breath releases. The whole room felt like a Vise Grip had been removed, creating more space, air, and light.

In order to clear these contracts, use the following process:

1. Simply envision a document that says "Planetary Contract" at the top. (Or write it out on a piece of paper if that is easier for you.)

2. At the bottom of the contract see your own name on one side and "All of the Women—or Men—on Earth" on the opposite side.

3. See the quoted words for your gender on the contract:

Men: "No woman can ever be trusted. All women want to control men and use them and hurt them. In order for you, as men, to protect yourselves and each other, you must agree to never trust any woman. You must keep women as an oppressed species or you will be oppressed. You must also agree to always keep the battle of the sexes going in order to prove that you are right and women are wrong."

Women: "No man can ever be trusted. All men want to control women and use them and hurt them. In order for you, as women, to protect yourselves and each other, you must agree to never trust any man. Men will always keep you oppressed because they are physically stronger than you are. Therefore, you must also agree to always keep the battle of the sexes going in order to prove that you are right and men are wrong."

4. Imagine that you have a big red marker in your hand and write "VOID" in large letters across the contract.

5. Rip the contract into at least two pieces.

6. Imagine a roaring fire in a fireplace or furnace and toss the pieces of torn paper into the fire. Watch it until all traces of the paper are indistinguishable.

7. Affirm in your own words, or as follows: "In the name of my I Am Presence that I Am, I am ready, willing, and able to take responsibility for restoring trust, understanding, respect, dignity, and true love to all of my relationships with women—or men. I am also ready, willing, and able to use discernment in all of my relationships with members of the opposite sex. I am determined and filled with courage and will no longer play games with members of my own gender that

in any way demean, humiliate, blame, or judge members of the opposite sex or categorize them as 'all the same'."

8. If you still feel a lot of emotional charge around this issue, sit and run energy while blowing roses and breathing deeply until you feel released. (These techniques are given in chapter 5 of *The Pleiadian Workbook*.)

Anger/Blame Release and Forgiveness

Forgiveness cannot be forced when it is not what you genuinely feel. If you still feel very angry, blaming, and deeply hurt by former lovers or other members of the opposite sex, then continue working on releasing those emotions before doing the forgiveness meditation given later in this section. For now, I do recommend that you do a meditation during which you call in your Higher Self of Light and guides and at least one Ascended Master, and tell them that you fully intend to come to a place of forgiveness with members of the opposite sex even though you are not yet ready to do so. Ask them for assistance with clearing and coming to a place of readiness. If you do feel ready to forgive, skip to page 144 and do the forgiveness meditation. Otherwise, continue with the following techniques for clearing anger and blame.

Writing a letter to the person, persons, or all men or women will help you release your emotions and mental charge. Make this a letter you do not intend to send. Use the following steps:

1. Ground yourself.

2. Surround your aura, and fill the room, with violet flame.

3. Call on Saint Germain and your own Higher Self of Light. Ask them to hold the violet flame in the room until you are complete. Tell them that you do not wish to psychically or otherwise harm the person or persons with whom you are angry. Your purpose is only to clear yourself of built-up emotions so that you can come to a place of forgiveness.

4. Invoke the Pleiadian Emissaries of Light. Tell them your purpose and ask them to place an Interdimensional Cone of Light above the entire room to assist you in the release, and in holding your boundaries.

5. Write your letter—or letters—to whatever members of the opposite sex you feel the need to clear. You can also make it to "all men" or "all women" if that is more appropriate for you. Make it as angry, blaming, hate-filled, and venomous as you can in order to help yourself release the charge. This is not to justify these emotions and attitudes; it simply helps deepen your release.

6. When you are through writing, read it out loud if possible. Imagine the person or persons with whom you are angry and speak directly to them. If you absolutely cannot do it verbally, then silently imagine saying the words to them. Put as much emotion into it as you can. If you need to, beat pillows or imagine physically attacking them in order to release the charge. If you followed the beginning steps for establishing boundaries and protection for the person or persons with whom you are angry, this process will be safe to do.

7. If you are still really angry, either read it again, or simply ad lib and continue.

8. When you are as complete as you can be for this time, put the letter away.

9. Ask your Higher Self, Saint Germain, and the Pleiadians to assist you by making sure that you do not psychically harm the person or persons until this process is complete.

10. Repeat the reading of the letter and releasing of emotions each day for two more days. Each time create your safe space before beginning.

11. At the end of the third time of reading the letter, burn it in a fireplace or sink. Watch until all traces of the writing and paper are burned.

12. Affirm, "It is done. So be it."

13. Take a bath or shower. In a bath, imagine that the water is pulling any residues of anger, blame, and hate from your body as you breathe deeply. When you feel really relaxed and complete, drain the tub and rinse off with fresh water. In a shower, imagine the shower is washing through—as well as around—your body, washing away all remainders of anger, hate, and blame. When you feel relaxed and complete, you are through with the shower.

14. Sit or lie down and go into a meditative state. Breathe fully and in a relaxed manner.

15. Visualize a large sun above your aura shining down into and filling your aura. Imagine it filling your body completely with golden light. Ask your guides and Higher Self to help you fill all of the places from which you have released anger, hate, and blame with this golden sunlight. Continue as long as you wish to do so, or for a minimum of five minutes.

16. Open your eyes and continue with your day.

Of course this process can be used for anyone, same sex or opposite sex, whenever you have the need. You may at times find it necessary to repeat the process with the same person as more or new issues arise.

You are now ready for the forgiveness meditation as follows:

1. Sit or lie down in a comfortable position. Ground yourself.

2. Ask your Higher Self of Light, the Pleiadian Emissaries of Light, Ascended Masters Jesus Christ and Mother Mary, and any others you wish to have present to join you.

3. Ask the Pleiadians to place an Interdimensional Cone of Light above your aura.

4. Tell your Higher Self and guides the name of the person you are ready to forgive and ask them to assist you in doing so as fully as possible.

5. Take a few deep breaths all the way to the base of your spine,

allowing your torso to release any tension held there and to simultaneously feel more alive.

6. Take a few deep breaths down into your arms and hands and allow them to become both more alive and relaxed.

7. Take a few deep breaths down into your legs and feet. Assist them in releasing any held tension and in feeling more vital and alive.

8. Imagine yourself walking through a beautiful meadow on a sunny day. The breeze is just cool enough to make the air temperature very pleasant. The scent from the multicolored wildflowers all around you fills the air. Butterflies and bees are flying from one flower to another. You hear and see a small stream gently flowing nearby. Take in the setting until you feel a deep sense of pleasure at being in this wonderful place.

9. At the far side of the meadow is a circular clearing about eight feet in diameter. You can just see it from where you are. You know that this is a sacred medicine circle expressly for forgiving yourself and others.

10. You begin to walk toward the East gateway of the circle. As you walk slowly toward the circle, you gather wildflowers along the way. You pick several flowers of each color you see, maybe even several varieties of each color. When you reach the outside of the circle you have a large, fragrant, and beautiful multicolored bouquet to use as a giveaway to this sacred place.

11. You stand at the entry to the circle in the East extending the bouquet of flowers first in the air and then gesturing toward the earth as an offering. You ask your spirit to be fully embodied and with you. You ask for transformation by fire and light as you enter this circle of forgiveness. When you feel complete at the East, move clockwise to the South.

12. Standing in the South, inside the circle, offer the flowers again to the sky and to the earth. Ask your body, your earth-self, to be fully alive and with you. Ask for transformation and rebirth by earth. Then walking clockwise, move on to the West.

13. Offer the flowers to the sky and to the earth as you stand in the West. Ask your emotional body and your astral body to be fully alive and present with you. Ask for purification and transformation by water. When complete, walk clockwise toward the North.

14. In the North offer your flowers to the sky and to the earth. Ask that your mental body, your mind, be fully alert, clear, and present with you. Ask for cleansing and transformation by air. Then walk back to the East completing the circle.

15. Next walk toward the center of the circle where there is a large flat rock, about two feet high. Place the flowers on the rock as an offering. Ask for your own wholeness and centeredness to be present in this sacred circle.

16. Call forth the person you are ready to forgive. See him or her appear on the opposite side of the rock from you.

17. Greet the person you have called upon and tell him or her why you have called and what your purpose is in the circle. Tell the person what you have previously blamed him or her for, why you have been angry and/or hurt, and that you are ready to let it go and forgive.

18. As you complete telling the person about what it is you are here to forgive, you will notice an iron bar between your bodies. It will most likely be located between your heart or solar-plexus chakras. This iron bar represents the hardness that has been between you in the form of anger, hate, hurt, or blame. Firmly grip the iron bar and loosen it from between you.

19. There is a fire pit just to the north side of the rock. Toss the iron bar into the fire with the intent that all of the hardness and negative feelings be transmuted in the fire as you watch the iron bar melt and disappear.

20. Tell the person you are sorry that you blamed him or her in the first place.

21. Walk around the rock and open your arms to embrace the person. Say, "I forgive you. I know that you have a Divine Essence made of Light just as I am. And I honor the self that you truly are."

22. Give the person a hug and send him or her as much love and forgiveness as you can. As you hug the person, he or she will slowly fade and disappear, returning to pure essence.

23. Next feel the area of your body where you found the iron bar. You will find any shame, regret, or anger that you did not let go and forgive sooner. Pull the hard rock from that place that represents your shame, regret, or anger at yourself. Toss it into the fire and watch it dissolve, while you breathe deeply into the area from which you removed the rock.

24. Ask your Higher Self to join you in the circle and give you a gift to replace the hard rock that you removed.

25. Receive the gift. Feel it. Then place it into your chakra as you affirm, "I completely forgive myself for not forgiving this person sooner."

26. Lie down on the ground by the fire. As you lie there the warmth of the fire makes you very drowsy and you drift into a gentle sleep. As you fall asleep you dream you are back in the room where you began this meditation. Your eyes open and you awaken in the dream, back where you began.

27. You are complete and ready to go on with your day.

This meditation process may be used as often as you feel the need. It may be used for self-forgiveness as well as with others. When using it for self-forgiveness, at step 16 you will see yourself appear on the other side of the rock. This other "you" will be the same age that you were when you did whatever you have been angry about, or have hated or blamed yourself for. When you embrace yourself and your other self dissolves, it is like reconnecting and reabsorbing a part of yourself from whom you have felt separate.

Male and Female Energy

Males and females alike have energy channels through which engendered energy is carried through specific glands and organs in your body. This energy helps regulate your endocrine system and balance your upper and lower body energies. It is the energy that you put out to others when you are nurturing and giving to them—how they experience your energy. When you are being sexual with another person, the other person feels not only your sexual passion and love, but also your male or female energy. Rarely do humans use their own engendered energy as a source of self-nurturing and self-esteem. That is what you will experience through the following exercises.

By clearing your male or female energy channels and learning to "run male or female energy," you can appreciate and love yourself more deeply, feel more fulfilled from within, bring vitality to your endocrine system and body, and increase your confidence in your own divine creative ability. When you begin to feel the quality of energy that you are usually giving away to others, you begin to recognize the beauty and value of that gift. Your male or female energy, when directed toward giving or sharing with others, is indeed a gift. As you experience your own energy more deeply, you may find yourself becoming more discerning about where you choose to gift this energy. You may realize how much you deserve to be with people who genuinely appreciate you. This realization is very vital to true self-esteem and self-love.

You may also become more aware of why you enjoy being around some people more than others. When a person feels good about himself as a man or herself as a woman, the engendered energies naturally flow more. The individual exudes a specific kind of confidence and ease that is very appealing. These individuals exude, or radiate, more than others. And, of course, you like being around them.

Certainly it is important to appreciate your own gender as well. You may be very giving to others, but not use your own energy to give to yourself. Or you may lack confidence and withhold from others because you do not feel that you have anything worthwhile to give. Whatever your personal situation may be, running your male or female energy can only make it better.

Running Male Energy (for males only)

The first exercise is a prerequisite to actually running your male energy. It is used to clear your male energy channels and your male creative energy reservoir. In illustration 13 on page 150, you will notice that the male energy channel begins at your pineal gland and then travels via a figure 8, or infinity symbol, to your pituitary gland and back. The figure 8 is used to create a reciprocal flow not only between these two glands, but also between your pineal gland and the rest of your channel. Your male energy channel extends from your pituitary down through your thyroid gland in your throat, then through your thymus gland, located in your heart chakra, and down through your adrenal glands and kidneys to your prostate.

Your male creative energy reservoir is shown in the illustrations on pages 151-152. This reservoir is a container for your male generative, creative energy. Clearing and activating this reservoir will be the last stage of this exercise.

The process for clearing your male energy channel is as follows:

1. Give yourself a small grounding cord from your prostate gland to the center of Earth. If you need a new, larger grounding cord at your first (or Earth) chakra, give yourself one at this time.

2. Check your aura boundary colors and aura size and make any needed adjustments.

3. Visualize a golden sun about eighteen inches above your head.

4. Begin to visualize, or intend, that the golden sunlight streams in through your crown and fills your pineal gland to overflowing. (See illustration 13 on page 150.) When your pineal gland is overflowing, go to the next step.

5. Now direct the golden sunlight through the figure 8 and into your pituitary gland. When your pituitary gland is overflowing and sending energy back to your pineal gland, go to the next step.

6. Send the golden sunlight from your pituitary gland into your thyroid gland. When your thyroid gland is overflowing, continue

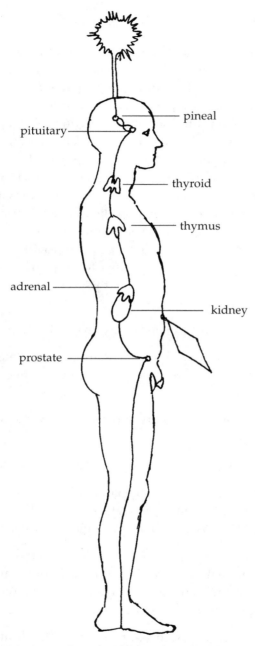

13. Male energy channel with his male creative diamond tilted down to run his creative energy through his channels

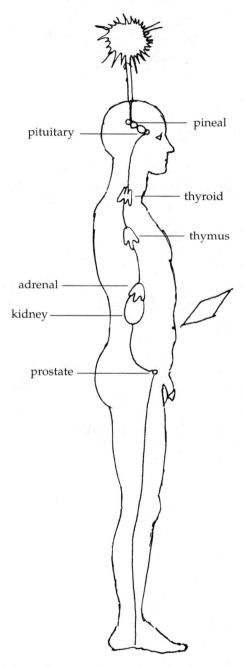

14. Male creative energy diamond tilted up (step 1)

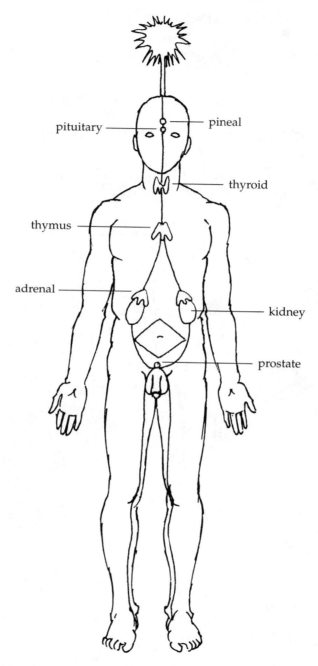

15. Male energy channel and creative diamond, front view

with the next step. Note: The energy is running through your pineal to your pituitary and will continue to do so throughout this clearing exercise.

7. Visualize, or intend, that the golden sunlight continues flowing down to your thymus gland in the center of your chest. Do not overflow the thymus gland at this time. Simply continue directing the sunlight through the rest of the channel: into your adrenal glands, then your kidneys, and finally your prostate.

8. Sit for at least five to ten minutes allowing the golden sunlight to flow through your entire male energy channel. Put this on "automatic" while continuing with the next step.

9. Place a grounding cord on the bottom tip of your male energy reservoir. This grounding cord need only go into the Earth a foot or two.

10. Imagine an "on/off" gauge on the reservoir and turn it on. At first the colors may be muddied or variegated. Sit running the golden sunlight and keeping your male energy reservoir grounded until the color in your reservoir settles to one solid color. This color is your male energy color.

11. Stop running the golden sunlight and continue with the next exercise.

The following is the exercise for running your male creative energy for self-nurturing:

1. Tilt your male energy reservoir downward as shown in illustration 14 on page 151. Placing your physical hands around the reservoir to do this will strengthen your experience.

2. Direct the energy in your reservoir to flow into your prostate gland area and into your male energy channels. Your male energy will flow upward through the entire channel until it reaches your pineal gland; at this point the energy will cycle back through the figure 8 to your pituitary gland, then back through your channels until it reaches your prostate. Continue holding your reservoir tilted downward and filling your male energy channel.

3. As your male energy flows back out of your prostate, having come full circle, remove the grounding cord on your prostate only. Leave the cord on your reservoir.

4. Begin to direct the energy that is overflowing your male energy channel at your prostate area to spread out along the outside of your entire body. As the energy touches your skin all around your body, imagine your skin breathing in the energy. Continue this as long as it takes to feel filled with your own male energy.

5. Remember, this wonderful energy you are feeling is what others feel when they are receiving from you. You may shut off the energy flow and return your reservoir to its normal position facing away from your body. Whether you choose to leave the grounding cord on your reservoir or not is up to you. Experiment with leaving it on and then removing it and decide which you prefer.

This exercise may be done as often as you would like. If you do it regularly, simply begin with the second exercise for running male energy. If you do it infrequently, you may need to clear your channels and reservoir before running your male energy.

Running Female Energy (for females only)

The first exercise is a prerequisite to actually running your female energy. It is used to clear your female energy channels, and your female creative energy reservoir. In illustration 16 on page 155, you will notice that your female energy channel begins at your pineal gland and then travels via a figure 8, or infinity symbol, to your pituitary gland and back. The figure 8 is used to create a reciprocal flow, not only between these two glands, but also between your pineal gland and the rest of your channel. Your female energy channel extends from your pituitary down through your thyroid gland in your throat; then the channel splits and goes behind both breasts. From your breasts it moves down through your adrenal glands, kidneys, and finally into your ovaries.

Your female creative energy reservoir is shown in illustration 17 on page 156. This reservoir is a container for your female generative,

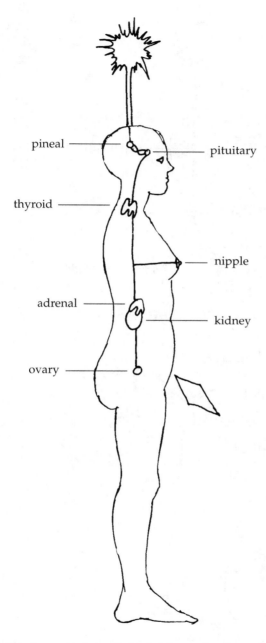

16. Female energy channel with female creative diamond tilted downward (step 4)

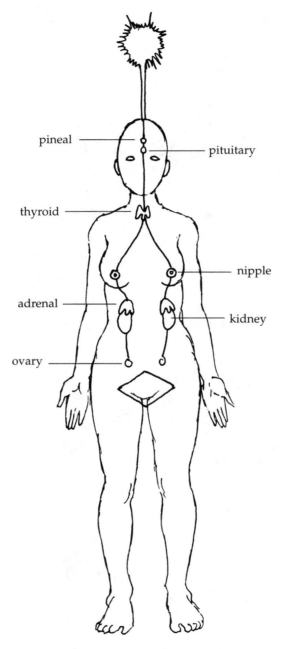

17. Female energy channel and creative diamond, front view

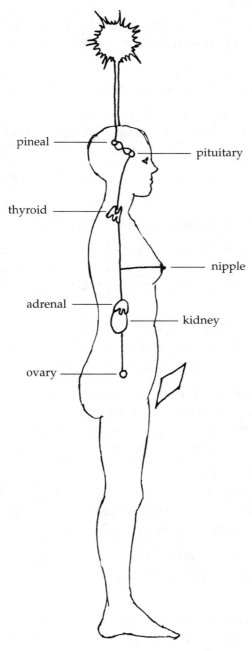

18. Female energy channel, side view, tilted up to run her female energy through her channels (step 1)

creative energy. Clearing and activating this reservoir will be the last stage of this exercise before actually running your female creative energy.

The process for clearing your female energy channel is as follows:

1. Give yourself two small grounding cords: one from each ovary to the center of Earth. If you need a new larger grounding cord at your second chakra, give yourself one at this time.

2. Check your aura boundary colors and aura size and make any needed adjustments.

3. Visualize a golden sun about eighteen inches above your head.

4. Begin to visualize, or intend, that the golden sunlight streams in through your crown and fills your pineal gland to overflowing. (See illustration 16 on page 155.) When your pineal gland is overflowing, go to the next step.

5. Now direct the golden sunlight through the figure 8 and into your pituitary gland. When your pituitary gland is overflowing and sending energy back to your pineal gland, go to the next step.

6. Send the golden sunlight from your pituitary gland into your thyroid gland. When your thyroid gland is overflowing, continue with the next step. Note: The energy is running through your pineal to your pituitary and will continue to do so throughout this clearing exercise.

7. Visualize, or intend, that the golden sunlight continues flowing into the two channels that go behind your breasts. Overflow the energy out through your nipples for a minute or two before moving on.

8. Continue directing the sunlight through the rest of the channel: into your adrenal glands, then your kidneys, and finally into your ovaries.

9. Sit for at least five to ten minutes allowing the golden sunlight to flow through your entire female energy channel. Put this on "automatic" while continuing with the next step.

10. Place a grounding cord on the bottom tip of your female energy reservoir. This grounding cord need only go into the earth a foot or two.

11. Imagine an "on/off" gauge on the reservoir and turn it on. At first the colors may be muddied or variegated. Sit running the golden sunlight through your female energy channels and keeping your female energy reservoir grounded until the color in your reservoir settles to one solid color. This color is your female energy color.

12. Stop running the golden sunlight and continue with the next exercise.

The following is the exercise for running your female creative energy for self-nurturing:

1. Tilt your female energy reservoir upward as shown in illustration 18 on page 157. Placing your physical hands around the reservoir will strengthen your experience.

2. Direct the energy in your reservoir to flow into your ovaries and into your female energy channels. Your female energy will flow upward through the entire channel until it reaches your pineal gland; at this point the energy will cycle back through the figure 8 to your pituitary gland and back through your channels until it reaches your ovaries. Continue holding your reservoir tilted upward and filling your female energy channels.

3. As your female energy flows back out through your ovaries, having come full circle, remove the grounding cord on your ovaries only. Leave the cord on your reservoir.

4. Begin to direct the energy that is overflowing your female energy channel at your ovaries to spread out along the outside of your entire body. As the energy touches your skin all around your body, imagine your skin breathing in the energy. Continue this as long as it takes to feel filled with your own female energy.

5. Remember, this wonderful energy you are feeling is what others feel when they are receiving from you. You may shut off the energy

flow and return your reservoir to its normal position fac-ing away from your body. Whether or not you choose to leave the grounding cord on your reservoir is up to you. Experiment with leaving it on and then removing it, and decide which you prefer. 🖭

This exercise may be done as often as you would like. If you do it regularly, simply begin with the second exercise for running female energy. If you do it infrequently, you may need to clear your channels and reservoir before running your female energy.

Dolphin Brain Balancing Chamber of Light

After running your male or female energy is a wonderful time to do this chamber session, although it may be done at any time. As you probably know, most humans only use one side of the brain at a time. However, you are intended to be a whole-brain creature, like the dol-phins. The dolphins operate from both sides of their brains at all times, except when sleeping. Then they shut off one side at a time while remaining awake on the other side. This is their version of sleeping. It has been said that when dolphins see human beings they think we are asleep because only half of our brains are functioning at any given time.

Therefore, as you move toward whole-brain function, the dol-phins are the natural teachers and assistants in doing so. As I said in *The Pleiadian Workbook*, the dolphins are Christ-conscious beings from Sirius who hold the energy of what we are becoming. Without them we would not stand much chance of ever attaining Christ conscious-ness. Of course, there are etheric dolphin spirit guides as well as the physical ones; you will be calling on these guides during this cham-ber session.

During this session, the Pleiadian Emissaries of Light, the Sirian Archangelic League of the Light, and Ascended Masters Jesus Christ and Mother Mary will be working with you as well. In the process of assisting you in activation of whole-brain function, clearing of block-ages may be required. Therefore, allow forty-five minutes to an hour for the chamber session. You will need to do this chamber many times before you are able to retain whole-brain function, unless you have already been working on this with other methods. Do this chamber as often as you like. Allow the full time the first three times you do it. After that, unless you sense a need for more time, ten minutes should suffice. It is recommended that you do this chamber session early in the day or at a time when you feel awake and do not plan to go to sleep.

Following are the steps for doing a Dolphin Brain Balancing Chamber of Light:

1. Lie down with a pillow beneath your knees and your feet shoulder-width apart.

2. Give yourself a grounding cord and pull in your aura, if needed.

3. Call in your own Higher Self of Light to activate your silver cord and fill your tube of light. When this is done, proceed.

4. Invoke the Pleiadian Emissaries of Light.

5. Ask the Pleiadians for an Interdimensional Cone of Light for clearing and divine alignment.

6. Ask the Pleiadians to place you inside a Dolphin Brain Balancing Chamber of Light.

7. Invoke the Sirian Archangelic League of the Light.

8. Ask the Sirians to place an Evolutionary Cone of Light above you.

9. Ask the Sirians to assist you in this Dolphin Brain Balancing Chamber session by realigning and reworking your brain patterning and sacred geometry to facilitate whole-brain function that is in alignment with your highest good.

10. Call in the Ascended Masters Jesus Christ and Mother Mary. Ask them to hold the male/female balance and to assist you in coming to whole-brain function.

11. Invoke the dolphin spirit guides and ask them to assist you in coming to whole-brain function.

12. Lie comfortably and relax for forty-five minutes to an hour, or until you feel or sense the chamber session is complete.

13. Sit up slowly. You may need to reground before standing and going on with your day. 🖻

The Black Witch and the Satanic Male

For those who sense a need to take their healing and clearing to a deeper level, who sense something angrier, or more hidden than what this chapter has covered, there is a next level. The Pleiadians and I have gone back and forth in our conferences about the information and clearing processes concerning dark astral connections with black witchcraft and the Satanic realms. We mutually agreed, at last, that it did not feel appropriate or safe to include the teachings and clearing processes in written form. First of all, before approaching these issues, you must have done the Sword of Truth and Holy Grail initiation in chapter 10 and be very comfortable with using the Sword of Truth.

The Pleiadians also decided that those who wish to do this further clearing would have to do it either in person with a Pleiadian Lightwork practitioner or on tape with my voice. A human being who has cleared these issues and has a direct pipeline to the higher-dimensional guides of Light is needed to hold a safe space while you work on dark astral witch and satanic clearings. Even though a tape is not quite the same as being in person, the energy and sound of my voice leading you through the process and doing the invocations will establish an extra protection that cannot be assured in written processes only. Therefore, much to my chagrin, I am able to offer the black witch and satanic clearings and teachings only on tape, or with a level II Pleiadian Lightwork graduate practitioner. This is not for promotional purposes. It is simply a matter of integrity of material and safety for those of you who desire to do clearing on this level. Tape ordering information is in the back of this book, as is the address to get on our mailing list and receive a list of practitioners.

Chapter 7

CELLULAR CLEARING

In order for your sexual energy to flow tantrically throughout your body, your cells must be available for this energy. When your cells are clear enough for tantric energy to flow fully through them, then the frequency of your body is gradually and steadily increased. When it reaches the point that your spirit and Ka may remain in your body consistently during waking hours, your cells will have been cleared enough that they are spinning clockwise in synchronization with the orbits of the planets and the Sun. This is a necessary prerequisite for full-body enlightenment and ascension. In this case, the goal for ascension is not one in which you finally and completely leave your body, transcending the physical realm. The goal is full cellular embodiment of your Higher Self, or Christ Presence. To raise the vibration of your body and all of physical existence until the third dimension is no longer synonymous with limitation is the bigger goal. Imagine becoming a Master being like Christ or Quan Yin and still considering the third dimension limiting, frightening, and to be avoided. It sounds ridiculous, does it not? By the time you have truly become a Master being, or Christ Presence, on Earth you will have transcended every fear, every limiting thought and circumstance, and will have nothing to avoid. Cellular clearing is another accelerated step toward that goal.

The Pleiadian Workbook states, "Tantric sexual energy runs intercellularly, as well as with the kundalini, up the spinal channel and through the chakras. It is pure creation energy. It is the stuff cosmic ecstasy is made of, and one of the energies that has been most damaged and distorted on Earth." As discussed in the previous chapter, return to innocence, spontaneity, and loving sexual behavior is essential to spiritual evolution and full embodiment of spirit. Now let us look at the further preparation for running tantric energy and kundalini intercellularly.

The Four-Cell Process

As you have learned to clear and release other people's energies, beliefs, karmic issues, contracts, cords, and judgments from your chakras and localized problem areas in your body, now it is time to clear these energies on a cellular level. Not all issues are carried in your etheric body on a cellular level, but those that are have a lot of control over your thought processes, emotional reactions, and life in general. For example, when I was first introduced to cellular clearing by the Pleiadians, they showed me that I was carrying disappointment cellularly. This means that I literally had disappointment energy in *every* cell of my body. It made me really afraid to ever get my hopes up too much about anything lest I be disappointed again. My greatest dread was the thought of even more disappointment because it seemed endless. The more I got into my body, the more I felt it. Therefore, when cellular clearing was introduced to me, clearing this disappointment and its sources in my cells was very important. In order to do so, I was guided to do a complete healing and clearing on four cells of my body, which would trigger the automatic release in the rest of the cells. This is the first and most primary rule for clearing cellular issues: Always clear the same energy in a total of four cells and the rest will follow suit.

When I did the clearing on myself, the first thing I saw was a spot of black, dead, pain energy in each cell. I used an ultraviotet Quantum Transfiguration grid on each of four cells, one at a time, until the pain was gone. (Using the Quantum Transfiguration grid on localized areas is explained on pages 251-256 of *The Pleiadian Workbook*.) Underneath the pain I found whitish-gray globs of my mother's disappointment energy accompanied by her belief that life is always painful and disappointing for women. I ran gold light into each of the four cells one at a time while pulling roses with my mother's face in them through each cell. The combination of the gold and the roses extracted her energy and belief from each cell, after which I blew up the roses outside my aura, returning the neutralized energy to her.

Then I found several life experiences in the form of tiny memory pictures in each cell. These pictures constantly reminded me that I should only expect disappointments and not to get my hopes up about anything, especially relationships. Being a Sagittarian optimist and idealist with daydreamy, naive Pisces rising, I had always had a tendency toward high aspirations and fancifulness. But eventually when my dreams and ideals had become shattered enough times, I became pessimistic and crushed by the weight of my unfulfilled dreams. Disappointment on a cellular level was a cliche about my astrological personality type. I proceeded to use roses and gold energy to pull out all of the memory pictures from each of four cells. After that I thoroughly cleansed each of the cells with violet flame in order to transmute my own emotional energies of disappointment and hopelessness. These energies continued to release from my physical and emotional bodies for about a month before I felt a sense of true freedom from them. You see, once you clear the four cells, the rest of the cells are triggered to release the same energies that you actively clear during the healing session on yourself. At times this gradual release has been experienced by clients and by me as a continual relief and relaxation in the body. At other times, sporadic releases of emotions, or kriyas—energy releases that cause the body to twitch, quiver, or shake—have continued for days or even several weeks after the healing. In any case, the eventual result is freedom from the problem—in this case my fear of hoping and the continual feelings of let down and disappointment.

Of course when you are holding energies on a cellular level, the magnetism toward situations and people to create more of that same energy is ever present. Like attracts like. So when I was holding disappointment about relationships and life as a woman, I continually magnetized people and situations that made it even worse. Since I have cleared this issue, I have found it necessary to also consciously work at breaking the behavioral patterns and changing my attitudes as they arise out of habit. The tendency toward expecting less in order to avoid disappointment was so deep that I had to monitor myself for many months as the habit would resurface. At first I tended to catch myself after the fact—sometimes days after. Gradually the time frame shortened until I finally came to the point that I would catch myself while having the feelings and attitudes. By changing these feelings and attitudes "midstream" a few times, I began to catch myself at the inception point of the feelings and attitudes and take charge of creating my life in a new and more positive way. By learning to use more discernment I could trust myself to be enthusiastic and hopeful in more realistic and less naive ways. The rewards have been a steady increase in joy, positive outlook, enthusiasm, creativity, and new and wonderful openings in many areas of my life. Sometimes I still find myself feeling surprised when situations in life go extremely well. Then I am reminded that I still may hold some reserves on how much goodness I believe is possible for me. To be delighted when good things happen is great. But when I am shocked that something so good could be happening to me, I stop and reaffirm, "Of course this is happening to me. Life is intended to work out in positive ways and I deserve it." I do not take the good things for granted, but I do openly affirm them and let them in.

Your own cellular issues will be unique to you. They could consist of: cellular anger and revenge; shame and low self-worth; humiliation; parental control energies and contracts; your own beliefs, judgments, or perfect pictures; pain or painful memory pictures; karmic patterns from this or past lives; denial and repressed emotions; fear of trusting yourself and/or others; or any other core issues you have not yet cleared in yourself. I use the term "core issues" because if something is in your energy field on a cellular level it will have a core, or all-encompassing, effect on your life.

The process for clearing cellular issues given to me by the Pleiadians includes visualization and self-healing. You may also choose to get together with a friend and do the process for each other if you find it too difficult to do for yourself. First you will go into a deeply relaxed state. Then you will imagine a miniature you in the center of your head. You will pull as much of your consciousness into this miniature you as possible. Then you will ask that your Higher Self and a Pleiadian Emissary of Light travel with you through a Cellular Magnification Chamber. You will see yourself walking through double doors into a room where all of the individual cells are as big as you are. As you examine the cells, you will look for common areas of blockage in them. For instance: Pain will appear as black, dead splotches; foreign energy will be milky and opaque, usually white, but any color is foreign if it is milky; contracts will look like legal papers saying "Contract" at the top; pictures will look like photographs; memories will either look like photos or little holographic bubbles with scenes inside them; programming will appear like strings of beads or connected dots that can be cleared in a Quantum Transfiguration grid. When you find a block to be cleared in the cells, you will clear it in all four cells before going on to the next energy to be healed or cleared. When you find painful emotions of your own, you may wish to run violet flame through four cells while blowing roses about whatever issue or memory is causing the pain. When complete, you will come back out of the chamber room to the center of your head and be guided to more full-body awareness again.

Following is the step-by-step procedure for cellular clearing:

1. Ground yourself.

2. Pull your aura in to within two to three feet of your body in every direction. Check your aura boundary colors and surround your aura with violet flame.

3. Blow up any old roses outside your aura and give yourself new ones.

4. Welcome your Higher Self of Light to activate and connect your silver cord to the top of your head and to fill your tube of light with your own Higher Self's energy and love. Ask your Higher Self to remain with you throughout the session.

5. Invoke the Pleiadian Emissaries of Light to come forth. Tell them you intend to do a cellular clearing and healing; ask them to give you an Interdimensional Cone of Light. Now ask the Pleiadians to place you inside a Cellular Clearing Chamber of Light until the session is done. (This will create safer boundaries, magnify your cellular awareness, and allow them to assist in your process.)

6. In order to relax your body and assist you in accessing deeper awareness, begin to breathe deeply and fully into your body as follows:

- Breathe all the way down to your toes, expanding the skin around your toes with your breath. Tell them to relax.

- Breathe and expand both feet with your breath, telling them to relax.

- Breathe and expand your calves and shins while telling them to relax.

- Repeat the breathing into and expansion of the rest of your body while telling each part to relax: knees, thighs, buttocks, groin, pelvis, solar plexus, small of your back, ribs, chest, shoulder blades, entire length of your spine, shoulders, arms, hands and fingers, neck and throat, face, scalp, and eyes.

7. Imagine a miniature you in the center of your head. Bring all of your awareness into this miniature self.

8. Ask your Higher Self and a Pleiadian Emissary of Light to go with you into a Cellular Magnification Chamber.

9. Envision double doors on which is written "Cellular Magnification Chamber." Go through the doors into the room. All that you will see there are many cells that are roughly the same size as your body. There will be a walkway with guard rails upon which you will walk while moving through the chamber.

10. Examine the cells, comparing them to each other. Look for common areas that need to be cleared. When you find something to be cleared, clear it thoroughly in four cells. Then move on to the next block to be cleared or area to be healed with healing light. Continue until you have cleared all that you are being shown to clear at this time. Ask the Pleiadians and your Higher Self for advice and assistance as you feel the need.

11. Go back out through the double doors to the center of your head.

12. Breathe deeply, expanding your consciousness with your breath down to the base of your spine; then down your arms and hands; then down into your feet and legs. Release the image and feeling of the miniature you and expand your awareness to full-body aliveness and consciousness again.

13. Ground yourself again if you feel the need.

14. Blow up your aura roses and give yourself new ones.

15. Open your eyes and continue with your day.

If you are feeling emotional or disoriented afterward, a hot bath with Epsom Salts, minerals, or peppermint oil would be ideal to assist you in the further release. A hot tub works well also. It is recommended that you not repeat this process any more often than once a month, or even longer, to allow for full integration after each clearing. It is also recommended that you wait at least one week before doing the next process, for clearing the original eight cells of your body. [cassette icon]

Clearing and Healing Your Original Eight Cells

According to the Pleiadians, the blueprint for your body was created in your original eight cells. This original eight-cell complex still exists in your perineum center. Thse cells maintain your original DNA encodings—as did your original eight cells—until you have cleared any mutations and blocks within those cells. The mutations and blocks in this area are literally ones with which you were born. They may be chemical, etheric, mental, or emotional in nature. When I use the word "etheric" I refer to your etheric body, which is the energy double of your physical body and through which healing of your physical body takes place.

Chemical deposits in this eight-cell structure generally appear as metallic or rocklike. To clear them requires use of the ultraviolet Quantum Transfiguration grid. You must also ask the Overlighting Devas of the Mineral Kingdom to return these chemical elementals to Earth where they belong. These chemical pollutants in your cells may originate from: drugs your mother took during pregnancy or during the birth process; toxins from nonorganic foods in your mother's body; neurotoxins contained in perfumes, commercial detergents, shampoos, and soaps; pesticides used in the house or garden; hair sprays, spray starch, or other aerosol sprays; cigarettes; house paints; plastics; new carpets; wood sealer and other surface sealers; chemical adhesives; or other building materials. Some of them may have been built up in your mother's body prior to her pregnancy with you, others during the pregnancy. Regardless of their source, if they were present in your original eight cells, they created a propensity in your body to collect these pollutants in your cells. They can also create substance addictions and allergies.

Etheric body pollutants and blocks may be caused by damage to your mother's etheric body such as a clogged liver, holes in her etheric intestinal track, amorphous buildup from negativity and hatred in the area of her physical heart or any other areas of her body in which she held repressions, traumas, or negativity. These may show up in your original eight cells as dark spots, milky patches, little holes, tears, or discoloration. If the spots are black and dead-looking you can use the ultraviolet Quantum Transfiguration grid as before to dissolve the pain. If you find milky patches, gold light and roses should work well for clearing them. Holes and tears require two stages of healing: First you will use the ultraviolet Quantum Transfiguration grid for clearing the pain or scar tissue around the edge of the holes or tears. This stage is like cleaning the debris from a cut prior to putting on an antiseptic and having it stitched back together. In order to stitch it back together—which is actually a process of weaving back together the broken light fibers of which the cells are made—you will use a Ki Quantum Transfiguration grid. (Ki is an ancient Egyptian word for the tiny fibers of light that make up your holographic body.) When using the grid for reweaving your broken Ki, you simply ask the Pleiadians to assist you in weaving together the damaged fibers of light in the area with a hole or tear. Then you envision the Ki Quantum Transfiguration grid of all golden light around the area to be healed. You will hold it in place until the area with the hole or tear is completely restored to normal with no more signs of damage. For discolored areas, the most commonly used healing colors are gold, violet flame, or rose gold. If you find thick, brownish-red discoloration that feels like resistance, use fire-engine red flame to break down this resistance energy.

Blocks in the mental body of your original eight cells will be in the form of your mother's or father's beliefs, judgments, memories, or programming (the connected dots or beads as mentioned previously). You may also find your own past-life beliefs, judgments, or programming you brought into this lifetime to clear. If these appear as two-dimensional photographlike pictures or holographic bubbles containing scenes, then you can simply use the "cancel, tear, and violet flame" method for clearing beliefs. If they appear as blobs of energy in which you sense or "hear" the words, then you will need to create an image to represent the belief, superimpose it over the energy, and then cancel, tear, and violet flame it. Programming may be dissolved in the ultraviolet Quantum Transfiguration grid as before.

Emotional energies contained in these orignial eight cells may belong to either of your parents. They will generally appear as swirls of milky colored energies that have an obvious feeling quality to them. For example: Mom's or Dad's shame may appear as sluggish-feeling swirls or masses of sulfur-yellow-green energy; their anger will look like opaque red or reddish-brown energy and it will feel hot; fear is generally cold-feeling, contracted, and stark white or yellow like the color of pus; resentment is generally a putrid orange color and sometimes has streaks of red or charcoal gray in it; hate is charcoal gray or black; envy, jealousy, and greed are varying shades of dull peridot to pea green; grief and sorrow are usually a dull olive green varying from pale to very dark. When these emotional energies belong to others, they are always milky and opaque looking. Even though the color may be dull, if it is clear looking as opposed to milky, the energy is your own. Emotions belonging to others are most easily removed by running sunlight gold or rose-gold light into the areas to be cleared while pulling roses with the person's face in them through the area. Continue until the foreign energies are gone. If emotions of your own are blocking the cells, once again use violet flame, as before, until the area looks clear. Roses may be used to clear the issues causing the emotional pain if the source is known.

Working with the original eight cells is a little different than cellular clearing in that you must clear energies in all eight cells. These energies may or may not be repeated in more than one cell. But the entire eight-cell matrix affects your body as a whole. Therefore, programming or a belief that appears in just one of the eight cells can impact you cellularly. Clearing it in the eight cells will trigger release in all your cells even if only one cell contains any given issue. When a block or mutation exists on the original eight-cell level, it is even more "core level" than other cellular issues. This is because these eight cells contain the blueprint for your entire body: etherically, elementally, mentally, and emotionally. These cells also greatly impact your spirit's ability to embody fully. Therefore, issues, mutations, and blocks in your original eight cells are part of your own creation of this lifetime. It is the stuff of which limited paradigms are made. When you clear these cells, you will literally give yourself the opportunity to undergo a paradigm shift.

One client on whom I did this clearing had a lifetime pattern of feeling obligated and indebted to her family, lovers, and close friends. She always carried the weight of guilt with her when others gave to her or were kind to her in any way. When I realized this was a birth paradigm, I looked at her original eight cells. Her mother had programmed her daughter en utero to be indebted to her for giving birth to the daughter. The pain and sacrifice of this gift of birth were carefully laid out in the programming to assure that the child would feel guilty, and therefore beholden to the mother—forever. By removing the programming in these cells, my client had the opportunity to make paradigm shifts in these areas and was able to embrace guilt-less receiving, giving from love instead of guilt, and codependence with family and friends. I told her that it would be easier for her to change these behaviors and attitudes after the programming was cleared, but that she would also need to consciously choose to break the habit patterns that had been created through the life-long paradigm. She had worked on this issue some but usually had given up, feeling hopeless to ever respond differently with loved ones. After the session I began to see quantum leaps in her self-confidence, independence in decision making, and ability to say "No" when that was her truth. She has continued to make progress on increasingly subtler levels as the grosser and more obvious aspects of the paradigm have changed. As with cellular clearing, your own ability and willingness to change your habits commensurate with your new awareness makes all the difference in your actual life changes. The eight-cell clearing makes this much easier to do.

The process for this clearing is very similar to the one for cellular clearing. Steps 1 through 7 are almost identical. The only exception is that when you ask the Pleiadians to place you inside a chamber it will be a "Original Eight-Cell Clearing Chamber of Light." After completing those steps you will go down a long spiral staircase from the center of your head all the way to your perineum. There you will find a set of double doors on which is written "Original Eight-Cell Chamber." When you go through the doors you will be inside a holographic observatory that looks somewhat like illustration 19 on page 174. The splotches, dots, and other blocks shown are hypothetical examples of what you might find. There will be a pathway with handrails for you to hold while you walk through the eight-cell matrix. As you find foreign energies, pictures, programming, pain, tears, holes, or whatever else needs to be cleared, you will simply stop and do the healing and/or clearing. Unlike in the cellular clearing process earlier in this chapter, you may not find the same energies in each of the cells. As I mentioned previously, these eight cells operate as a whole entity unto itself. Each cell, therefore, is part of an overall matrix and not necessarily identical to any other cell in the matrix. Duplicates sometimes do occur in which case you will clear them everywhere they are found. When you are through with the session, the eight cells should be clear of blocks as in illustration 20 on page 175.

After completing the clearing part of the session, you will be guided to ask to be placed inside a PEMS—Physical, Emotional, Mental, and Spiritual—Synchronization Chamber of Light as described in *The Pleiadian Workbook*. This part of the session will take between twenty and forty minutes, and the full time should be allowed. The entire process will take between forty-five minutes and one-and-a-half hours.

19. *Original Eight-Cell Chamber with hypothetical examples of energy blocks in need of clearing*

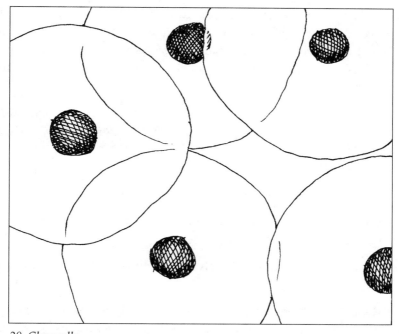

20. Clear cells

The process for clearing and healing your original eight cells is as follows:

1. Ground yourself.

2. Pull your aura in to within two to three feet of your body in every direction. Check your aura boundary colors and surround your aura with violet flame.

3. Blow up any old roses outside your aura and give yourself new ones.

4. Welcome your Higher Self of Light to activate and connect your silver cord to the top of your head and to fill your tube of light with your own Higher Self's energy and love. Ask your Higher Self to remain with you throughout the session.

5. Invoke the Pleiadian Emissaries of Light to come forth. Tell them you intend to do a clearing and healing of your original eight

cells and ask them to give you an Interdimensional Cone of Light above your aura. Now ask the Pleiadians to place you inside an Original Eight-Cell Clearing Chamber of Light until the session is done. (This will create safer boundaries and magnify your cellular awareness.)

6. In order to relax your body and assist you in accessing deeper awareness, begin to breathe deeply and fully into your body as follows:

- Breathe all the way down to your toes, expanding the skin around your toes with your breath. Tell them to relax.

- Breathe and expand the whole of both feet with your breath, telling them to relax.

- Breathe and expand your calves and shins while telling them to relax.

- Repeat the breathing into and expansion of the rest of your body while telling each part to relax: knees, thighs, buttocks, groin, pelvis, solar plexus, small of your back, ribs, chest, shoulder blades, entire length of your spine, shoulders, arms, hands and fingers, neck and throat, face, scalp, and eyes.

7. Imagine a miniature you in the center of your head. Bring all of your awareness into this miniature self.

8. In your miniature body you will see a spiral staircase going down from the center of your head. Walk down it with your Higher Self and a Pleiadian Emissary of Light until you have reached your perineum center. There you will see double doors on which is written "Original Eight-Cell Chamber." Go through the doors.

9. Once inside you will see the eight-cell holographic structure and walkways with handrails going around each cell. Begin to walk to the nearest cellular hologram and clear and heal anything that is blocking or mutating it. Continue around all eight cells, clearing and healing as you go. Make a mental note of the nature of the energies you are clearing for future reference.

10. When you are through, go back to the double doors but do not leave yet. Ask the Pleiadians to place a protective cocoon around the eight-cell structure until the integration from the clearing and healing is complete. Envision strands of golden light wrapping around the entire chamber like wrappings around a mummy. When this is complete, go back out through the doors.

11. Walk up the spiral stairs until you are back in the center of your head.

12. Breathe deeply, expanding your consciousness with your breath down to the base of your spine; then down your arms and hands; then down into your feet and legs. Release the image and feeling of the miniature you and expand your awareness to full-body aliveness and consciousness again.

13. Ground yourself again if you feel the need.

14. Blow up your aura roses and give yourself new ones.

15. Ask the Pleiadians to place you inside a PEMS Synchronization Chamber of Light. Allow twenty to forty minutes for the session.

16. When you sense the chamber session is complete, open your eyes and continue with your day.

It is recommended that you do this process no more often than every three to six months. After the first time of clearing and healing your original eight cells, it is advised that you should only do it again as you feel guided to do so. The information and techniques in the next chapter will assist in your integration of the processes in this chapter. Therefore, you may move on whenever you feel so inclined. 🖭

Sacred Geometry Chambers of Light for Your Pineal and 108-faceted Prism

The process for clearing, realigning your sacred geometry, and activating your pineal gland and the 108-faceted prism is almost identical to the one for your perineum center, given in chapter 5. The only difference is that when that exercise instructed you to focus on your perineum area, in this case you will focus on your pineal gland and then your 108-faceted prism instead. When you get to the last phase, in which the Interdimensional Chamber of Light is used, you will simply visualize a smaller version of that chamber in a grid around your pineal gland and then your 108-facted prism as pictured in illustration 21 on page 181.

First, I would like to explain a little more about your pineal gland's function relative to Pleaidian Lightwork. *The Pleiadian Workbook* describes your Ka Template as having four channels that connect it to your pineal gland. That is because your pineal gland is responsible for downstepping the energies that come into your body from other dimensions. This gland then transduces the energy into utilizable form and disperses it throughout your body in whatever way it is needed. Every human is continually receiving light and color from one of the seven rays as well. This energy enters your crown chakra and goes directly into your 108-faceted prism as shown. This prism receives and refracts the light and sends it into your pineal gland. The color and frequency of the light that enters your pineal gland depends upon which facets of the prism it passed through. When this energy reaches your pineal gland it activates a corresponding point on the Fibbernache spiral of your pineal. (See illustration 21 on page 181.) This creates a chain reaction in which the light strikes a musical tone, color, and frequency within the Fibbernache spiral, then moves with a domino effect through the rest of that spiral and its corresponding spiral in the opposite direction. From there the light and energy have been transduced and naturally flow out to the organ, gland, blood stream, or wherever in the body corresponds to the aspect of the Fibbernache spiral that has been activated.

A practical example is: Imagine that you have just eaten lunch. When the ray energy passes through your 108-faceted prism into your pineal gland, a tone and neurological message will have already been sent from your digestive tract to your brain. So your pineal gland takes the ray energy into the part of the Fibbernache spiral that regulates your stomach to secrete hydrochloric acid. As the pineal sends the appropriate harmonic, color, and electrical energies to your stomach, it responds.

Another example is: You have just greeted your partner after being apart all day. You look at each other, hug, kiss, and begin to blend your energies. The ray energy coming into your crown reaches your 108-faceted prism, which has already been impulsed by your neurological and chakra responses to your partner. So the ray energy moves through the aspects of the prism in just the right combination to activate your heart chakra to open more, your body to secrete pre-sexual lubricating fluids, and your sexual channels to open. The ray energies move into your pineal gland, striking just the right harmonics there to trigger these desired body and emotional responses. Internally, a chorus of sounds synchronizes with a prismatic light show and activation of your bodily sexual response. Externally, you move into a deeper kiss, pressing into your partner's body, and so on.

When the refracted rays of light from your 108-faceted prism reach their corresponding points on your pineal gland's Fibbernache spiral, it is as if a xylophone has been struck on a single note which triggers the ringing of the notes on the rest of that arm of the spiral. When that arm of the spiral has been activated, the light and sounds jump over to the corresponding spiral arm that goes in the opposite direction. (See illustration 21 on page 181.) When that arm of the spiral has been harmonically sounded and illuminated, it moves into the aspect of your pineal gland that holds the sacred geometry for individual organs, glands, chakras, and so on. The pineal gland holographically contains microcosmic sacred geometry forms for every chakra and body system. Therefore, the colors and tones ring and illuminate whatever chakras and body systems need to be activated at any given time.

Your pineal gland also receives messages from throughout your body and chakras continually. The neurological impulses from each organ and gland carry the sacred geometry and tone of that part of your body. Therefore, when the neurological impulse reaches your pineal gland, your pineal gland can pull in the needed ray and Ka energies to fulfill the function being requested of it at any given time.

This may seem a little complicated and off the subject. But clear function of your pineal gland and 108-faceted prism is essential to full-body tantric energy flow, enlightenment, and ascension. These two centers in your brain literally enable your body to receive not only the energies and messages with which to sustain physical function, but they also keep the sacred geometry of every cell capable of achieving full-body tantric ecstasy—the frequency necessary for ascension and Christ consciousness. Therefore, you might say that complete health and enlightenment of your pineal gland is a prerequisite to ascension and Christ consciousness.

During a tantric release in which you bring the sexual energy all the way up from your genitals through your perineum to your pineal gland, you literally have the capacity to ring the harmonic tones of every spiral arm of the Fibbernache spiral in your pineal gland. This fully opens your chakras, pulls your ray and Ka energies in at your current maximum capacity, and can open you to powerful spiritual experiences. You may feel yourself becoming one with the Milky Way, or the Tree of Life, or the rain forest, or with Earth or the Sun. You may simply expand into a color-and-light show that is ecstatically blissful, or joyful. The degree to which you can experience these heightened spiritual states is a direct result of the health and sacred geometry of your soul, perineum, pineal gland, and 108-faceted prism. Therefore, the next step in preparing you for full-body tantra, and later for ascension, is the restoration of the sacred geometry of your pineal gland and 108-faceted prism. You will do the chambers for these two centers individually, beginning with your pineal gland.

Following are the steps for experiencing the Sacred Geometry Chamber of Light for your pineal gland:

1. Lie down comfortably with a pillow beneath your knees and your feet shoulder-width apart.

2. Give yourself a new grounding cord.

3. Pull in your aura to within two to three feet around your body in every direction. Check and adjust your aura boundary colors as needed.

4. Invoke your Higher Self of Light to come forth and be with you throughout the session.

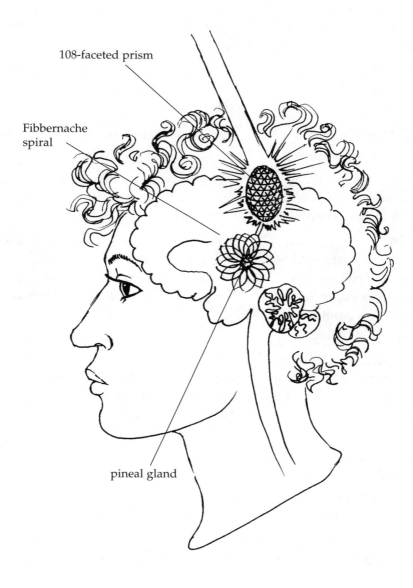

108-faceted prism

Fibbernache
spiral

pineal gland

21. Energy enters crown and activates 108-faceted prism which activates the pineal-gland Fibbernache spiral

5. Invoke the Pleiadian Emissaries of Light and ask them to place an Interdimensional Cone of Light above you for clearing and divine alignment.

6. Invoke the Sirian Archangelic League of the Light and ask them to place an Evolutionary Cone of Light above you so that this session may be used to achieve the highest good.

7. Invoke Ascended Masters Jesus Christ and Mother Mary to assist in the session.

8. Tell your guides that you are ready to be placed inside a Sacred Geometry Chamber of Light for your pineal gland. When you feel the shift in your energy field, proceed.

9. For the first level of activation, envision an ultraviolet Quantum Transfiguration grid around your pineal gland. Ask the Pleiadians to assist in placing and holding this grid for the next ten minutes. After two minutes of focusing on the grid, relax until the ten minutes is over. Then continue.

10. Next ask that the sacred geometry of your pineal gland be restored to whatever degree is possible at this time. Envision a Fibbernache spiral inside a small sun at the location of your pineal gland. After two minutes of holding that focus, relax for twenty to forty minutes until you feel that the work is done.

11. Next ask that your newly restructured pineal gland be placed inside an Interdimensional Chamber of Light grid for ten more minutes. Envision the golden white light streaming into the center of your pineal for about a minute. Then relax, breathe gently and deeply, and allow the expansion and light activation to occur fully.

12. When you feel the chamber session is done, sit up very slowly. Reground yourself if you feel the need. Then continue with your day.

You will need to wait at least forty-eight hours before continuing with the Sacred Geometry Chamber of Light for your 108-faceted prism. The process is identical to the one above except that you will substitute the 108-faceted prism for the pineal gland. Step 10 will be revised as follows:

10. Next ask that the sacred geometry of your 108-faceted prism be restored to whatever degree is possible at this time. Envision your 108-faceted prism inside a small sun. After two minutes of holding that focus, relax for twenty to forty minutes until you feel that the work is done. (Then complete steps 11 and 12 from the previous chamber session.) ▭

Sacred Geometry Chambers of Light for Your Organs and Glands

If you wish to continue with the restoration of your sacred geometry, you may do so by using the same Chamber of Light process given above for your pineal gland. It is important that you do no more than one chamber per week for organs and glands. If you notice detoxification symptoms or any other physical changes such as mild spasms in an organ, more sensation in the designated area, or tenderness, you will need to wait until these side effects have subsided completely before moving on to the next part of your body you wish to clear. A suggested approach to the continuation of these particular Sacred Geometry Chambers is as follows:

Make a list of all of the organs and glands you wish to clear and realign geometrically. One week after completing the chamber for your 108-faceted prism, do a Sacred Geometry Chamber of Light for whatever organ or gland is first on your list. At step 10, do the following:

10. Next ask that the sacred geometry of your chosen organ or gland be restored to whatever degree is possible at this time. Envision that particular gland or organ inside a ball of golden sunlight. Hold that vision for two minutes and then relax for twenty to forty minutes until you sense this step is complete. ▭

Another alternative is to do a cellular clearing for the organ or gland prior to doing the Sacred Geometry Chamber. If you choose this alternative, you will use the Four-Cell Process given on pages 167-169. At steps 8 and 9, do the following:

8. Ask your Higher Self and a guide from the Pleiadian Emissaries of Light to go with you into the particular organ or gland you wish to clear. Imagine walking down through your body to that organ or gland.

9. Envision double doors leading into that organ or gland. Go through the doors into your organ or gland. You will see there many cells that are roughly the same size as your miniature body. There will be a walkway with guardrails, upon which you will walk around.

Then resume the instructions as given for the Four-Cell Process.

If you choose to do the Four-Cell Process prior to doing the Sacred Geometry Chamber of Light for specific organs and glands, please wait at least one month in between each organ and gland that you clear and realign.

Chapter 8

CLEARING AND ACTIVATING YOUR KUNDALINI AND SEXUAL CHANNELS

In order to fully run your sexual energy tantrically throughout your body, there are several channels, that must be cleared, through which this energy is intended to flow.

In addition, the free flow of your kundalini (as described in the first subsection of this chapter) is important as well. Kundalini helps in the rising of the sexual energy through your chakras, and even cellularly in its more advanced stages of activation. The tantric channels carry sexual energy from your genital area to other parts of your body that are keys to grounding, deeper soul bonding with your partner, and mutual nurturing and arousal. Therefore, before beginning the tantric exercises in the next chapter, you will be given exercises for clearing these channels.

Kundalini Channels

Kundalini has been discussed, taught, and described in many religious and spiritual paths and by many teachers and authors throughout the world. I will not be covering the subject thoroughly since there are so many sources in print. However, since the kundalini flow is so vital to the deeper activations of the Ka, flow of tantric energy, and spiritual growth in general, I will give a brief overview before going into the clearing techniques in this chapter.

First of all, the kundalini with which most people are familiar is that which runs along your spine in an intertwining snakelike pattern as shown in illustration 22 on page 186. Electrical energy that is created by the spinning of your cells is stored in a kundalini reservoir at the base of your spine. This kundalini energy is released into those channels and moves through your spinal channels, clearing and activating your chakras along the way. This energy may only make it as far as your second chakra if you need a lot of clearing there or in its more advanced stages it will travel all the way through your crown chakra. Kundalini is stimulating to your physical, emotional, mental, and spiritual bodies. It is intended to begin its spinal journey at puberty for the purpose of clearing any energy blockages from childhood, as well as activating your hormones and sexual energy in your first and second chakras. Teenage rebellion is most often a product of kundalini triggering the release of pent-up emotions relative to parents and other authority figures. If it is not activated as fully as it is intended to be at that time, energy blocks intensify and wait for later opportunities for release, or eventually cause illness.

At various stages in life, kundalini is intended to make its way up your spinal channels, crawling, sizzling, clearing, and enlightening you along the way. During these varying activations, you experience changes in your psyche and your health (mentally and physically), as well as overall empowerment at whatever level the kundalini is freely moving. This is in an ideal situation. However, you may not have experienced the ideal. Perhaps at puberty you were shamed about sexual feelings, or afraid of them. You may have been afraid to feel your emotions and express them, and therefore contracted and shut down your kundalini flow. At other passages in your life when kundalini should have been activated, you may have continued shutting down for whatever reason. And by the time you reached the age you are now, you are behind on a few kundalini rights of passage. Do not despair, because you can still catch up. The time frames for kundalini activation are not set in stone. For instance, my kundalini spontaneously "blew open" with gale force when I was 29 years old, during

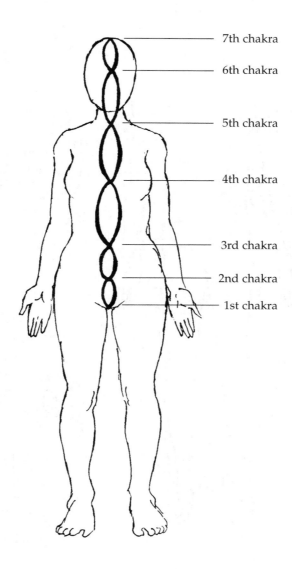

7th chakra

6th chakra

5th chakra

4th chakra

3rd chakra

2nd chakra

1st chakra

22. *Central kundalini channels running through the seven chakras*

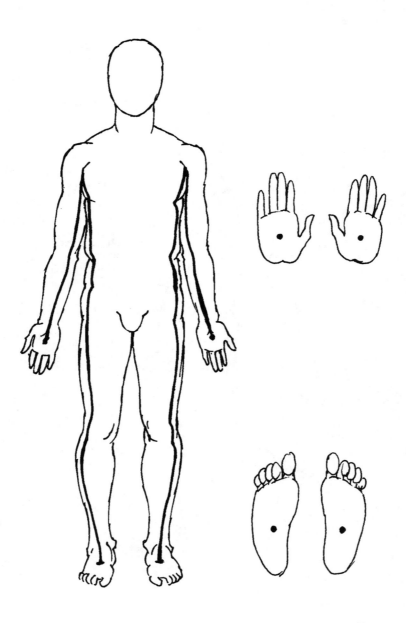

23. *Kundalini channels in legs and arms, showing chakras on palms of hands and soles of feet*

my spiritual awakening and my first fast. And now it is activated at levels that some teachers would say are not activated until you are in your fifties. I am 45 years old.

The point is that wherever you are with your kundalini, the exercises in this chapter are a safe, easy, and gracious way of clearing the pathways for your own kundalini activations to begin. These techniques do not result in the violent blasting open of channels, craziness, back problems, or other dilemmas often associated with kundalini awakening. The reason for this is simple. Most kundalini awakening that happens later in life happens to people whose kundalini channels are clogged with repressed energies. Therefore, when the kundalini is awakened, it has to storm the barricades just to begin to flow. Excess emotional activation causes emotional and psychic instability. Thick energy blocks in the channels cause a logjam effect when the kundalini suddenly rises. Peoples' backs are thrown seriously out of alignment. It can be confusing, painful, and even terrifying.

However, by systematically cleaning out the channels first, then activating them gently, the awakening is usually experienced as subtle, energizing, gracious, and spiritually stimulating. The processes given for kundalini clearing and activation that follow are intended to make kundalini awakening as simple and nonthreatening as possible. After reading the exercises first, if you feel frightened or ambivalent about opening your kundalini channels, then simply move on to the next chapter. You will still be able to do all of the exercises in this book, but without kundalini activation the results will simply be somewhat diminished.

There are three types of kundalini: body kundalini, Earth kundalini, and cosmic kundalini. This chapter will deal only with the body kundalini. The others will be discussed and activated in chapter 10.

As I mentioned previously, most of you are familiar with the spinal kundalini channels shown in illustration 22 on page 187. However, there is a second set of physical body kundalini channels that are intended to flow freely in correspondence with your spinal channels. These channels are shown in illustration 23 on page 188. They begin in your foot chakras, at the center of the soles of your feet, and extend through your legs, up the outside of your body, through your armpits, down your arms and out your hand chakras in the center of the palms of your hands. The flow in these channels is directly caused by the flow in your spinal channels.

The process for clearing these two pairs of channels will be accomplished simultaneously. You will be inside a Kundalini Clearing Chamber of Light while the Pleiadians, Mother Mary, and Jesus Christ work on your channels. You will need to assist them by visualizing healing light of different colors going through your channels at varying intervals. The first color you will use is rose gold. This color is the same as the rose-pink gold you see in the Black Hills gold jewelry. It is like yellow gold with a little copper color added. You will be using the rose gold in the Quantum Transfiguration grid pattern in both sets of kundalini channels simultaneously. The rose-gold energy has the ability to *melt down* thickened or calcified energies. It softens and warms, and makes it possible for the energies to be flushed from your channels.

After the rose-gold grid, you will visualize liquid silver light flowing from your foot chakras up through the entire length of the channels and out the palms of your hands. You will alternate tracing that line of flow with visualizing the liquid silver light flowing from the base of your spine through both intertwining channels around your spine and out through your crown. When you can feel a smooth full flow out your hands and crown, you will then visualize golden sunlight pouring into the bottoms of your feet and the base of your tailbone at the same time. This golden sunlight will run until it is freely flowing out through your palms and crown.

Once the channels have been cleared, you will do some simple breaths to activate your own kundalini. When the exercise refers to a deep sucking breath that means you literally pucker your lips and suck breath in as if you were slurping the last drops of a drink through a straw. You will do this while directing your inhalation through the base of your spine at the kundalini reservoir. Then when you exhale you will do so as if you are blowing out lots of birthday candles while directing your exhale up your spine and out your crown. Two or three of these breaths will be enough to activate your kundalini at its present-time flow level. Then you will repeat the breathing technique, inhaling through the bottoms of your feet and exhaling the full length of the channels up and out through your hands. Two or three breaths again will be enough.

After you have experienced the kundalini flow, you will be instructed through two different processes for shutting the kundalini off and one for adjusting the flow level. This is an important part of the exercise in that you may need to know how to adjust or shut off your kundalini at times in order to sleep. There are stages of kundalini activation when it begins to clear so much emotional or psychic energy blockage that it can become overwhelming. At those times, knowing how to regulate it is a godsend. Some people have difficulty sleeping while kundalini is flowing, and in that case turning it all the way off is ideal. When the gauge does not seem to work, or the kundalini immediately comes back on, ice-blue light is usually more reliable. These steps are described fully in the exercise.

Allow up to an hour and fifteen minutes for this exercise although it may not take quite the full time. If you tend to space out in chambers, you will need a timer or alarm clock for this exercise.

Following is the process for clearing and activating your kundalini channels:

1. Sit or lie down with your hands and feet uncrossed. If you choose to lie down, place a pillow beneath your knees.

2. Remove your old grounding cord and give yourself a new one. Take your time visualizing the grounding cord going to the center of Earth. You need to be very grounded.

3. Pull your aura in to within two feet around your body in all directions and check and adjust your aura boundary colors and roses as needed.

4. Ask your Higher Self of Light to come forth and be with you throughout this session.

5. Invoke the Pleiadian Emissaries of Light to come forth and to place an Interdimensional Cone of Light above you.

6. Invoke Ascended Masters Jesus Christ and Mother Mary to be with you.

7. Tell the Pleiadians, your Higher Self, and your guides that you would like to be placed inside a Kundalini Clearing Chamber of Light. When you feel your energy field shifting as the chamber is brought in, continue.

8. Visualize, feel, or think about where your spinal kundalini channels are located, and your foot-to-hand kundalini channels.

9. Ask that a rose-gold Quantum Transfiguration grid be brought around both sets of channels. Visualize, feel, or think about this as best you can. This will assist the guides in the implementation of this grid. Hold the vision for about two minutes until it is fully anchored, then relax for fifteen minutes while the grid is held there and worked with by your guides. Set a timer or alarm if you feel the need.

10. When the grid has been removed, visualize liquid silver light flowing into the base of your tailbone area and direct it into your spinal kundalini channels. It will not flow all the way through right away. It will take a few minutes. Put this on "automatic" and continue.

11. Visualize liquid silver light flowing in through the bottoms of your feet and into your kundalini channels in your legs. It will eventually flow all the way through the channels and out your hands, but again, it will take a few minutes.

12. If you can visualize both channels simultaneously with the silver light flowing through, then do so. Otherwise, alternate visualizing the flow in first one set of channels and then the other. Continue this until you can feel the energy freely flowing out through the palms of your hands and out your crown chakra. This could take up to fifteen minutes so be patient.

13. When the silver has flushed both sets of kundalini channels thoroughly, visualize a golden sun between your legs and visualize and inhale the sunlight into your spinal kundalini channels. Put this on "automatic."

14. Next visualize a large golden sun beneath your feet and visualize and inhale golden sunlight flowing into your foot chakras and into your leg channels. If you can hold the vision or intent for both sets of channels being filled and overflowing with golden sunlight simultaneously, then do so for the next fifteen minutes. Otherwise, alternate visualizing the golden light flowing into and through first one set of channels and then the other.

15. When the golden sunlight has thoroughly flushed and filled the channels, sit with your feet and hands uncrossed. Your spine needs to be straight but not rigid.

16. Focusing on the base of your tailbone area, take two or three deep sucking breaths in through your tailbone area. As you do this, ask your kundalini to turn on. With each exhale push the energy up your spine as if you are blowing out birthday candles. When you feel gentle energy beginning to move upward from your tailbone, breathe normally while keeping your awareness on the flow in your spinal channels for a couple of minutes.

17. Focus on the bottoms of your feet while taking two or three deep sucking breaths in through the bottoms of your feet. As you do this, ask your kundalini to activate in these channels. Exhale as if you are blowing out birthday candles while pushing your breath up through the entire length of the channels and out your palm chakras. When you begin to feel the energy moving through your channels, breathe normally while keeping your awareness on the flow in your foot-to-hand channels for a couple of minutes.

18. Sit and meditate while allowing your kundalini to flow as long as you wish.

19. Next visualize a gauge that reads from 0 to 100. This is your kundalini gauge. Notice how much is flowing. Now turn the gauge up 5 percent and feel the difference. Then turn it down 10 percent and feel the difference. Now turn the gauge all the way off to 0 percent and feel the change.

20. Do the kundalini breaths as described in steps 16 and 17. When the kundalini is flowing again, feel the flow for about two minutes.

21. Now visualize a ball of ice blue light the width of your shoulders but above your head. Slowly move the ice blue ball down around and through your entire body to beneath your feet. Then let the ice blue light go down your grounding cord. This will turn off your kundalini.

22. If you want to leave your kundalini on for now, repeat steps 16 and 17. Otherwise, simply continue with your day.

Leg Tantric Channels

The tantric energy channels in your legs are shown in illustrations 24 and 25 on pages 195 and 198. As you can see on the illustration, the channels are the same for men and women although the inception point of the channels in the genital area is different. All of the male tantric channels begin at the end of the prostate where the tube from the prostate connects with the penis. There is a neurological connection between the tip of the penis and the inception point, but the actual channel begins at the base of the penis as indicated on the illustration. All of the female tantric channels begin at the G-spot. There is a neurological connection between the clitoris and the G-spot; however, the actual channel begins with the G-spot.

These leg tantric channels are the source of grounding for your sexual energy. They also serve to carry the sexual energy into your legs and eventually even into the cells of your legs. Why is this important? Tantric energy is the energy of ecstasy. It is this energy that allows your spirit to come more deeply and fully into your body. When tantric energy is flowing cellularly you are in your most heightened state in which to embody your Higher Self. Remember that your Higher Self cannot live in a contracted, low-frequency energy field. Your Higher Self's natural state of being is that of love, light, and ecstatic joy. As your body and consciousness are filled with more love, light, and ecstatic joy, your body becomes a clear temple in which your Higher Self can dwell, and your consciousnesses blend into one

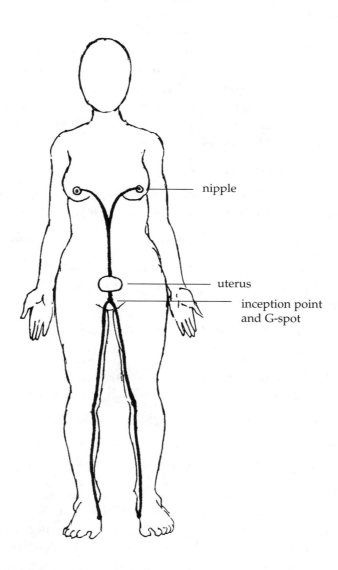

nipple

uterus

inception point
and G-spot

24. Female tantric leg and breast channels

consciousness. Eventually you will no longer distinguish yourself and your Higher Self as individuated. You will be one on all levels. Clearing these channels is just a step in that direction.

In the following sections, you will be given instructions for clearing these channels one at a time. The technique for all of the channels will be the same as is used in this section for the leg channels. You will simply substitute the appropriate channel as you are ready to do each one. The process is similar to that for clearing your kundalini channels in that it uses the same series of colors: rose-gold Quantum Transfiguration grid, liquid silver light, and golden sunlight. The process will take about forty-five minutes. Allow for the full time each time you do this process on a new channel.

The directions for clearing your leg tantric channels are as follows:

1. Sit or lie down with your hands and feet uncrossed. If you choose to lie down, place a pillow beneath your knees.

2. Remove your old grounding cord and give yourself a new one.

3. Pull your aura in to within two feet around your body in all directions and check and adjust your aura boundary colors and roses as needed.

4. Ask your Higher Self of Light to come forth and be with you throughout this session.

5. Invoke the Pleiadian Emissaries of Light to come forth and to place an Interdimensional Cone of Light above you.

6. Invoke Ascended Masters Jesus Christ and Mother Mary to be with you.

7. Tell the Pleiadians, your Higher Self, and your guides that you would like them to assist you in clearing your leg tantric channels.

8. Ask that a rose-gold Quantum Transfiguration grid be brought around your leg channels. Visualize, feel, or think about this as best you can. This will assist the guides in the implementation of this grid. Hold the vision for about two minutes, until it is fully anchored, then

relax for fifteen minutes while the grid is held there and worked with by your guides. Set a timer or alarm if you feel the need.

9. When the grid has been removed, visualize liquid silver light flowing into the inception point of your leg tantric channels and down through the entire length of the channels. This will take a few minutes. (Inception point for men is at the base of the penis. Inception point for women is at the G-spot.)

10. When the silver has flushed your channels thoroughly, visualize a golden sun between your legs and visualize and inhale the sunlight into your tantric channel inception point and then into your leg channels. Hold this vision until you feel the golden sunlight flowing all the way through your channels smoothly and out through your feet.

11. Open your eyes and continue with your day.

Breast Tantric Channels

Males and females alike have tantric channels that run from their inception points in the genital area up the midline of the torso, then fanning out to both nipples. (See illustrations 24 and 25.) These channels both stimulate the breasts and allow for deeper nurturing of one another during a sexual experience. Clearing of these channels will be done using the same process as for clearing your leg channels.

Following is the process for clearing your breast tantric channels:

1. Sit or lie down with your hands and feet uncrossed. If you choose to lie down, place a pillow beneath your knees.

2. Remove your old grounding cord and give yourself a new one.

3. Pull your aura in to within two feet around your body in all directions and check and adjust your aura boundary colors and roses as needed.

4. Ask your Higher Self of Light to come forth and be with you throughout this session.

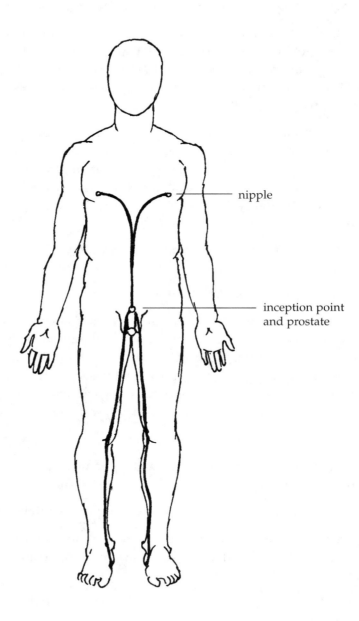

nipple

inception point
and prostate

25. Male tantric leg and breast channels

5. Invoke the Pleiadian Emissaries of Light to come forth and to place an Interdimensional Cone of Light above you.

6. Invoke Ascended Masters Jesus Christ and Mother Mary to be with you.

7. Tell the Pleiadians, your Higher Self, and your guides that you would like them to assist you in clearing your breast tantric channels.

8. Ask that a rose-gold Quantum Transfiguration grid be brought around your breast channels. Visualize, feel, or think about this as best you can. This will assist the guides in the implementation of this grid. Hold the vision for about two minutes until it is fully anchored, then relax for fifteen minutes while the grid is held there and worked with by your guides. Set a timer or alarm if you feel the need.

9. When the grid has been removed, visualize liquid silver light flowing into the inception point of your tantric channels, up through the entire length of your breast channels, and out through your nipples. This will take a few minutes. (Inception point for men is at the base of the penis. Inception point for women is at the G-spot.)

10. When the silver has flushed your channels thoroughly, visualize a golden sun between your legs and visualize and inhale the sunlight into your tantric channel inception point and then into your breast channels. Hold this vision until you feel the golden sunlight flowing all the way through your channels smoothly and out through your nipples.

11. Open your eyes and continue with your day. 🖭

Genital/Soul Tantric Channel

When you make love, whether it is with a partner or through self-pleasuring, you always have an impact on your soul. This is because of this specific channel. As you can see in illustration 26 on page 200, your soul is connected directly to your genital area through this genital/soul tantric channel. The effects of lovemaking on your soul are deeper and potentially more damaging for a woman than for a man because of the nature of woman as the receptive vessel. When a

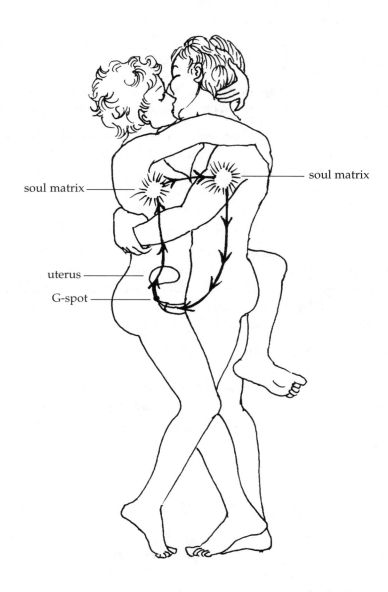

soul matrix

soul matrix

uterus

G-spot

26. Genital / soul tantric channels with energy flowing from the male's soul to his genitals, into her vagina and through her tantric channel to her soul. Then her soul sends energy to his soul, which creates a circular flow between them.

woman is having a sexual sharing with a partner, she runs energy from her G-spot through her womb and up to her soul. She is intended to feel her partner's love and passion flowing into her all the way up to her soul. When the lovemaking is indeed a loving and honoring one, the partner's love and passion energies literally flow through her into her soul and illuminate and activate her soul. This results in deeper trust, receptivity, and love for the partner. Her soul energy reaches out to his (in a heterosexual encounter), his soul responds by opening to more trust, love, and giving of adoration. They bond deeply and may experience something akin to feeling as if they were in one body with no separation between.

The male sexual energy is intended to be activated by love and adoration for the female. This triggers a flow of his soul energy down into his penis via this same channel and out to her genital area. In other words, their energy flows form a circular flow: From his soul to his penis, from his penis to her vagina, from her G-spot inside her vagina through her womb and upward to her soul, which expands and sends love out to his soul, then downward through his genital/soul channel out through his penis and back to her again. In a world where lust after the body has taken precedence over love and adoration, these channels often become blocked. When this happens, your experience of connectedness to your own soul essence and love is stifled, eventually blocked altogether, and at worst your soul is deeply damaged. This will be discussed in more depth in the next chapter, but it is good to have a basic understanding of the function of this channel before beginning to clear it.

The process for clearing the genital/soul channel is the same for men and women and is as follows:

1. Sit or lie down with your hands and feet uncrossed. If you choose to lie down, place a pillow beneath your knees.

2. Remove your old grounding cord and give yourself a new one.

3. Pull your aura in to within two feet around your body in all directions and check and adjust your aura boundary colors and roses as needed.

4. Ask your Higher Self of Light to come forth and be with you throughout this session.

5. Invoke the Pleiadian Emissaries of Light to come forth and to place an Interdimensional Cone of Light above you.

6. Invoke Ascended Masters Jesus Christ and Mother Mary to be with you.

7. Tell the Pleiadians, your Higher Self, and your guides that you would like them to assist you in clearing your genital/soul tantric channel.

8. Ask that a rose-gold Quantum Transfiguration grid be brought around your genital/soul channel. Visualize, feel, or think about this as best you can. This will assist the guides in the implementation of this grid. Hold the vision for about two minutes until it is fully anchored, then relax for fifteen minutes while the grid is held there and worked with by your guides. Set a timer or alarm if you feel the need.

9. When the grid has been removed, visualize liquid silver light flowing into the inception point of your tantric channel and up through the entire length of the channel to your soul area in the center of your chest. This will take a few minutes. (Inception point for men is at the base of the penis. Inception point for women is at the G-spot.)

10. When the silver has flushed your channels thoroughly, visualize a golden sun between your legs and visualize and inhale the sunlight into your tantric channel inception point and then into your genital/soul channel. Hold this vision until you feel the golden sunlight flowing all the way through your channel smoothly and out through your heart chakra.

11. Open your eyes and continue with your day.   [▭]

Infinity Channel

The infinity channel connects your second, fourth, and sixth chakras, allowing an interrelationship between them, and an

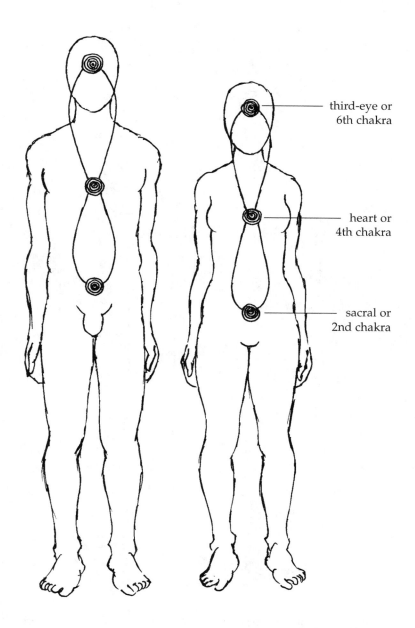

third-eye or
6th chakra

heart or
4th chakra

sacral or
2nd chakra

27. Front view of man and woman showing location of infinity channel

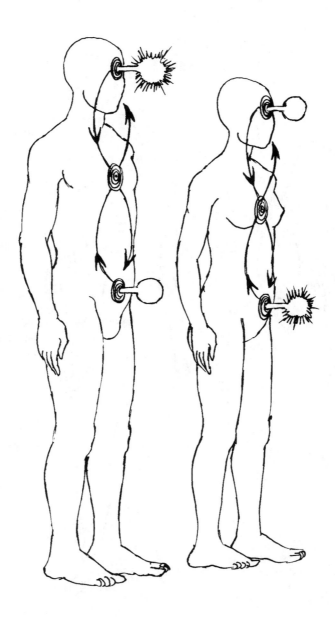

28. 3/4 view of man and woman showing them running energy through their infinity channels

exchange of energy. (See illustration 27 on page 203.) When this channel is clear and flowing properly in lovers, it allows a deeper and more balanced flow of energy between them not only physically, but also emotionally, mentally, and spiritually. Even when you are not making love, having this channel open and flowing creates more balance between your own physical, emotional, mental, and spiritual aspects. The second chakra rules your gender identity, sexual energy, ability to give and receive nurturing, and how and what you feel. Your fourth, or heart, chakra, of course is the home of your soul. It is also the chakra of love and the outward flow of the emotional nature of love. Your sixth chakra, beyond its most commonly known function as the third eye, rules your self-image and how you see others. It also rules your spiritual and mental attitudes.

If you look at the nature of these three chakras, you can understand how having them in communication and harmony with one another makes you a more balanced person. It also creates more interconnectedness in your relationships with others. In other words, instead of just relating sexually from a second chakra and physical level, when this channel is open and flowing in both partners, you can more easily feel connected spiritually, mentally, and emotionally during lovemaking as well as at other times. This is all much clearer experientially. What you feel when you are opening and running energy in this channel will help you understand it more fully.

The process for clearing and activating this channel is slightly different for males and females. Males will run silver energy into the second chakra, then upward through the channel, crossing at the heart chakra and on up to the third eye. Simultaneously, males will send golden sunlight energy into their third-eye areas down through the infinity symbol, crossing at the heart chakra and on down to the second chakra. Women will follow the same procedure except they will run golden sunlight into their second chakra and up to the third eye, and silver into the third eye and down to the second chakra. (See illustration 28 on page 204.)

For both males and females, when the silver and gold energies have filled the full length of one side of the infinity symbol, the energies will make a loop and flow up or down the opposite side. For example, in a woman, when the gold has made it all the way up to her third eye from her second chakra, it loops around the top of the infinity symbol and begins to flow down toward the heart on the opposite side. Since that side is filled with silver energy flowing downward already, the gold and silver mix with one another. Simultaneously, the silver energy from her third eye will have filled the opposite channel all the way down to her second chakra, and then looped upward on the other side of her channel that is already filled with gold. The gold and silver eventually become equally blended throughout the entire infinity symbol. This exercise only takes about ten minutes, unless you prefer to do it longer.

Following is the exercise for clearing and activating your infinity channel:

1. Sit or lie down with your hands and feet uncrossed. If you choose to lie down, place a pillow beneath your knees.

2. Remove your old grounding cord and give yourself a new one.

3. Pull your aura in to within two feet around your body in all directions and check and adjust your aura boundary colors and roses as needed.

4. Ask your Higher Self of Light to activate your silver cord and fill your tube of light with your own Higher Self energy. When this is done, continue.

5. Envision the location of the infinity channel beginning at the center of your second chakra, arcing upward in both directions and crossing at your heart chakra. From your heart chakra it arcs upward in both directions to your third eye. The infinity channel is self-contained and forms a closed-loop energy flow.

6. *Men only*: Envision a ball of silver light in front of your second chakra flowing into your second chakra and entering your infinity channel. From there the silver light flows upward, crossing over at your heart chakra to the opposite side and then upward to your third eye and back down again on the opposite side. Simultaneously envision a ball of golden sunlight in front of your third eye flowing into

that chakra. From there the golden light flows into your infinity channel downward toward your heart chakra. After crossing over at your heart chakra, it flows down the opposite side of the channel to your second chakra. From there it loops back up the other side, blending with the silver. (See illustration 27 on page 207 for exact flow pattern.) Continue with step 7 below.

Women only: Envision a ball of golden sunlight in front of your second chakra, flowing into your second chakra and entering your infinity channel. From there the golden light flows upward, crossing over at your heart chakra to the opposite side and then upward to your third eye and back down again on the opposite side. Simultaneously envision a ball of silver light in front of your third eye flowing into that chakra. From there the silver light flows into your infinity channel downward toward your heart chakra. After crossing over at your heart chakra, it flows down the opposite side of the channel to your second chakra. From there it loops back up the other side, blending with the gold. (See illustration 27 on page 204 for exact flow pattern.)

7. Continue running these energies for at least ten minutes with the gold and silver blending equally throughout the entire infinity channel.

8. When you are complete, release the gold and silver balls of light in roses.

9. Open your eyes and continue with your day. 📼

Chapter 9

DOLPHIN TANTRA

Dolphin Tantra is the name the Pleiadian Emissaries of Light and the Sirian Archangels of the Light have given to uninhibited, innocent, loving, intercellular flow of sexual energy. The following is a passage from *The Pleiadian Workbook* about why the dolphins are such important teachers and guides to humans:

Dolphins operate from both sides of their brains at the same time, whereas most humans at this time act from one or the other side of their brain, but rarely both sides together. It has been said that dolphins see humans as being asleep. This is because dolphins sleep by turning off first one side of their brains, then the other, keeping one side functional at all times. It is also fairly commonly understood that average human beings only utilize about 5 to 10 percent of their brain capacity. This is an evolutionary factor and not a normal condition in humans. You are intended to become a "whole brain" being like the dolphins who are "elder brothers and sisters" to the human race.

Dolphins were sent to Earth prior to human colonization to prepare the evolutionary frequencies and patterns. They are highly evolved Light Beings who are lovingly dedicated to the fulfillment of human spiritual evolutionary goals. So, why do you need to become a "whole brain" being? Without whole brain function, you remain split off from your own spiritual wholeness, your connection through oneness with God/Goddess/All That Is. In order to attain whole brain function, you must both spiritually evolve and heal the electrical system in your brain and body. This electrical system is literally the communication link through which your spirit speaks and creates in the physical world. Any blockage in your electrical system inhibits your spirit and Master Presence from fully embodying.

Think about the way dolphins move in the water: they have no

29. Dolphins podding and sonaring a newborn

kinks in their spines, or sluggishness in their neurological response time. They live in spontaneous harmony with themselves and their surroundings, their bodies fluidly responding to every need and situation. When they move their fins, the effects of that small movement flow like gentle waves through their bodies via their nervous systems, devoid of kinks or contractions. This is what the Pleiadians call the Dolphin Wave Effect. It is only possible because dolphins are uninhibited, whole-brain, spiritually evolved beings who are aligned through their bodies and spirits with the Earth, the Sun, the stars, and with the collective consciousness that is God/Goddess/All That Is. They are the blueprint for what the human race is destined to become; they hold the vibrational patterns and frequencies for human evolution on Earth. Their very presence on Earth is a vital boon to human spiritual development.

When a dolphin baby is born, it is nuzzled and touched first by its mother, and then one by one by the other dolphins of the pod who are nearby. A call is sent out through the waters for those who wish to welcome the young one and "pod it." The dolphins who respond "pod the baby" by forming a circle around it and the mother. They swim around the circle first in one direction and then in the other, calling out greetings and blessings to the newborn with their sonar. These sounds also serve to create the harmonic tones needed to bring the full consciousness of the dolphin spirit into its body and activate its Ka Body, which links the newborn energetically to the stars through axiatonal lines, or Ka Channels. The sonar waves create a Dolphin Wave Effect with sound that is similar to what dolphin body movement creates tactilely. It activates the baby's electrical system and body response and enables the dolphin spirit to operate through the baby's brain and electrical system. The adult dolphins then take turns nuzzling and rubbing the baby with their bodies. This is continued until the baby dolphin's soul is fully anchored and looking out from behind the newborn's eyes.

What this means to you as a human being is that the dolphins have created, and still maintain, an etheric map or blueprint within their consciousnesses and bodies that you can follow. The Dolphin Tantra processes contained in this chapter were given to me by the Pleiadians and Sirians working together. The Sirians align and maintain the sacred geometry needed to create integrity of form in the

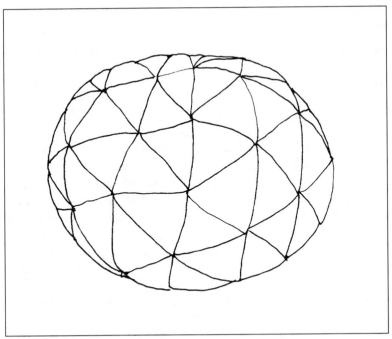

30. Geometric pattern of joined triangles in the physical heart

lower dimensions. For instance, the Sirians once worked on the sacred geometry of my physical heart in order to help it heal and be available for my Ka and Higher Self to embody more permanently. They showed me that the geometric pattern for the molecular structure of my heart consists of equilateral triangles conjoining one another in a holographic manner. (See illustration on this page.) Early heart chakra damage from abuse, as well as genetic imbalances, had mutated the cells and molecular structure somewhat.

When step-by-step processes for healing and spiritual alignment are needed, the Pleiadians furnish the technical details. They also assist in the acclimation of the sixth-dimensional geometric forms and relationships to the third- through fifth-dimensional aspects of human existence. In other words, when the Sirians realign the sacred geometry in the body, the Pleiadians may give a movement process that is needed to integrate the changes neuromuscularly, or else a meditation to do. The Sirians tend to hold higher-dimensional forms in place while the Pleiadians give us techniques to help us align with those forms. This collaboration will be present throughout the rest of this book in all exercises related to Dolphin Tantra techniques and aligning with your Christed Self.

As you move through the following sections, you will be putting puzzle pieces together. Perhaps you will combine the equivalent of all of the sky pieces in one exercise and all of the trees in another. By the time you are through, you will have put those pieces into their appropriate sections of the puzzle and then put the sections together until the puzzle is complete. The various aspects of Dolphin Tantra are like a puzzle that will be finally put together in the sections on self-pleasuring. So as you work with each one, you are coming closer to the completed puzzle: Dolphin Tantra.

Dolphin Wave Chamber of Light

The first section of this puzzle is the Dolphin Wave Chamber of Light. In the Dolphin Moves described in *The Pleiadian Workbook*, the Dolphin Wave Effect was introduced. This is the name given to the movement of energy and form when it is uninhibited and free flowing from inception point throughout your body. For example, if you raise one arm a few inches, the movement translates through your nervous system, skeleton, and muscles. If you are not blocked in any of these areas of your body, the raising of your arm will be easy and flowing, and will translate into your shoulder, neck, cranial bones, spine, hips, and finally into your legs. Try it.

1. Close your eyes and center yourself.

2. Lift one arm slowly about six inches from its resting position. Lower your arm slowly. Then repeat this movement as many times as you need to in order to observe the effects of the movement on the following areas of your body: both shoulders; neck; cranial bones; upper spine; mid-spine; lower spine; both hips; both legs.

3. What did you notice? Could you track the movement throughout your body? Were there places where the translation of movement was blocked by contraction or pain in parts of your body?

Wherever contraction and pain inhibit translation of movement, you will also experience some limitations on the movement of sexual energy in a tantric sexual release. When your body is free of these contractions and pain, you will be able to experience the Dolphin Wave Effect and full-body tantric sexual ecstasy. Doing this chamber session will assist in giving your body an etheric reference point in what the Dolphin Wave Effect is, and prepare it for further opening and clearing.

The Dolphin Wave Chamber of Light will take fifteen minutes. Instructions for this chamber are as follows:

1. Lie down in a comfortable position with a pillow under your knees and your feet shoulder-width apart.

2. Ground yourself and pull your aura to within two to three feet of your body.

3. In order to relax your body and assist you in accessing deeper awareness and sensation, begin to breathe deeply and fully into your body as follows:

- Breathe all the way down to your toes, expanding the skin around your toes with your breath. Tell your toes to relax.

- Breathe and expand the rest of both feet with your breath, telling them to relax.

- Breathe and expand your calves and shins while telling them to relax.

- Repeat the breathing into and expansion of the rest of your body while telling each part to relax: knees, thighs, buttocks, groin, pelvis, solar plexus, small of your back, ribs, chest, shoulder blades, entire length of your spine, shoulders, arms, hands and fingers, neck and throat, face, scalp, and eyes.

4. Ask your Higher Self to be with you and to activate your silver cord and fill your tube of light with your own divine love and light.

5. Ask the Pleiadian Emissaries of Light to come forth and place an

Interdimensional Cone of Light above you for clearing and divine alignment.

6. Call upon the Sirian Archangelic League of the Light to join you.

7. Call upon Ascended Masters Jesus Christ and Mother Mary to join you.

8. Tell all of the guides and Masters to place you inside a Dolphin Wave Chamber of Light. Ask the Sirians to assist in realigning your sacred geometry to be in total self-affinity and to implement the Dolphin Wave Effect throughout your body and aura.

9. Breathe fully and in a relaxed manner for fifteen minutes as the Dolphin Wave Effect is activated throughout your aura and body.

10. *Optional:* If you would like to ask for a Dolphin Brain Balancing Chamber of Light at this time, it will deepen the effects of the Dolphin Wave Chamber session you just completed. Five minutes in this chamber should be enough because of just having finished the other one.

11. Sit up while slowly reorienting yourself to the room. Ground yourself before standing and going on with your day.

Dolphin Moves

Now that you have experienced the Dolphin Wave Chamber session, you will add movements to the Dolphin Wave Effect. These movements, when done inside a Dolphin Wave Chamber, assist in freeing your body of holding patterns that inhibit full sexual energy flow. Later you will be combining these while using the Dolphin Tantra process for self-pleasuring. When you use those techniques, you need to be already familiar with the techniques in this section.

You will be guided through a series of infinity movements. Infinity movements are body movements done in a figure 8, or infinity, pattern. In illustration 31 on page 216, you will see the infinity symbol superimposed over the areas of the body you will be moving. Your body movements will trace the entire infinity symbol first in one

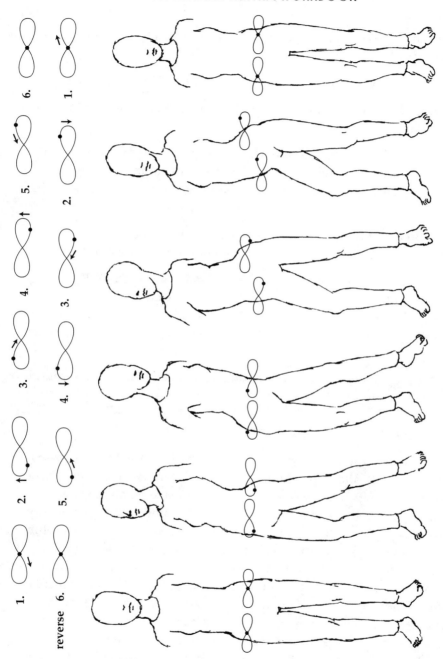

31. *Infinity Dolphin Moves: horizontal infinity symbols in the pelvic region*

direction, as shown in steps 1 to 6, then in the opposite direction, as shown in steps 6 to 1. Do these moves slowly. Adopt an attitude of pleasure in moving your body in such a natural and sensual way. If unpleasant emotions come up during the movements, continue to move while breathing deeply to release the old emotions. Try not to identify with the emotions. Remind yourself that these are simply old emotions that were waiting for an opportunity to leave your body. Remind yourself that it is a great gift to have the opportunity to release these emotions in order to make way for more ecstasy and for your Higher Self in your body. While doing the movements, allow yourself to feel all of your bodily and emotional sensations fully. However, do not touch yourself sexually, or fantasize. The purpose of this exercise is to free yourself of holding patterns and contractions. To add sexual focus will diminish these effects. Later you will be using the Dolphin Waves and Dolphin Moves along with sexual pleasuring.

If you do not have the tape set that accompanies this book, I would suggest that you make a tape of this process, allowing enough time for each movement to be completed before going on to the next. You may do them while reading each step as well; it is just not quite as effective.

When you have studied the illustrations and feel ready to begin, use the following process for Dolphin Moves:

1. Wear only loose, stretchy clothing. Remove any jewelry, bras, jock straps, belts, glasses, and contact lenses. Keep your eyes closed throughout the duration of this session unless you are reading the steps. Close your eyes while doing each movement.

2. Repeat steps 1 through 8 for placing yourself in a Dolphin Wave Chamber of Light. Lie on a carpeted floor, thick rug, or yoga mat only.

3. When you feel the Dolphin Wave Effect beginning, continue to breathe deeply and freely. Have your mouth open just slightly to allow more movement in your neck and jaws.

4. Silently state the affirmation, "I now establish reciprocal balance between my pineal gland and the pineal gland of my enlightened future self relative to overall body, mind, spirit, and emotional

balance and makeup." This affirmation aligns you with your natural evolution for the purpose of releasing holding patterns and becoming free.

5. Begin to move your pelvis in the pattern of a horizontal infinity symbol, or a figure 8, from side to side (horizontal as if you were standing). It is as if your hips are tracing the infinity shape with the cross-over point at your pubic mound. (See illustration 31 on page 216.) Make this movement a half dozen times in one direction and then in the other. Move your body *slowly* and sensually. Leave your arms at your sides. While doing the movements track the effects of this movement on other areas of your body: your lower spine; knees; ribs; mid-spine; upper spine; chest; both shoulder blades; both upper shoulders; neck; cranial bones; eyes; both cheeks. Without trying to change it, just observe where your body contracts or holds pain, or where there are kinks or glitches in the translation of the movements.

6. Rest in a still position for about one minute while continuing to observe the Dolphin Wave Effect in your body and emotions.

7. Next imagine that only your perineum is making the infinity pattern. Of course other parts of your body will move involuntarily, but isolate your inception point of movement in your perineum. (See illustration 32 on page 219.) Make this movement a half dozen times in one direction and then in the other. Move your body *slowly* and sensually, keeping your arms at your sides. While doing the movements, track the effects of this movement on other areas of your body: your lower spine; knees; ribs; mid-spine; upper spine; chest; both shoulder blades; both upper shoulders; neck; cranial bones; eyes; both cheeks. Without trying to change it, just observe where your body contracts or holds pain, or where there are kinks or glitches in the translation of the movements.

8. Rest in a still position for about one minute while continuing to observe the Dolphin Wave Effect in your body and emotions.

9. Now move your pelvis in vertical (relative to standing) infinity symbols up and down. Make this movement a half dozen times first in one direction and then in the other. (See illustration 33 on page 220.)

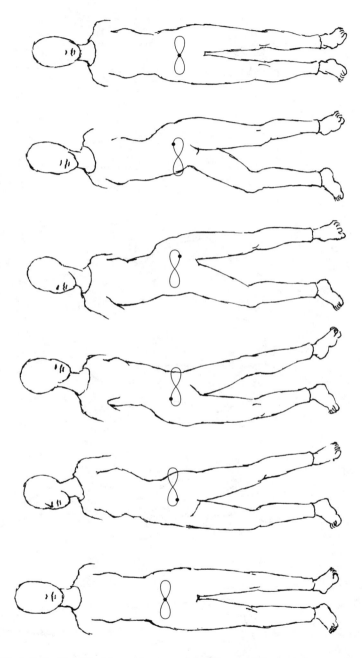

32. Infinity Dolphin Moves: horizontal infinity symbols at the perineum

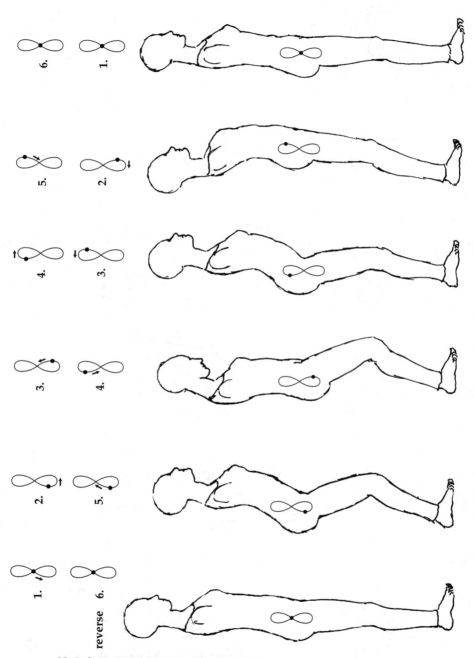

33. *Infinity Dolphin Moves: vertical infinity symbols in the pelvic region*

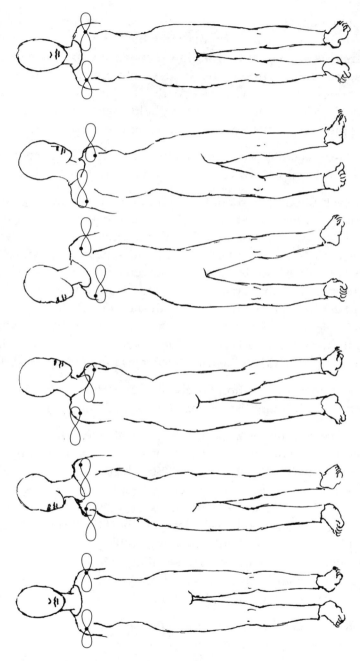

34. Infinity Dolphin Moves: horizontal infinity symbols at the shoulders

Move your body *slowly* and sensually, keeping your arms at your sides. While doing the movements, track the effects of this movement on other areas of your body: your lower spine; knees; ribs; mid-spine; upper spine; chest; both shoulder blades; both upper shoulders; neck; cranial bones; eyes; both cheeks. Without trying to change it, just observe where your body contracts, or holds pain, or where there are kinks or glitches in the translation of the movements.

10. Rest in a still position for about one minute while continuing to observe the Dolphin Wave Effect in your body and emotions.

11. Next move your shoulders in a horizontal (relative to standing) infinity pattern side-to-side. Make this movement a half dozen times first in one direction and then in the other. (See illustration 34 on page 221.) Move your body *slowly* and sensually, keeping your arms at your sides. While doing the movements, track the effects of this movement on other areas of your body: your lower spine; knees; ribs; mid-spine; upper spine; chest; both shoulder blades; both upper shoulders; neck; cranial bones; eyes; both cheeks. Without trying to change it, just observe where your body contracts or holds pain, or where there are kinks or glitches in the translation of the movements.

12. Rest in a still position for about one minute while continuing to observe the Dolphin Wave Effect in your body and emotions.

13. Move your upper spine in a vertical (relative to standing) infinity pattern up and down. Make this movement a half dozen times first in one direction and then in the other. (See illustration 35 on page 223.) Move your body *slowly* and sensually, keeping your arms at your sides. While doing the movements, track the effects of this movement on other areas of your body: your lower spine; knees; ribs; mid-spine; upper spine; chest; both shoulder blades; both upper shoulders; neck; cranial bones; eyes; both cheeks. Without trying to change it, just observe where your body contracts or holds pain, or where there are kinks or glitches in the translation of the movements.

14. Rest in a still position for about one minute while continuing to observe the Dolphin Wave Effect in your body and emotions.

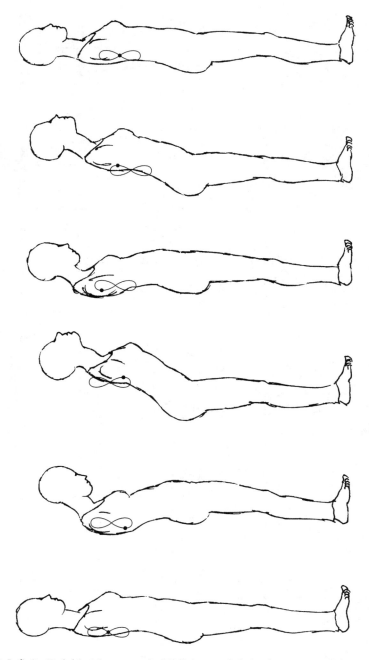

35. *Infinity Dolphin Moves: vertical infinity symbols in the upper spine*

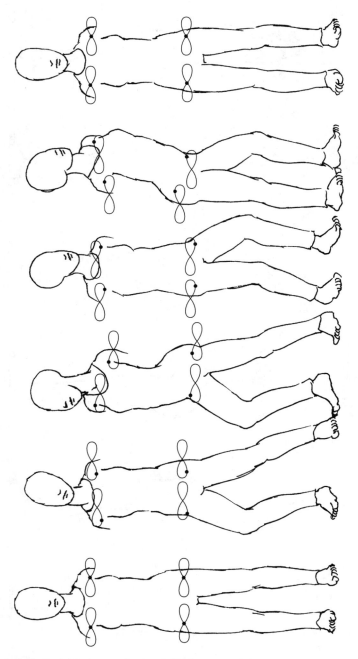

36. *Infinity Dolphin Moves: horizontal infinity symbols synchronized in the pelvis and shoulders*

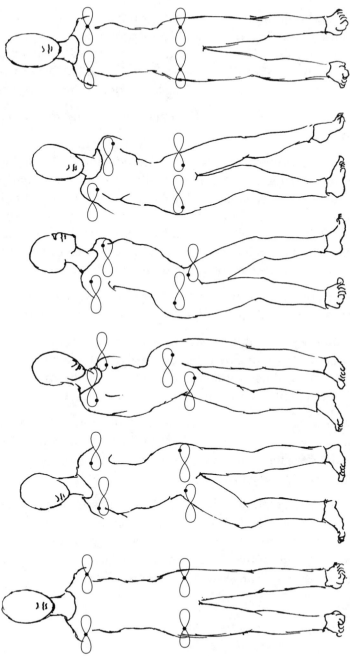

37. Infinity Dolphin Moves: horizontal infinity symbols in the pelvis and shoulders moving in opposite directions at the same time

15. Now combine the horizontal infinity patterns at your pelvis and shoulders moving your shoulders and pelvis in the same direction at the same time. Then reverse directions. Move in each direction a half dozen times. (See illustrations 36 on page 224.) Scan the rest of your body, as you did before, while slowly doing these movements.

16. Rest about one minute while continuing to observe the Dolphin Wave Effect.

17. Finally, move your pelvis and shoulders in horizontal infinity patterns at the same time but in opposite directions. In other words, while your pelvis is tracing the right half of the infinity symbol, your shoulders will be tracing the left side, and vice versa. After doing this differentiated move a half dozen times, repeat it in the opposite directions. (See illustration 37 on page 225.) Scan the rest of your body as you did before, while slowly doing these movements.

18. Rest quietly for at least two more minutes while integrating the learning your body just did about how to move more freely.

19. Silently say, "I affirm that my body, emotions, mind, and spirit will integrate this movement lesson easily and graciously without replay of any healing trauma. I welcome the Dolphin Wave Effect throughout my entire body and nervous system. So be it."

20. Get up slowly without stretching. Walk around the room a few times slowly while feeling your feet on the floor as you walk. Walk backward a few steps. How does your body feel when you move? Do you notice any changes?

21. You may go on with your day. Leave glasses, bras, jock straps, belts, and contact lenses off a minimum of one hour, longer if possible. Do not stretch for at least one hour. A half-hour-to-an-hour walk within twenty-four hours is recommended to assist your body in integrating the neurological, skeletal, and muscular changes. 🔲

Tantra and Toning

The next section of our Dolphin Tantra puzzle is comprised of toning your sexual energy channels. Toning, in this case, means: the use of sound for clearing energy, activating desired parts of your body or chakras, moving or grounding energy, or raising vibrational frequencies. What you will be guided to do is tone, or sing, one note at a time, directing the sound into a particular part of your body or energy channel in order to open and activate the area and prepare to run sexual energy there. Toning is very experiential and works best when done whole-heartedly—as opposed to in a self-conscious, barely audible manner. In other words, you need to open up and let the sounds resonate and flow fully in your body. When in a situation in which you must remain fairly quiet, you can still achieve the desired effect as long as you use your breath fully and freely, and simply control the volume of the output.

First try this exercise for opening to toning:

1. Sit or stand with your back straight but not tight. If you choose to stand, have your feet shoulder-width apart and your knees bent slightly.

2. Feel your feet firmly planted on the floor. Ask Mother Earth to send her loving and nurturing Earth light through your feet and up through your body. Inhale as if your breath is coming into your body through the soles of your feet, pulling Earth energy in with it.

3. Give yourself a new grounding cord and adjust your aura to within two to three feet around your body in every direction.

4. Change your breathing pattern to the following:

• Inhale deeply into your solar plexus, expanding your diaphragm toward your abdomen;

• exhale very slowly while regulating the movement of your diaphragm back up to the center of your solar plexus. Continue exhaling until you can feel your diaphragm pushing all of the air out of your lungs;

- immediately inhale deeply into your solar plexus, again expanding your diaphragm toward your abdomen. Repeat the exhalation very slowly as in the step above. Continue this type of breath for about four breath cycles all together;

- breathe normally for a few breaths before moving on.

5. Now you will add sound to the above breathing process. Choose any note that is easy for you to sing. Sing it with a syllable such as "ah" or "oo" or "Om" as follows: a) Inhale deeply into your solar plexus, expanding your diaphragm toward your abdomen; b) exhale very slowly while singing your tone and regulating the movement of your diaphragm back up to the center of your solar plexus. Continue exhaling and singing until you can feel your diaphragm pushing all of the air out of your lungs; c) immediately inhale deeply into your solar plexus, again expanding your diaphragm toward your abdomen. Repeat the exhalation with toning very slowly as in step b. Continue this type of breath and toning for about four or more breath cycles altogether; d) breathe normally for a few breaths before moving on to step 6.

6. If the toning and breathing in this manner are still difficult or awkward, practice step 5 until you feel comfortable.

7. Repeat step 5, only this time press your tongue gently into the roof of your mouth while toning.

8. Practice directing the tone into your heart chakra. Use the syllable "ah" as you repeat step 5, pressing your tongue into the roof of your mouth and directing the sound into your heart chakra in the center of your chest. Try different tones until you find the one to which your heart chakra opens the most.

9. Next practice directing the tone into your genital area. Practice using different tones and syllables until you find the ones that vibrate and open that area the most.

10. When steps 8 and 9 are easy for you, you may continue. 🔲

Now that you have learned how to direct tones into specific areas of your body, you will use this process to activate and run energy through your sexual channels, which you cleared in chapter 8. This entire process will be done while inside a Dolphin Tantra Chamber of Light to facilitate more energy movement throughout your body. You may find it helpful to read the exercise steps first and then do them.

The process for toning your sexual energy channels is as follows:

1. Sit, lie down, or stand with your back straight but not tight. If you choose to stand, have your feet shoulder-width apart and your knees bent slightly. If lying down, your feet should be shoulder-width apart and your knees elevated with a pillow. If you sit, have your knees a comfortable distance apart so that your hips are fully relaxed.

2. Feel your feet. Ask Mother Earth to send her loving and nurturing Earth light through your feet and up through your body. Inhale as if your breath is coming into your body through the soles of your feet pulling Earth energy in with it.

3. Give yourself a new grounding cord and adjust your aura to within two to three feet around your body in every direction.

4. Ask your Higher Self of Light to be with you and to activate the silver cord and fill your tube of light with your own divine love and light.

5. Ask the Pleiadian Emissaries of Light to come forth and place an Interdimensional Cone of Light above you for clearing and divine alignment.

6. Call upon the Sirian Archangelic League of the Light to join you.

7. Call upon Ascended Masters Jesus Christ and Mother Mary to join you.

8. Tell all of the guides and Masters to place you inside a Dolphin Tantra Chamber of Light for the duration of this process. Ask the Sirians to assist in realigning your sacred geometry to be in total self-affinity and to implement the Dolphin Wave Effect throughout your body and aura and to further open your sexual energy channels.

9. Gently press your tongue into the roof of your mouth and maintain it there throughout each of the remaining steps in this process.

10. First you will tone your leg channels. Inhale, pushing your diaphragm down toward your abdomen. This time continue the inhalation until you have breathed all the way down into your leg channel activation point. (*Women:* This is your G-spot. *Men:* This is the point between your prostate and the tube leading to your penis. See illustrations 24 and 25 on pages 195 and 198.) When you exhale, loudly direct a tone down through your leg channels all the way down to your feet. Repeat this step until you feel that this channel is fully open and vibrating. You may need to experiment until you find the best tone for this area. You will probably notice your sexual energy beginning to flow as well.

11. Next you will tone your breast channels. Once again, inhale, pushing your diaphragm down toward your abdomen. This time continue the inhalation until you have breathed all the way down to your breast channel activation point. (This is the same area for both men and women as described in step 9 of the Breast Tantric Channel clearing exercise on page 199. See illustrations 24 and 25.) When you exhale, loudly direct a tone up through your breast channels all the way up to your nipples. Repeat this step until you feel that this channel is fully open and vibrating. Again, you may need to experiment until you find the best tone for this area. You will notice your sexual energy flowing more fully.

12. Your soul channel is the next one to be toned. Once again, inhale, pushing your diaphragm down toward your abdomen.

Women: Continue the inhalation until you have breathed all the way down to your soul channel activation point, your G-spot. When you exhale, loudly direct a tone up through your soul channel all the way to the center of your heart chakra where your soul is located. Repeat this step until you feel that this channel is fully open and vibrating. Experiment until you find the best tone for this channel. Your sexual energy will continue to flow more fully. (See illustration 26 on page 200 for the location of the soul channels.)

Men: Continue the inhalation until you have filled your soul area with your breath. When you exhale, loudly direct a tone down through your soul channel all the way to the activation point between your prostate and the tube to your penis. Repeat this step until you feel that this channel is fully open and vibrating. Experiment until you find the best tone for this channel. Your sexual energy will continue to flow more fully as you continue. (See illustration 26 on page 200 for the location of the soul channels.)

13. Now you will tone the three chakras involved in your infinity channel. Find the best tone for each chakra. Once again, inhale, pushing your diaphragm down toward your abdomen. Continue the inhalation until you have breathed all the way down to your second chakra. When you exhale, loudly direct a tone up through your second chakra and out into your aura. Intend to open this chakra fully. When it feels open, repeat this process for your heart chakra, and then for your third eye. (See illustration 27 on page 203 for the infinity channel.)

14. Now that each of your three chakras involved is open, you will tone the entire infinity channel. Inhale, pushing your diaphragm down toward your abdomen. Continue the inhalation until you have breathed all the way down to your sexual activation center in your genital area. As you exhale, send a tone from your sexual center up to your second chakra, following the infinity pattern to your heart chakra, and then to your third eye. Find the best tone for this channel. Inhale again. This time as you exhale, send a tone from your third eye back down to your heart chakra, and then to your second chakra. Repeat this cycle of breaths until you feel that the channel is open and flowing, and the energy between your three chakras is balanced.

15. Relax your tongue. Remain in the Dolphin Tantra Chamber for at least two or three more minutes, or as long as you would like, breathing in a relaxed manner. If the sexual energy flow is strong, you may need to do infinity movements in your pelvis, spine, and/or shoulder areas to further encourage the flow.

16. When you feel complete, continue with your day.

Dolphin Tantra

Whether you are in a relationship or not, it is recommended that you do the exercise alone before moving to the section called Dolphin Tantra for Couples. If you have resistance to, or judgments about, self-pleasuring, or masturbation, you may need to work on clearing your beliefs and emotions before proceeding. In any case, I highly encourage you to at least read this entire section before deciding whether you are ready to do it or not.

This is the point at which you will put all of the completed sections of the puzzle together and experience Dolphin Tantra. First of all, the intent, as mentioned, is to bring your sexual energy up through your spinal area, your sexual energy channels, your chakras, and eventually, your cells. Rather than an orgasmic release that occurs only in your genital area—which is better than none at all—you will learn a new way to move that energy with your breath, Dolphin Wave Effect, infinity movement, toning, and self-pleasuring throughout your body. Tantra, for these purposes, can be practiced alone or with a partner. (Many religious groups, and even some spiritual groups, have condemned masturbation for a long time on Earth. The old adage of "never spilling your seed upon the ground" applies not only to men. It also shames women who would seek sexual pleasure for purposes other than reproduction with a man. This certainly leaves those who choose single life or homosexuality out in the cold, so to speak. However, there are also spiritual traditions that exonerate the use of sexual energy for elevating spiritual awakeness, opening chakras, raising frequencies, activating kundalini fully, and even producing transcendental states. The Inca, Tibetans, Buddhists, Maya, many Native American tribes, ancient Druids and Egyptians, and members of Goddess-based spiritual traditions are among the many who actively practice some form of tantra in order to enhance their spiritual journeys.)

What is truly wonderful about tantric energy, and in this case Dolphin Tantra particularly, is that it simultaneously elevates your lower chakra energies through the alchemical fires of transmutation, grounds you more fully, and makes way for your spirit to live more fully in your body—and all the while you are naturally loving yourself more and experiencing ecstatic energy states and spiritual opening. The dolphins are the only other creatures upon Earth, besides humans, known to have orgasms. They are certainly guilt-free, loving, ecstatic, spontaneous, and joyful beings! If the true nature of the human soul and spirit is to be as the dolphins in these ways, then it is important to liberate ourselves by learning to be as guilt-free, loving, ecstatic, spontaneous, and joyful as they are.

In the Dolphin Tantra sections for females and males which follow, you are encouraged to try the exercises somewhat narcissistically at first. Do not imagine a partner with you; be your own partner. Enjoy the feelings, sensations, love, and energy movement in and of themselves without the need for mental and visual stimulation about an imaginary partner. The exercises themselves are structured in such a way as to encourage you in this. Later you can practice Dolphin Tantra for Couples. But for now, allow it to be an opportunity to get to know yourself and your body better, love yourself more deeply, and redefine what sexual energy is for you.

Once you have done the self-pleasuring exercise a few times, you will be able to be more spontaneous in your approach while still incorporating the basic purpose and energy flows into your sexual expression. For instance, the figure-8 movements will become more natural so that you will not need to think about them so intently. The toning and breathing will evolve into your most natural order and flow instead of following the step-by-step process.

As you experience the following self-pleasuring exercise for your gender, you will be instructed to use various techniques that you have used previously to begin, and enhance, the flow of sexual energy. Therefore, read the instructions first, making sure that you are fully familiar with each process used before you actually begin. Then enjoy. You may wish to create a loving and sacred space before beginning. Candles, flowers, aroma therapy, or anything else that you might normally do if inviting a lover to your bed, are also perfect ways of setting the space for your time with yourself.

Self-Pleasuring Dolphin Tantra for Females

The self-pleasuring Dolphin Tantra exercise for females is as follows:

1. Lie down naked in your bed. Make yourself comfortable with just the right pillows, covering, or whatever else you need. If you prefer the use of a vibrator to using your own hands, have that on the bed beside you where it will be easy to reach.

2. Ground yourself and adjust your aura to within two to three feet of your body in every direction.

3. Ask your Higher Self of Light to be with you and to activate your silver cord and fill your tube of light with your own divine love and light. When you feel the energy flowing, continue.

4. Ask the Pleiadian Emissaries of Light to come forth and place an Interdimensional Cone of Light above you for clearing and divine alignment.

5. Call upon Ascended Masters Jesus Christ and Mother Mary, and/or any other higher-dimensional male and female Light Beings, to join you and to hold male/female balance.

6. Tell all of the guides and Masters to place you inside a Dolphin Tantra Chamber of Light. This is similar to, and includes, the Dolphin Wave Effect. However, it is more expanded to assist in activation of your sexual energy channels and flow specifically.

7. Press your tongue into the roof of your mouth and begin to tone from your soul down to your G-spot and back up again within your soul channel. Alternate between breathing and toning the energy from your soul down and from your G-spot up.

(*An alternate breathing and toning pattern:* With your tongue pressed into the roof of your mouth, inhale from your clitoris to your G-spot and then all the way up to your soul. When you exhale send your breath and tone upward from your clitoris and G-spot to your soul as well. This alternative method will sustain a flow upward from your G-spot to your soul, as opposed to the back-and-forth flow pattern given earlier.)

Choose the breathing and toning pattern that works best for you. Feel free to experiment with this throughout the exercise except during the near-orgasm times when the instructions are very specific. If it feels good, add Infinity Dolphin Moves in your pelvis, perineum, shoulders, spine, or combined. (See illustrations 31-37 on pages 211-225 for recommended figure-8 movement patterns.)

As you begin to feel the love and sexual energy filling the channel move on to the next step.

8. Continuing to gently tone your soul channel, add body touching. Begin by stroking your own face the way you like a lover to do. Gently stroke your neck, arms, chest, including your breasts, your hips and pelvis areas, your outer legs down to your feet, then back up the inside of your legs to your groin area. As you come up the inside of your legs direct your toning and breath through your leg channels. Take your time. Feel the suppleness of your own skin. Appreciate all of the contours and various areas of your body fully. Your shape and size are insignificant where this is concerned. Simply turn off your mind and be as loving, tender, and appreciative of your uniqueness as possible. As you begin to feel sexually aroused, you may wish to add Infinity Dolphin Moves to enhance and sustain your full-body sensations or to help the energy move in blocked areas. When you reach your groin area, go to the next step.

9. Some people find at this stage that it is impossible to keep the toning going. Just deep breathing is all they can manage. If this is true for you, then keep your breath flowing up and down in your soul channel, but cease the toning. Otherwise, use toning and breath within the channel while touching your genitals in the way you find most pleasurable. Avoid fantasizing about a partner. Enjoy the sensations, love, and energy of your own body. (If you prefer a vibrator, begin to use it whenever you feel ready.) You may find it helpful to alternate tightening and relaxing of your vaginal muscles. Some women do that automatically, while others do not. When tightening your vaginal muscles, you may find it easier to feel the area of your G-spot and strengthen the sensation there—even without physically touching it. Sustain the flow and activation of sexual energy for as

long as you can. When you are near the point of having an orgasm, stop touching yourself and deeply inhale your sexual energy from your G-spot up into your soul area and back down again. Infinity Dolphin Moves may be used here as well. As the energy diminishes a little, resume touching your genitals again.

10. As your energy builds toward orgasm again, stop touching yourself and breathe and tone the energy up to your soul area with as much breath and sound as you are capable of at this time. Then breathe the soul energy and sexual energy mixture back into your G-spot and genitals again, continuing to alternate the direction of the flow until your energy subsides somewhat. Infinity Dolphin Moves may help. Continue.

11. This time when you are nearing the point of orgasm, stop touching yourself, then tone and breathe the energies down through your leg channels to your feet. Do not inhale them back up the channel. This channel grounds your sexual energy. Any body movements that assist in this process may be used. When the energy dies down a little, continue.

12. Resume touching yourself, stopping just prior to orgasm again. This time run the energy up from your G-spot through your breast channels. Do not run the energy back down again. This step opens and activates your breast channels more fully. The vertical Infinity Dolphin Moves may help you move the energy. When the energy has died down a little, continue.

13. Resume touching your genital area while breathing deeply, and toning if you can. When you are near the point of orgasm this time, continue touching yourself until you climax. If you prefer to avoid a full orgasm, then stop touching your genitals at the last moment just before orgasm. Otherwise, at the exact climactic point, take a deep sucking breath into your soul area from your genitals. You will not send your breath back down to your genitals any more. Continue breathing and/or toning your tantric energies while touching yourself, until your heart chakra is as full and open as it can be at

this time. (Use Infinity Dolphin Moves to facilitate further and more powerful movement of your sexual energy through your body if it feels right to do so. Some people prefer to become still at this point.)

14. *If your energy has died down at this point*, simply allow your body and breath to relax. Be with yourself in a quiet, loving way. You may experience continuing Dolphin Waves for awhile, light inside your body or third eye, or other spiritual experiences or revelations. Be fully present in a receptive, relaxed, and gently alert way for as long as it feels appropriate to you.

If your tantric energy is still flowing after your heart is fully open, then continue breathing and/or toning your sexual energy beyond your soul and up to your crown. When your crown is fully open, you may wish to breathe the energy down your arms, legs, or through any other chakra that you feel needs to open more at this time.

15. When you feel complete, ask the Pleiadians to remove the Dolphin Tantra Chamber, then continue with your day, go to sleep, or whatever you choose. ▨

The next time you do this exercise, substitute the following alternate step 13 in place of steps 13 and 14 above:

13. Inhaling deeply into your perineum, pull your sexual energy from your groin area to your perineum center. (See illustration 33 on page 220.) Continue breathing in this way until your perineum is full of energy and feels ready to overflow. At this point take a deep sucking breath and pull the energy you have built up in your perineum all the way up to your pineal gland in the center of your head. Continue breathing and toning the energy from your perineum to your pineal until your pineal gland is fully activated and your perineum center has been emptied of the built-up sexual energy. Relax and enjoy the energy and light flowing through your body.

The third time you do this exercise, use the following alternate step 13. You may choose to alternate between the three choices after that, or simply choose to work with the one that feels most correct for you personally.

13. Resume touching your genital area while breathing deeply, and toning if you can. When you are near the point of orgasm this time, continue touching yourself until you climax. If you prefer to avoid a full orgasm, then stop touching your genitals at the last moment just before orgasm. Otherwise, at the exact climactic point, take a deep sucking breath into your perineum. When you have breathed all of the energy into your perineum that it will hold, continue breathing deeply and tone (if possible) your orgasmic tantric energies up your spine to your crown and down to your third eye. When your third eye is filled with as much tantric energy as it will hold, use the deep sucking breaths and toning (if possible) to pull the energy into your heart chakra/soul area until your heart chakra is as full and open as it can be at this time. Continue this pattern of breathing the sexual energy into your perineum, up your spine to your crown and down to your third eye, and into your heart/soul area until your body has completely relaxed, and the energy has been moved fully into your heart. (Use Infinity Dolphin Moves to facilitate further and more powerful movement of your sexual energy through your body if it feels right to do so. Some people prefer to become still at this point.)

Self-Pleasuring Dolphin Tantra for Males

The self-pleasuring Dolphin Tantra exercise for males is as follows:

1. Lie down naked in your bed. Make yourself comfortable with just the right pillows, covering, or whatever else you need.

2. Ground yourself and adjust your aura to within two to three feet of your body in every direction.

3. Ask your Higher Self of Light to be with you and to activate your silver cord and fill your tube of light with your own divine love and light. When you feel the energy flowing, continue.

4. Ask the Pleiadian Emissaries of Light to come forth and place an Interdimensional Cone of Light above you for clearing and divine alignment.

5. Call upon Ascended Masters Jesus Christ and Mother Mary, and/or any other higher-dimensional male and female Light Beings, to join you and to hold male/female balance.

6. Tell all of the guides and Masters to place you inside a Dolphin Tantra Chamber of Light. This is similar to, and includes, the Dolphin Wave Effect. However, it is more expanded to assist in activation of your sexual energy channels and flow specifically.

7. Press your tongue into the roof of your mouth and begin to breathe and tone from your soul down to your sexual activation spot at the base of your prostate and on down through your penis to its tip. Alternate between breathing and toning the energy from your soul down and from your penis and activation spot up to your soul.

(*An alternate breathing and toning pattern:* With your tongue pressed into the roof of your mouth, inhale from your soul all the way down to your sexual activation point and then down through and to the tip of your penis. When you exhale send your breath and tone downward from your soul to your sexual activation point and through and to the tip of your penis as well. Continue breathing and toning in this direction only.)

Choose whichever breathing and toning pattern works best for you. Feel free to experiment with the direction of flow of your breathing and toning, except at near-orgasm points when the directions are very specific. If it feels good, add Infinity Dolphin Moves in your pelvis, shoulders, spine, or combined. (See illustrations 31 through 37 for specifically recommended figure-8 movement patterns.) As you begin to feel the love from your soul filling the channel and stimulating your penis, move on to the next step.

8. Continuing to gently tone your soul channel and the full length of your penis in your chosen directional pattern, add body touching. Begin by stroking your own face the way you like a lover to do. Use the amount of pressure you consider sensual and pleasurable. Gently stroke your neck, arms, chest, including your nipples, your hips and pelvis areas, your outer legs down to your feet, then back up the inside of your legs to your groin area. As you stroke from your feet

back up the inside of your legs, direct your breath and toning down your leg channels. Take your time. Feel the texture of your own skin. Appreciate all of the contours, muscles, and various areas of your body fully. Your shape and size are insignificant where this is concerned. Simply turn off your mind and be as loving, tender, and appreciative of your uniqueness as possible. As you begin to feel more sexually aroused you may wish to add Infinity Dolphin Moves to enhance and sustain your full-body sensations or to help the energy move in blocked areas. Avoid thrusting types of movements as these involve more contraction and localizing of your energy. When you reach your groin area, go to the next step.

9. Some people find at this stage that it is impossible to keep the toning going. Just deep breathing is all they can manage. If this is true for you, then keep your breath flowing up and down in your soul channel, but cease the toning. Otherwise, use toning and breath within the channel while touching your genitals in the way you find most pleasurable. Avoid fantasizing about a partner. Enjoy the sensations, love, and energy of your own body. Sustain the flow and activation of sexual energy for as long as you can. When you are near the point of having an orgasm, stop touching yourself and, using a deep sucking breath, inhale your sexual energy from your penis into your sexual activation point and up into your soul area and back down again. Infinity Dolphin Moves may be used here as well. As the energy diminishes a little, resume touching your penis.

10. As your energy builds toward orgasm again, stop touching yourself and breathe and tone the energy up to your soul area with as much breath and sound as you are capable of at this time. Then breathe the soul energy and sexual energy mixture back into your activation point and penis again, continuing to alternate the direction of the flow until your energy subsides somewhat. Infinity Dolphin Moves may help. Continue.

11. This time when you are nearing the point of orgasm, stop touching yourself, then tone and breathe the energies down through your leg channels to your feet. Do not inhale them back up the channel.

This channel grounds your sexual energy. Any body movements that assist in this process may be used. When the energy dies down a little, continue.

12. Resume touching yourself, stopping just prior to orgasm again. This time run the energy up from your penis and sexual activation spot through your breast channels. Do not run the energy back down again. This step opens and activates your breast channels more fully. The vertical Infinity Dolphin Moves may help you move the energy. When the energy has died down a little, continue.

13. Resume touching your penis while breathing deeply, and toning if you can. When you are near the point of orgasm this time, continue touching yourself until you know you will ejaculate if you continue. Stop and immediately take a deep sucking breath from your penis all the way up and into your soul area. You will not send your breath back down to your genitals any more. Continue breathing and/or toning your tantric energies until your heart chakra is as full and open as it can be at this time. (Use Infinity Dolphin Moves to facilitate further and more powerful movement of your sexual energy through your body if it feels right to do so. Some people prefer to become still at this point.)

14. *If your energy has died down at this point,* simply allow your body and breath to relax. Be with yourself in a quiet, loving way. You may experience continuing Dolphin Waves for a while, light inside your body or third eye, or other spiritual experiences or revelations. Be fully present in a receptive, relaxed, and gently alert way for as long as it feels appropriate to you.

If your tantric energy is still flowing after your heart is fully open, then continue breathing and/or toning your sexual energy beyond your soul and up to your crown. When your crown is fully open, you may wish to breathe the energy down your arms, legs, or through any other chakra that you feel needs to open more at this time.

15. When you feel complete, ask the Pleiadians to remove the Dolphin Tantra Chamber, and then continue with your day, go to sleep, or whatever you choose. [icon]

The next time you do this exercise, substitute the following alternate step 13 in place of steps 13 and 14 above:

13. Inhaling deeply into your perineum, pull your sexual energy from your groin area to your perineum center. (See illustration 33 on page 220.) Continue breathing in this way until your perineum is full of energy and feels ready to overflow. At this point take a deep sucking breath and pull the energy you have built up in your perineum all the way up to your pineal gland in the center of your head. Continue breathing and toning the energy from your perineum to your pineal until your pineal gland is fully activated and your perineum center has been emptied of the built-up sexual energy. Relax and enjoy the energy and light flowing through your body.

The third time you do this exercise, use the following alternate step 13. You may choose to alternate between the three choices after that, or simply choose to work with the one that feels most correct for you personally.

13. Resume touching your genital area while breathing deeply, and toning if you can. When you are near the point of orgasm this time, stop touching your genitals at the last moment just before ejaculation, and with a deep sucking breath pull all of the energy from your penis up and into your perineum center. When you have breathed all of the energy into your perineum that it will hold, continue breathing deeply and tone (if possible) your tantric energies up your spine to your crown and down to your third eye. When your third eye is filled with as much tantric energy as it will hold, use the deep sucking breaths and toning (if possible) to pull the energy into your heart chakra/soul area until your heart chakra is as full and open as it can be at this time. Continue this pattern of breathing the sexual energy into your perineum, up your spine to your crown and down to your third eye, and into your heart/soul area until your body has completely relaxed, and the energy has been moved fully into your heart. (Use Infinity Dolphin Moves to facilitate further and more powerful movement of your sexual energy through your body if it feels right to do so. Some people prefer to become still at this point.)

Dolphin Tantra for Couples

Now it is time to practice moving your sexual energy tantrically with a partner. Once you have done the exercise a few times, you will be able to incorporate the activations and touch in a more spontaneous and natural way into your lovemaking. It is not intended that every sexual act must involve toning and step-by-step process. This tantric exercise is intended to assist you in learning how to move your sexual energy in a way that achieves maximum tantric movement of energy into all of your cells, and those of your partner. After you have mastered this process, you will find innovative ways of incorporating the techniques you continue to find helpful into more spontaneous sexual exhanges.

If you are in a homosexual relationship, simply determine who will first be in the male and female roles. You may choose to interchange these roles at your discretion. When the exercise specifies "male" or "female" simply apply that term to the one who is serving in that role.

Follow the step-by-step outline given below for Dolphin Tantra for couples:

1. Lying naked in bed with your partner, give yourselves grounding cords and pull your individual auras in to two to three feet around your bodies in every direction.

2. Call in your Higher Selves of Light to fill your individual tubes of light and activate your silver cords.

3. Call in the Pleiadian Emissaries of Light. Ask them to place an Interdimensional Cone of Light above your bed.

4. Call in Ascended Masters Jesus Christ and Mary Magdalene to hold the male/female balance. If there are other higher-dimensional male and female Light Beings with whom you both prefer to work, or in addition, call them in now.

5. Ask to be placed inside the Dolphin Tantra Chamber of Light for couples.

6. *The female will receive first:* Press your tongue into the roof of your mouth and begin to breathe and tone from your G-spot up to your soul. Alternate between breathing and toning the energy from your soul down and from your clitoris and G-spot up to your soul. Feel free to experiment with the direction of flow of your breathing and toning, except at near-orgasm points when the directions are very specific. If it feels good, add Infinity Dolphin Moves in your pelvis, shoulders, spine, or combined. (See illustrations 31 through 37 for specifically recommended figure-8 movement patterns.)

Male partner who is giving: Lie on your side propped on your elbow, or sit beside your partner. Focus on sending your partner your love and adoration while placing a fingertip each on her clitoris and G-spot. With your other hand cover her heart chakra. If you cannot reach her G-spot and clitoris at the same time with the same hand, then touch her G-spot only. Match her tone while imagining the tone going out through your fingertips and hands into her clitoris, G-spot, and soul. As she begins to feel the love from your soul and her own sexual energy filling the channel and stimulating her, move onto the next step.

7. *Male:* Continuing to gently tone her soul channel, add body touching. Begin by stroking her face tenderly. Allow your touch to be an expression of your love and adoration, and sensual enjoyment of her skin. Gently stroke her neck, arms, chest, including her nipples, her hips and pelvis areas, outer legs down to her feet, then back up the insides of her legs to her groin area. As you stroke from each foot back up the inside of her leg, leave one hand holding the end point of the leg channel at her foot. When you reach her groin area with your other hand, place a fingertip each on her clitoris and G-spot. If you cannot reach both at the same time, touch the G-spot only. Gently massage her clitoris and G-spot while toning from her G-spot down to her feet.

Female: Tone your own leg channels while your partner is doing so.

Male: Take your time. Feel the texture of her skin. Appreciate all of the contours, muscles, and various areas of her body fully. Shape and size are insignificant where this is concerned. Simply turn off your mind and be as loving, tender, and appreciative of her uniqueness as possible.

Female: As you begin to feel more sexually aroused you may wish to add Infinity Dolphin Moves to enhance and sustain your full-body sensations or to help the energy move in blocked areas. Avoid thrusting types of movements as these involve more contraction and localizing of your energy. When your leg channels feel well-activated, continue with the next step.

8. *Male:* Alternating from her left to right breast at about one-minute intervals, massage and stimulate her breasts, clitoris, and G-spot simultaneously. Using your mouth in any way that feels natural to you is appropriate at this time. If you choose to use your mouth on her breasts or clitoris area, place a finger inside her vagina and massage her G-spot simultaneously.

Female: Some women find that it is impossible at this stage to keep the toning going. Just deep breathing is all they can manage. If this is true for you, then keep your breath flowing up and down in your breast channels, but cease the toning. Otherwise, use toning and breath within the channels while your partner touches your breasts, clitoris, and G-spot. Enjoy the sensations, love, and energy of your own body and those coming from your partner. Sustain the flow and activation of sexual energy for as long as you can. When you are near the point of having an orgasm, ask your partner to stop touching you. Using a deep sucking breath, inhale your sexual energy from your genitals up into your breasts. Infinity Dolphin Moves may be used here as well. As the energy diminishes a little, your partner can resume touching your genitals and wherever else he wishes to touch and stroke.

9. As your energy builds toward orgasm again, ask him to stop touching your body. Breathe and tone the energy up to your soul area with as much breath and sound as you are capable of at this time. Then breathe the soul energy and sexual energy mixture back into your G-spot again, continuing to alternate the direction of the flow until your energy subsides somewhat. Infinity Dolphin Moves may help. Continue.

10. *Male:* Resume massaging and stroking of her clitoris, G-spot, and the insides of her legs.

38. Woman activating her male partner's tantric soul channel

Female: This time when you are nearing the point of orgasm, ask him to stop touching your body. Tone and breathe the energies down through your leg channels to your feet. Do not inhale them back up these channels. These channels ground your sexual energy. Any body movements that assist in this process may be used. When the energy dies down a little, continue.

11. You will conclude this tantric exercise with penetration after the male has been given to, unless he prefers to use his hands and oral connection to bring the female to orgasm now.

If you prefer to complete with penetration at the end, move on to step 12 now. The female partner will begin giving to the male, in this case.

If the male prefers to bring the female to orgasm with hands and oral touch, he resumes touching her in whatever way she chooses. When she is at the point of orgasm this time, he continues touching her through the orgasmic release unless she asks him to stop.

Female: As you begin to orgasm take a deep sucking breath and pull the energy from your genital area up to your soul. Continue this until your soul feels full and overflowing with love and energy. Then begin to inhale deeply into your perineum center from your genitals until your perineum feels full. Then, with a deep sucking breath, or several if needed, pull the energy from your perineum straight up your spine and into your pineal gland until it is full and overflowing. Ask your partner to stop stimulating you when it feels appropriate. At that point, ask him to hold you until the tantric waves have subsided enough that you can step into the giving role.

12. *Male:* Press your tongue into the roof of your mouth and begin to breathe and tone from the tip of your penis to the activation point at the base of your penis and up to your soul. Alternate between breathing and toning the energy from your soul down and from your penis up to your soul. Feel free to experiment with the direction of flow of your breathing and toning, except at near-orgasm points when the directions are very specific. If it feels good, add Infinity Dolphin Moves in your pelvis, shoulders, spine, or combined. (See illustrations 31 through 37 for specifically recommended figure-8 movement patterns.)

Female partner who is giving: Lie on your side propped on your elbow, or sit beside your partner. Place one fingertip each on the tip of his penis and at the base of his penis as per illustration on page 246. Place your other hand on his heart chakra. Send as much love and adoration for your partner through your hands, eyes, and heart as you can. Match his tone while imagining the tone going out through your fingertips and hands into his penis and soul. As he begins to feel the love from your soul and his own sexual energy filling the channel and stimulating him, move onto the next step.

13. *Female:* While he continues to gently tone his soul channel, add body touching. Begin by stroking his face tenderly. Allow your touch to be an expression of your love and adoration and sensual enjoyment of his skin. Gently stroke his neck, arms, chest, including his nipples, hips and pelvis areas, outer legs down to his feet, then back up the insides of his legs to his groin area. As you stroke from each foot back up the inside of his leg, leave one hand holding the end point of the leg channel at his foot. When you reach his groin area with your other hand, place a fingertip each on the tip and base of his penis. Gently massage his penis while toning from his penis down to his feet.

Male: Tone your own leg channels while your partner is doing so.

Female: Take your time. Feel the texture of his skin and hair. Appreciate all of the contours, muscles, and various areas of his body fully. Shape and size are insignificant where this is concerned. Simply turn off your mind and be as loving, tender, and appreciative of his uniqueness as possible.

Male: As you begin to feel more sexually aroused you may wish to add Infinity Dolphin Moves to enhance and sustain your full-body sensations or to help the energy move in blocked areas. Avoid thrusting type of movements as these involve more contraction and localizing of your energy. When your leg channels feel well activated, continue with the next step.

14. *Female:* Alternating from his left to right nipple at about one-minute intervals, massage and stimulate his nipples and penis simultaneously. Using your mouth in any way that feels natural to you is appropriate at this time. If you choose to use your mouth on his penis,

continue to massage his nipples simultaneously.

Male: Some men find that it is impossible at this stage to keep the toning going. Just deep breathing is all they can manage. If this is true for you, then keep your breath flowing up and down in your breast channels, but cease the toning. Otherwise, use toning and breath within the channels while your partner touches your nipples and penis. Enjoy the sensations, love, and energy of your own body and that which is coming from your partner. Sustain the flow and activation of sexual energy for as long as you can. When you are near the point of having an orgasm, ask your partner to stop touching you. Using a deep sucking breath, inhale your sexual energy from your penis up into your breasts. Infinity Dolphin Moves may be used here as well. As the energy diminishes a little, your partner can resume touching your genitals and wherever else she wishes to touch and stroke.

15. As your energy builds toward orgasm again, ask her to stop touching your body. Breathe and tone the energy up to your soul area with as much breath and sound as you are capable of at this time. Then breathe the soul energy and sexual energy mixture back into your penis again, continuing to alternate the direction of the flow until your energy subsides somewhat. Infinity Dolphin Moves may help. Continue.

16. *Female:* Resume massaging and stroking of his penis and the insides of his legs.

Male: This time when you are nearing the point of orgasm, ask her to stop touching your body. Tone and breathe the energies down through your leg channels to your feet. Do not inhale them back up this channel. This channel grounds your sexual energy. Any body movements that assist in this process may be used. When the energy dies down a little, continue.

17. You will conclude this tantric exercise with penetration after the male has been given to, unless the female prefers to use her hands and oral connection to bring him to orgasm now.

If you prefer to complete with penetration, move on to step 18 now.

If the female prefers to bring the male to orgasm with hands and oral touch, she resumes touching him in whatever way he chooses. When he is at the point of orgasm this time, she continues touching him until he tells her to stop.

Male: In order to maximize the tantric energy flow, it is important to avoid ejaculation if you can. When you are near the point of orgasm this time, ask her to stop at the point you know you will ejaculate if she continues. Immediately take a deep sucking breath from your penis all the way up and into your soul area. You will not send your breath back down to your penis any more. Continue breathing and/or toning your tantric energies until your heart chakra is as full and open as it can be at this time. Use Infinity Dolphin Moves to facilitate further and more powerful movement of your sexual energy through your body if it feels right to do so. Some people prefer to become still at this point.

Continue this until your soul feels full and overflowing with love and energy. Then begin to inhale deeply into your perineum center from your penis until your perineum feels full. Then, with a deep sucking breath, or several if needed, pull the energy from your perineum straight up your spine and into your pineal gland until it is full and overflowing. At this point, ask her to hold you until the tantric waves have subsided.

18. Choose whatever position you wish to be in, and begin penetration. Maintain eye contact, kissing, and any other touching that feels natural to you both. While moving together breathe as follows:

Male: Breathe from your soul down into your penis. When she exhales, you inhale, and vice versa. When you inhale, take in her love and nurturing energies from her heart and breasts. When you exhale send her your love and adoration down through your penis into her vagina.

Female: Breathe from your clitoris and G-spot up to your soul. When he exhales, you inhale, and vice versa. When you inhale, take in his love and adoration through your vagina up to your heart. When you exhale, send your love and adoration for him out through your heart and breasts.

NOTE: If either or both of you wish to tone the channels at any time, do so. If the male nears the point of orgasm before the female is ready, stop moving. *Male:* Breathe the energy up into your heart until the energy diminishes enough to continue movement without ejaculation. Then continue the breathing pattern above.

19. When you are both ready for the final tantric orgasmic release, deepen the penetration to capacity. Stop moving; then both of you inhale the energy with a deep sucking breath up to your souls. When your souls feel full and overflowing, inhale deeply from your genitals into your perineum centers until your perineums feel full. With a deep sucking breath pull the energy from your perineums up to your pineal glands.

NOTE: You may or may not be able to synchronize this step. If one partner releases prior to the other, it is okay. The one who releases will simply need to assist the partner in coming to completion once the first person's own tantric flow is full and complete.

20. When your mutual energy flows are full and moving into the "bliss stage," simply allow your bodies and breathing to relax. Be with one another in a quiet, loving way. You may experience continuing Dolphin Waves for a while, light inside your bodies or third eyes, or other spiritual experiences or revelations. Be fully present in a receptive, relaxed, and gently alert way for as long as it feels appropriate to you. Allow yourself to blend fully with your partner's aura. You may feel as if you have become one body or one galaxy, or other heightened experiences may occur. Follow your mutual flow to your own natural completion.

21. When you feel complete, ask the Pleiadians to remove the Dolphin Tantra Chamber, and continue with your day, go to sleep, or whatever you choose. ▭

The next time you do this exercise use the following alternate step 19. You may choose to alternate between the two choices after that, or simply choose to work with the one that feels most correct for you personally.

19. Continue moving together while breathing deeply, and toning if you can. It is ideal to work at timing this step together whenever possible. However, if one partner reaches his or her release point prior to the other, it is okay. The one who has released will simply need to assist his or her partner in coming to completion.

When one or both of you are near the point of orgasm this time, stop moving just before orgasm, and with a deep sucking breath pull all of the energy from your penis/vagina up and into your perineum center/s. When you have breathed all of the energy into your perineum/s that they will hold, continue breathing deeply and tone (if possible) your tantric energies up your spine/s to your crown/s and down to your third eye/s. When your third eye/s are filled with as much tantric energy as they will hold, use deep sucking breaths and toning (if possible) to pull the energy into your heart chakras/soul areas until your heart chakras are as full and open as they can be at this time. Continue this pattern of breathing the sexual energy into your perineum/s, up your spines to your crowns and down to your third eyes, and into your hearts/soul areas until your bodies have completely relaxed, and the energy has been moved fully into your heart/s. When your partner is doing the breathing of the tantric energies into the perineum, third eye, and heart, match his or her breathing to enhance both of your sense of unity and sharing. (Use Infinity Dolphin Moves to facilitate further and more powerful movement of your sexual energy through your body if it feels right to do so. Some people prefer to become still at this point.)

Chapter 10

BECOMING YOUR CHRISTED SELF

Cosmic and Earth Kundalini Activation

In addition to your body-based kundalini, which was activated in chapter 8 exercises, there are two more types of kundalini that are important to your ongoing multidimensional alignment and Christ consciousness. They are cosmic kundalini and Earth kundalini.

First, your cosmic kundalini is a much more refined, rarefied electrical energy than is your body kundalini. Cosmic kundalini also has a different flow pattern. Your tube of light is the channel in your body and aura through which cosmic kundalini flows. It is basically your Higher Self's electrical energy. When this energy begins to flow through your tube of light it brings in higher frequencies, accelerates your awakening, deepens your connection to your Higher Self, and heightens your full sensory perceptions. It increases and strengthens your cerebral spinal fluid production and flow throughout your central nervous system, and assists in bringing you to fuller brain activation. Cosmic kundalini also triggers deeper levels of Ka activation.

Your cosmic kundalini enters through your cosmic portal chakra at the top apex of your aura and runs into your crown, down through your spinal cord in the interior of your spine, and to your perineum. You will not need to clear the pathways since you have already been running Higher Self energy through your tube of light. During the meditation to run cosmic kundalini, you will be instructed to stop the flow at your pineal gland and brain and allow it to fill and overflow those centers. Around your atlas, or first vertebra, located just under your occipital ridge is a membrane. (See illustration on page 254.) This

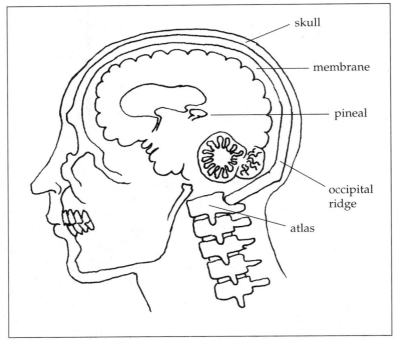

39. Bones of skull, and membrane that holds cerebral spinal fluid protecting the brain

membrane also surrounds your brain like a thin sack and contains cerebral spinal fluid that surrounds and protects your brain. You will be instructed to allow the flow of cosmic kundalini to activate this entire membrane. You will experience this as pressure, expansion, and more energy inside your head. When your brain feels fully activated, you will direct your cosmic kundalini down to your perineum center. Once this kundalini has reached your perineum center, time will be given for filling and overflowing that center as well.

Then when the tube of light in your body has been fully activated, you will be instructed to send a "burst" of cosmic kundalini down through the lower part of your tube of light to the center of Earth to the Earth Star crystal. This will activate and impulse the Earth Star crystal to send back Earth kundalini to your feet and first chakra. At that point you will simply be asked to breathe in through the bottoms of your feet and your first chakra in order to receive this Earth kundalini into your body. Earth kundalini will help balance your energy between your physical and spiritual bodies. It will also assist you in remaining more grounded while running your body and cosmic kundalini.

It is recommended that you do this meditation in the early part of the day. It may keep you awake otherwise. If you notice a lot of clearing and intensity during the day after doing this meditation, you may wish to do it no more than once per week in the beginning. Find your own right frequency of timing. Eventually it is intended to become part of your daily ascension meditation routine.

The meditation for activating your cosmic and Earth kundalini is as follows:

1. Give yourself a new grounding cord.

2. Pull in your aura to within two to three feet around you in every direction. Check your aura boundary colors and roses and make any needed adjustments.

3. Call in your Higher Self of Light to activate your silver cord and fill your tube of light.

4. Ask the Pleiadian Emissaries of Light and Ascended Masters Jesus Christ and Mother Mary to be with you.

5. Ask for an Interdimensional Cone of Light for clearing and divine axis alignment.

6. Ask your Higher Self to send its cosmic kundalini into and through your tube of light. Breathe deeply in through your crown chakra, pulling the cosmic kundalini into your pineal gland. Allow the flow to stop at your pineal gland until you sense that it is full and overflowing.

7. Now breathe the cosmic kundalini down to your atlas at the top of your spine, under your occipital ridge. (See illustration 39 on page 252.) The membrane around your atlas continues around and through your brain. Continue focusing on the cosmic kundalini as it activates this membrane throughout your brain. When this feels full, continue.

8. Breathe deeply in through your crown and down into your spinal cord. Continue breathing downward until your cosmic kundalini has come out the other end of your spine at your perineum center.

9. Continue breathing from your crown, down through your spine, and into your perineum until your perineum center is full and overflowing with light and cosmic kundalini.

10. Next send a brief burst of cosmic kundalini down through your tube of light, out through your Earth Star chakra at the bottom apex of your aura, and into the Earth Star crystal at the center of Earth.

11. Breathe in through the bottoms of your feet and your first chakra in order to welcome Earth kundalini into your body.

12. Relax and feel the new energies and light in your body for as long as you wish to do so.

13. When complete, ask your Higher Self to turn off your cosmic kundalini for now.

14. Ground yourself if you feel the need. Continue with your day.

After doing this meditation the first time, you need not stop at your pineal gland, atlas, and perineum centers unless you prefer. You can simply bring in the cosmic kundalini through your crown and breathe it all the way through your pineal, spine, and perineum without pausing to fill and overflow the three centers along the way.

Sword of Truth and Holy Grail Initiation

Before moving into the out-of-body meditation practice in the last section of this chapter, it is important to know that you can move through the dimensions without becoming entrapped in the astral planes and dark aspects of the fourth and fifth dimensions. In order to have this assurance, Archangel Michael/Michaella will initiate you into the use of the Sword of Truth and the Holy Grail. But first I will explain this archangel's higher-dimensional service to humans, and what the Sword of Truth and Holy Grail are.

Archangel Michael/Michaella is the head of the Legions of Light. The Legions of Light are those humans and higher-dimensional beings who have dedicated themselves exclusively to aligning with, and protection of, Divine Truth, which is Light. Most people have heard of Archangel Michael as a male being only. However, he has a divine counterpart, Archangel Michaella. Michael and Michaella are twin flames, who when in one light body only appear as Archangel Michael. This dual-natured archangel is also the protector of the Goddess, the divine feminine energy, and the *unio conjunctio,* or sacred marriage. Sacred marriage can be between the inner male and female in an individual, or between a man and woman in separate bodies.

The Sword of Truth is the symbol for alignment with and protection of Divine Truth. The female counterpart to the Sword is the Holy Grail, which is the symbol for the Goddess and for sacred marriage.

When you are initiated as a carrier of the Sword of Truth and the Holy Grail, you are required to make a commitment to honoring the sacredness in all things and people, to never use the Sword for harm, to protect innocence, and to be receptive to Divine Truth at all times. In carrying the Sword of Truth, you are enabled to clear dark and erroneous energies from your hologram, make clear discerning choices, and eliminate unwanted influences in a nonharmful manner. For example, if you were sleeping and suddenly awakened in fear because of a dark being attempting to harm you, you could pull out your Sword of Truth, point it at the invader, and command in the name of the Legions of Light that it be gone. Under the universal law of free will, the entity will have to obey. If you move the Sword of Truth around and through your aura while saying, "I command that all that is less than or other than I am be gone now from my body, my aura, and my entire hologram," any invasive and malevolent energies will be forced to leave. The only exception to this rule is that if you have a contract with a person or entity that allows it to be in your energy field, you may have to clear that contract first. The Sword of Truth can be used to clear psychic cords as well.

Another function of the Sword of Truth is that of making discerning observations and choices. You can practice holding your Sword of Truth pointed upward while saying things that are true and false. The Sword of Truth remains strong, and brightens, in the presence of truth. In the presence of deception, it dulls and/or may go limp. If you practice this process with statements that you know are true or false until you consistently get a recognizable response from the Sword, you will be able to use it in other ways. For instance, if you are unsure about a person's honesty, you can visualize the person in front of your Sword of Truth while imagining him or her talking to you. If the Sword remains strong and bright, this person is probably telling you the truth, but probably lying to you if it dulls. Regardless of the outcome, you are responsible for discernment, not judgment. In fact, if you begin to use the Sword to judge others or feel superior to them, it will be taken away from you. It is only intended to help you align with Divine Truth and make choices based on knowing the truth of your circumstances. If you are strongly invested in the answer you receive from the Sword, I would recommend not using it. When you are not 100 percent available for knowing the truth, if you are more invested in a desired outcome than you are willing to let go, you may sway your own interpretation of the Sword's answer. Misuse of the Sword in this, or any other way, will result in losing your right to carry and use it. The Sword will never harm an etheric attacker, but it will keep one at Sword's length, at the very least. At best, it will remove the threat completely and permanently.

In the ancient days of the knights and the quest for the Holy Grail, the young men went into the world carrying swords, which they agreed to use only in the protection of their country, women and children, themselves, and their fellowman. Until these men had become so selfless that they could not harm another except for the above reasons, they could not marry. They had to find the Holy Grail first. The Holy Grail in this case represented the knight's inner female self. To find the Holy Grail meant that he had surrendered in service to country and to spirit, was determined to know and protect Truth above his own desires, and *had learned to care more about not harming others than he did about meeting his own needs and wants*. "Beauty and the Beast" is the perfect story of a man overcoming his own desires to possess, control, save himself at the expense of others, and conquer. He learned to love more than he desired. He learned to respect and honor beauty and innocence, even at the expense of his own pain. He had found the Holy Grail within himself. When a man does this, he is ready to be with a woman in sacred marriage.

When a woman finds the Holy Grail inside herself, she must then balance with her own male side, which is the carrier of the Sword of Truth. She ceases to lure men for her own vanity and control. She opens herself fully to receive a man, but only if he is able to meet her halfway. She no longer settles for inappropriate companionship in lieu of loneliness or fear of harm. Her attachment and possessiveness are vanished in her deep commitment to love and honor of herself and her partner. Unless he comes willingly, humbly, and lovingly, she remains alone. She accomplishes this by surrendering to Truth, and holding herself and others in the light of Truth before acting.

The balance between the Holy Grail and the Sword of Truth is the balance between surrender and nonattachment, and action based on Divine Will and Truth, respectively.

The meditation for receiving your Holy Grail and Sword of Truth is really an initiation. Read the process thoroughly before doing it to be certain you are ready to take the vows required in order to become a member of the Legions of Light. Once you have determined that you are sincerely aligned with the process, you will meet Archangel Michael who will present you with your own Sword of Truth. Then Archangel Michaella will present you with the Holy Grail. Both symbols will find their natural place in your body or aura for safekeeping. Then you will use the Sword to move through your aura and body and do an astral clearing, and a clearing of anything less than or other than your own energy.

The meditation for receiving your Sword of Truth and Holy Grail and joining the Legions of Light is as follows:

1. Ground yourself and pull in your aura to within two to three feet around your body.

2. Call in your Higher Self of Light to activate your silver cord and fill your tube of light. (Cosmic kundalini activation is optional.)

3. Invoke Archangel Michael/Michaella of the Light. Ask that they come in their male and female aspects.

4. Tell Archangel Michael/Michaella the following: "I am ready, willing, and able to become an active member of the Legions of Light. I ask for absolute protection by the Legions of Light at all times and in all places. I understand that I am responsible in turn to carry the Sword of Truth and the Holy Grail. I now ask Archangel Michael to give me my own Sword of Truth. I am ready to surrender to Divine Truth, to release my own attachments and desires. I promise to never use the Sword of Truth to harm or judge myself or others. I agree to be responsible for caring more about not harming others than than I am about meeting my own needs and wants. I promise to never harm, but to always protect innocence and truth and to honor the sacredness of all things and all people."

5. Extend your hands and receive your Sword of Truth. Feel it in your hands. Move it around and accustom yourself to holding it.

6. Beginning at the bottom of your aura, move the Sword through your aura and upward through your body and aura while repeating, "In the name of the I Am That I Am, as a member of the Legions of Light, I command that all that is less than or other than I am be gone now from my body, my aura, and entire hologram throughout time and space." Continue until you have traced your entire auric field and body with your Sword.

7. Where does your Sword of Truth belong? Tune in and place it there. It may go inside your body or a chakra, hang from your waist, or be suspended in your aura somewhere. Wherever it goes, place it there until you are ready to use it again.

8. Now address Archangel Michaella as follows: "I am ready, willing, and able to receive my own Holy Grail. I am receptive only to the Divine Truth, and am ready to release all attachments to illusion. I honor the true beauty and sacredness of myself, and of others. I will

only share my body with partners who love, honor, trust, and respect me, and whom I love, honor, trust, and respect. My body is a sacred vessel that holds my Holy Spirit. I will always love it, protect it, and care for it unconditionally. I am ready to be fully alive, with nothing to hide from myself or others. I am blameless and unblaming. I am the beauty of my Holy Spirit embodied. So be it." Extend both hands to receive your Holy Grail from Michaella. Hold it, feel it, cherish it.

9. You will either feel guided to drink from your Grail or to pour from it over your body. Whichever is right for you, take your time to experience it fully. When complete, continue.

10. Tune in to where your Grail is to be kept inside your body or aura. Place it there.

11. Express your gratitude to, and honoring of, Archangel Michael/Michaella in your own way. When they are gone, open your eyes and continue with your day.

Sixth-Dimension Meditation

The purpose of this meditation is to bring symbols into each of your chakras that represent each chakra's highest purpose in this lifetime. In other words, the symbols for each chakra hold the energy of what that chakra will be when fully opened, enlightened, and en-Christed. In order to identify these symbols, you must go out to your own sixth-dimensional Higher Self. It is there that the sacred geometry for your body, and all its organs, glands, and chakras, is held. When you are in your tube of light alignment with your silver cord attached, your sixth-dimensional self can impulse you toward rebecoming what you truly are: a perfect and divine being of light, truth, and love. Your sixth-dimensional self is, in a manner of speaking, the blueprint and consciousness of your future Christed Self.

When you go out to the sixth dimension, you will first collect your consciousness into a miniature you in the center of your head. Then you will take your Sword of Truth into your hands to take with you. A Pleiadian Emissary of Light guide will go with you as you bring yourself out of your crown chakra in your body and rise above your body. Just above your body you will ask to be placed inside a light merkabah shaped like an octahedron, a double pyramid. This merkabah is a sacred geometry vessel for moving safely through dimensions and through time and space. Once you are inside, your guide will take you upward through the fourth and fifth dimensions to the sixth. You will clear any dark or foreign energies you find along the way by swinging your Sword of Truth in continuing circles around yourself.

When you have arrived in the sixth dimension, you will move up to the crown chakra of your Higher Self and experience that chakra exclusively. When you have basked in those energies, a symbol will be given to you that holds the energy of your crown chakra in your body in your highest potential and purpose for this life. After experiencing that symbol fully, you will move down to your Higher Self's third-eye chakra and repeat the process. Then you will move down through each of your Higher Self's chakras, one after another, until you have experienced all seven body chakras. Then you will downstep back through the fifth and fourth dimensions until you are back in your body. Once you are in your body's crown chakra, you will leave the symbol from your sixth-dimensional crown chakra there. Again you will move down through your chakras one at a time until you reach your first chakra. In each one you will leave the higher-dimensional symbol in order to impulse yourself toward your highest purpose and attainment. Then you will slowly spread your consciousness back through your body, put away your Sword of Truth, and the meditation will be complete. Have a note pad and pen nearby so you can write down your symbols as soon as the meditation is done. You may wish to occasionally reactivate your symbols by running light through them in meditation. This is recommended in order to assist in your ongoing awakening and in staying on purpose.

Following is the sixth-dimension meditation for bringing in your higher-dimensional chakra symbols:

1. Ground yourself and pull in your aura to two to three feet around you. Check and adjust your boundary colors and roses as needed.

2. Surround your aura in violet flame for the duration of this meditation.

3. Call your Higher Self of Light to activate your silver cord and fill your tube of light. (Optional: Activate your cosmic and Earth kundalini.)

4. Pull your consciousness as fully as you can into a miniature image of your body in the center of your head.

5. Take the Sword of Truth into your miniature self's hands.

6. In your miniature light body, lift yourself upward until you are above your head.

7. Ask that a Pleiadian Emissary of Light guide come to accompany you on your sixth-dimensional journey. Ask this guide to place you inside a double-pyramid merkabah for safe transport. When the merkabah is around you, continue.

8. You, inside your merkabah, and your Pleiadian guide will begin to lift upward, out of your aura into the fourth dimension. Slowly make circles with your Sword of Truth with the intent to clear anything "less than or other than I am." Continue moving upward until you feel an obvious shift in the energy. At this point you will be in the fifth dimension.

9. Continue slowly swinging your Sword of Truth around you while maintaining a clear intent as before. You will continue to move upward until you feel a notable increase in light. The energy will become much more rarefied and expansive. This is the lower part of the sixth dimension.

10. Hold the intent with your guide to go all the way up to the crown chakra of your sixth-dimensional Higher Self. When you stop moving, you are there.

11. Allow yourself to blend with your Higher Self's crown chakra. You will see a symbol there that holds the energy of your highest purpose and potential for this lifetime. Embrace the symbol and experience it fully.

12. Next move down to your sixth-dimensional third eye. Bask in the energy and receive your symbol. When complete, continue.

13. Move downward to your sixth-dimensional throat chakra. Blend with that chakra and feel it. You will receive a symbol for this chakra. Take time to experience it before moving on.

14. Now move into your Higher Self's heart chakra. Blend with that chakra and feel the purity and strength of your own higher love. Receive and experience fully the symbol for that chakra.

15. As you move down again, you will arrive at the third, or solar-plexus, chakra of your sixth-dimensional Higher Self. Blend there, receive your symbol and experience it fully.

16. Move down to your sixth-dimensional second, or sacral, chakra. Blend with the chakra, feel it, and receive your symbol.

17. Last, move into your Higher Self's first chakra. Blend with that chakra, receive your symbol, and take time to experience it fully.

18. Now you will move back down through the fifth and fourth dimensions until you find yourself arriving back at your physical body.

19. Descend into your body's crown chakra. Release your crown chakra symbol there.

20. Move down into your body's third eye, and place the appropriate symbol there.

21. Move down into your body's throat chakra, and place the appropriate symbol there.

22. Move down into your body's heart chakra, and place the appropriate symbol there.

23. Move down into your body's third, or solar-plexus, chakra, and place the appropriate symbol there.

24. Move down into your body's second, or sacral, chakra, and place the appropriate symbol there.

25. Move down into your body's first chakra, and place the appropriate symbol there.

26. Ask your Pleiadian guide to take away the merkabah.

27. Expand your consciousness into your whole body. Breathe deeply and feel your body.

28. Put away your Sword of Truth.

29. Give yourself a new grounding cord.

30. Open your eyes and immediately write down your symbols.

Chapter 11
DOLPHIN STAR-LINKING

Planetary/Stellar Alignment Chamber of Light

Now that you have linked your own chakras to your sixth-dimensional Higher Self, both by experiencing your chakras in the sixth dimension, and by bringing back the symbols for those chakras, the next step is to make chakra alignment with the Pleiades, Sirius, the Earth Star at the center of Earth, our Sun, and the Galactic Center of the Milky Way. The purpose in making these alignments is to assist you in feeling more connected with this solar ring, with the Pleiades, Sirius, and the entire galaxy. Within each human being is a microcosm of All That Is. Within that microcosm, there is a repeated patterning of seven basic chakra-type functions. These chakras work interdependently with the multidimensional roles in Creation. And Creation is physically actualized in the third dimension and grounded to the first dimension and second dimension via its mineral components and etheric body. There is also an essence connection, and a translator and organizer of energy that unites all systems. The Planetary/Stellar Alignment Chamber of Light works with these planets, stars, and cosmic bodies relative to those specific functions and how they innerrelate with the microcosm of the universe that you are.

The Seven Sisters of the Pleiades, or the seven suns or stars of that system, have a direct connection to each of your chakras. In the chamber, you will be guided through a specific process for linking these individual stars to individual chakras. This linkup is made by envisioning golden infinity symbols between your chakras connecting each chakra to the specific star, or sun, to which it is being linked. In

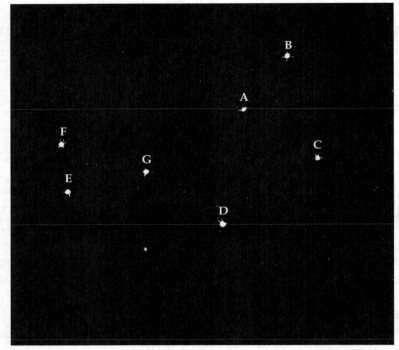

40: *Pleiades, The Seven Sisters, and their correspondence to your chakras. a-crown, seventh chakra; b-third eye, sixth chakra; c-throat, fifth chakra; d-heart, fourth chakra; e-solar plexus, third chakra; f-sacral, second chakra; g-root, first chakra*

illustration 40 above, you will notice that the stars of the Pleiades are labeled a,b,c,d,e,f, and g. In the meditation you will be guided to link star "a" with your crown chakra, star "b" with your third eye, and so on, all the way down through star "g" linking with your first chakra.

This linkup between the Seven Sisters of the Pleiades and your chakras has been practiced in other civilizations for at least the last hundred-thousand years, and probably more. The Maya, today, still know of these linkups between the chakras and the Pleiades. The aboriginal cultures, the Cherokee, and the ancient Egyptians, to name only a few, have known of their relationship to the Pleiades for a great long time. For you see, within this solar ring our Sun is part of a smaller microcosmic system, which includes the seven stars of the Pleiades. Our Sun holds the direct link to your soul, while the Pleiades hold the link to your individuated chakras. The nearest star or sun to the planet on which physical beings live is always the source of soul connection. When your soul was created, and when you were born in each lifetime, your consciousness and soul literally passed through the dimensional gateways of the Sun. As you moved through these gateways, four things happened. First, you were imprinted with your own soul creation energy and higher purpose relative to all of your incarnations on Earth. This encoding aligned you with your purpose for the individual lifetime, as well as your overall purpose for all lifetimes.

The second imprint was from your soul to the Sun. The encodings and messages for your lifetime that you had received prior to down-stepping to take on a body were imprinted into the Sun's matrix. In other words, your soul imprints the Sun with the encodings that you need it to reflect back to you throughout this lifetime.

The third purpose of moving through the Sun was for your soul to be imprinted with the collective consciousness encodings for the time period during which you would be living on Earth. This is a planet of co-creation. Therefore, when you come into an individuated lifetime, you must align with the overall purpose for the planet, the solar ring, the Pleiadian system, and the entire galaxy, as well as with your own purpose for being here. Therefore, any of the priorities—the currently agreed-upon solar ring and planetary laws, as well as goals for these systems—must be imprinted in such a way as to align your personal goals with those of the entire planet, solar system, and galaxy.

The fourth reason for moving through the Sun is that the Sun continually holds a relationship to all beings on Earth individually and collectively. From the collective standpoint, being merged with the Sun is the equivalent to being merged with the Divine Essence of every individual on Earth at the same time. Moving through the Sun prior to coming into a body gives you a last minute reference point, so to speak, in Oneness with All That Is. During that blending and movement through the Sun there is great harmony, love, devotion, and cooperation. It gives you an energy boost spiritually, from the stand-point of feeling inspired by Oneness while moving into individuation. It prepares you to experience individuation, with the minimal sense of separation that your soul is available to experience at that time.

In this chamber session, once you have experienced the linking of each of your seven chakras with the stars of the rest of the Pleiadian system, you will then link your soul to the Sun. After linking to the Sun, you will link the chakra area located just above your head, called the creative rings, to the star Sirius. (See illustration 41 on page 271.) Sirius is the next dimensional step up from the Pleiades, as has been mentioned previously. It is a sixth-dimensional system and is the bridge between the lower dimensions and the upper dimensions. It is the place where geometric form was first created to assist you in hold-ing your third-, fourth-, and fifth-dimensional forms in place. Without the star Sirius, or a star holding the same function that Sirius does, you literally would go out of form. Matter would simply start to fall apart and eventually become nothing but particles of light floating in the air randomly, much like dust particles being illuminated by sun-light. Therefore, the creative function of the star Sirius aligns directly with the creative rings of your chakra just above your head. When you make this alignment, you will be impulsed to remember your power to create your own reality, to heal yourself, and to literally restructure and destructure your form to move through dimensions, time, and beyond time and space. This experience may remain in your subconscious for a period of time, and yet the impulse to remember consciously will begin. This linkup accelerates your own awakening to remembering yourself as a co-creator with God/Goddess, as well. It also strengthens your ability to pull through past-life memories and strengths attained in other lifetimes that you are ready to utilize now. It accelerates your multidimensional linkup by creating not only a more direct linkup with your own sixth-dimensional Higher Self, but with the entire sixth-dimensional realm in which you are a co-creator.

After making the linkup to the star Sirius, you will then go to the chakra beneath your feet which is called the Earth chakra. As you can see in illustration 41 on page 271, the Earth chakra beneath your feet has three rings as does the creative ring chakra above your head. It is

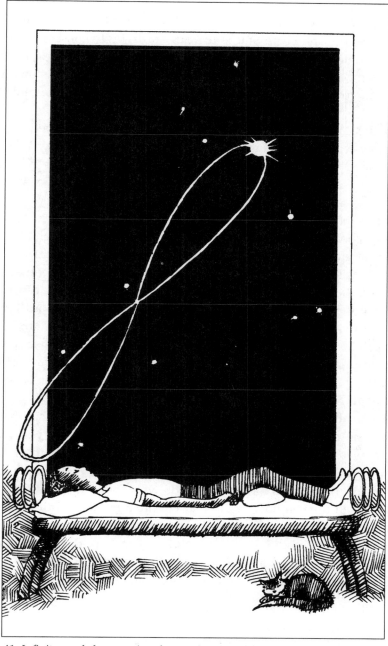

41. *Infinity symbol connecting the creative rings (chakra above the head) to the star Sirius*

the correlate to your creative ring chakra, you might say. As Sirius is to your spirit, the Earth Star is to your spirit/body consciousness. It helps you to ground, to connect with Earth kundalini, and to feel the continuity of purpose between the higher and lower dimensions. You will link your Earth chakra with the Earth Star crystal at the center of Earth.

After linking the Earth centers, the last to be connected in this chamber will be your pineal gland to the center of the Milky Way. As mentioned previously, this is a female galaxy. Its center is like a womb, or a void. When you connect the center of the Milky Way to your pineal gland, you are linking to the consciousness of the Goddess, and to the Divine Plan for this galaxy. You are also making a direct connection to the galactic beam that extends through the center of all galaxies back to the Great Central Sun of All That Is. This linkup assists you in experiencing unity in diversity, Oneness, and individuation simultaneously. Your pineal gland has many functions and many geometric forms within its singular structure. Your pineal gland is to your chakra system and spirit as galactic portals and gateways are to the universe and God/Goddess/All That Is. Therefore, it is appropriate that your pineal gland be linked to the center of the Milky Way, which is a portal between this galaxy, all other galaxies, the Great Central Sun, and God/Goddess/All That Is.

Once all of the linkups have been made within this Chamber of Light, you may spend as much time in that experience as you wish. You may use it in a meditative way while enjoying the impulsing from these star systems that will be taking place. It is recommended that, once the linkups have been made, you spend a minimum of a half hour in the chamber session. Therefore allow for a minimum of forty-five minutes to an hour and a half when doing this session. It is also recommended that you do this session early in the day as it can be very exhilarating, inspiring, and stimulating for some people, while relaxing and peaceful at the same time.

Following are the instructions for doing a Planetary/Stellar Alignment Chamber of Light:

1. Ground yourself and pull in your aura to within two to three feet around your body in all directions.

2. Check your aura boundary colors and roses and make any needed adjustments.

3. Invoke your Higher Self of Light to activate your silver cord and to fill your tube of light with your own divine essence.

4. Activate your cosmic kundalini by asking your Higher Self to send cosmic kundalini down your tube of light, while you breathe deeply in through your crown and down to your perineum.

5. Activate your Earth kundalini by sending a quick burst of cosmic kundalini down the lower portion of your tube of light all the way to the center of Earth to the Earth Star crystal. Breathe deeply in through the bottoms of your feet and first chakra to receive the Earth kundalini in your body.

6. Call on the Pleiadian Emissaries of Light, the Sirian Archangelic League of the Light, Ascended Masters Jesus Christ, Mother Mary, and Saint Germain.

7. Ask that Interdimensional and Evolutionary Cones of Light be placed above your aura for the duration of this chamber session.

8. Ask to be placed inside a Planetary/Stellar Alignment Chamber of Light.

9. Tell your Higher Self and all the higher-dimensional light beings that you are ready to activate and remember your stellar and galactic origins and to experience your personal relationship with these heavenly bodies and with God/Goddess/All That Is.

10. Envision a golden infinity symbol coming from your crown chakra out to the Pleiadian star labeled "a" in the illustration 40 on page 268.

11. Envision a golden infinity symbol connecting your third eye to the Pleiadian star labeled "b" on the illustration.

12. Envision a golden infinity symbol connecting your throat chakra to the Pleiadian star labeled "c."

13. Envision a golden infinity symbol connecting your heart chakra to the Pleiadian star labeled "d."

14. Envision a golden infinity symbol connecting your third chakra or solar plexus to the Pleiadian star labeled "e."

15. Envision a golden infinity symbol connecting your second, or sacral, chakra to the Pleiadian star labeled "f."

16. Envision a golden infinity symbol connecting your root chakra, or first chakra, to the Pleiadian star labeled "g."

17. Envision a golden infinity symbol connecting your soul, in the center of your heart chakra, to our Sun.

18. Envision a golden infinity symbol connecting your creative rings above your head to the star Sirius.

19. Envision a golden infinity symbol connecting your Earth chakra to the Earth Star Crystal at the center of Earth.

20. Envision a golden infinity symbol connecting your pineal gland to the center of the Milky Way.

21. Now relax for a minimum of half an hour and experience the frequencies of these stellar bodies as they continue to connect with you more deeply.

22. When you are ready, open your eyes and continue with your day. Give yourself a new grounding cord if you feel the need.

Feel free to do this Chamber of Light as often as you would like. In fact, it can be included in your meditations even if you do not have time to do an entire chamber session. After grounding, contacting your Higher Self, pulling your aura in, and so on, simply, one by one, connect your chakras, glands, and other body aspects to their corresponding stellar bodies and then relax in your meditation space for as long as you choose.

Temples of the Sun

As far back as the early days of Lemuria, Temples of the Sun have been built and honored as sacred spaces. Many indigenous cultures, and cultures that have long been departed from Earth, have called human beings children of the Sun, the sons and daughters of the Sun, or the solar family. Of course this relates to the information given in the last section about the function of the soul and the function of the Sun relative to the support and encoding of your soul for its lifetimes of journeying upon Earth. Temples of the Sun are unique ceremonial and energy sites at which you can feel those soul connections more deeply. For example, in my personal experience, when I visited the Temple of the Sun at Palenque, all of the memories of my lifetimes in that place and in that culture came flooding back to me. Many of them were unpleasant memories of times of sacrifice and invasion; and yet others were of a peaceful and innocent culture whose people lived in sacredness and harmony with all things. In the Temple of the Sun in Palenque, I felt an overwhelming sense of the duality and separation that were created between the priests and the "common people." There was a time when the spiritual leaders in that culture had become more like a dominating patriarchy over the women, children, and men of lesser stature. Yet within the temple there also remained the purity and the original purpose of uniting with, and connecting with, the Sun on a daily basis.

The Temples of the Sun, in various sacred sites around the world, today maintain a sacred and unique connection between Earth, her inhabitants, and the Sun. These temples have long been thought to assist Earth in maintaining her orbits around the Sun, her seasons, her day and night, as well as the spiritual connections mentioned above. Some of these temples still remaining as physical temples today have existed for thousands of years, while others are only etheric forms— perhaps someday to be brought into the physical. In the meditation that follows, you will be guided to connect your soul to the Temples of the Sun one by one. You will work with seven specific temple sites, though there are more. These are the seven that I have been guided to use by the Pleiadians and Sirians for the purpose of aligning your consciousness and your soul with the Sun and with Earth. These Temples of the Sun bring Earth and the Sun together, the mother and the father, the Oneness. The specific sites with which you will connect are described below:

Mount Shasta, in the Sierra Nevada Mountains of California, holds an etheric Temple of the Sun inside the main peak on its southern side. (See illustration 42 on page 277.) This etheric Temple of the Sun has a golden altar at one end of a twenty-by-forty-foot room. Just above that altar is a microcosmic hologram of our Sun. All of the Temples of the Sun contain, in various forms, this etheric microcosmic holographic sun. It is with this etheric Sun inside each temple that you will unite.

The second Temple of the Sun with which you will connect is in Palenque, in the Yucatan region of Mexico. This Temple of the Sun still stands atop a small knoll as shown in illustration 43 on page 278. As you can see, it is a very small structure. There is a large rock carving just opposite the entry. The picture shown on the stone is of two priests facing one another, wearing only loin cloths, standing on the backs of men on all fours and reaching toward the Sun. There is a sense of them reaching for it and holding it in place at the same time which reflects the dual meaning of the Temples of the Sun.

The third Temple of the Sun with which you will connect is in Machu Picchu. At Machu Picchu the location you will used is actually called the "Hitching Post of the Sun." (See illustration 44 on page 279 for location.) There is a wonderful carved seat in a large rock at the Hitching Post. When I sat on it I felt as if I were sitting on the throne of the Holy Mother and Holy Father in the center of the Great Central Sun. Because some of the indigenous people still follow the ancient Sun-based spiritual traditions and ascension teachings, this vortex area is more connected through the dimensions than some of the vortices where less awareness of the higher purpose of the area exists.

The fourth Temple of the Sun with which you will connect is actually an underground cave beneath the Tor in Glastonbury, England. In ancient times this cave was used for specific initiatic purposes and for clairvoyant observations of other parts of the planet. It was in this

42. *Mt. Shasta, California: Temple of the Sun shown interior to the base of the snow-capped area of the mountain. A lenticular cloud formation adorns the peak—often reputed to be camouflage for light ships coming in and out of the mountain*

43. *Palenque, Mexico: Temple of the Sun (Templo del Sol)*

44. Machu Picchu, Peru: The Hitching Post of the Sun is located directly to the left of the small rectangular building on the highest terrace

45. *Tor in Glastonbury, England: The Temple of the Sun, (also known as Merlin's initiatic cave) is shown beneath Archangel Michael's tower*

Temple of the Sun cave that the Druid priests and the oracular priestesses would fast and do ceremonies to keep their people abreast of
what was happening on the planet. This included climatic changes
that might forewarn of Earth changes in England. They also kept
abreast of spiritual trends, arrivals of new beings on Earth, and any
other events they deemed important. On the northeast side of the cave
there is a slow steady drip so that one wall remains wet at all times. There
is a spring that comes in with just a slight trickle. A pool forms at the bottom and exits through a hole in the ground that goes very deep into Earth.
In the center of this cave the etheric sun resides toward the ceiling. It was
also in this cave, often called Merlin's Cave, that the Sword of Truth of
Archangel Michael was precipitated from the higher dimensions into
physical form. This became the sword known as Excalibar. It was used by
King Arthur until he betrayed his commitment to Divine Truth. It was
then dematerialized back through the dimensions. (See illustration 45 on
page 280.)

The fifth Temple of the Sun with which you will connect is the
Great Pyramid. Many of you may be aware that the Great Pyramid is
a sacred temple for aligning with Sirius, Orion, and the Pleiades. It
also maintains the relationship between our Sun, the Pleiades, Orion,
and Sirius. The etheric sun is inside a chamber in the upper portion
of the Great Pyramid as shown in illustration 46 on page 283. The
Temple of the Sun chamber is a small, sealed, pyramid-shaped room
above the room that is currently called the King's Chamber. However,
according to the Pleiadians and Sirians, this chamber was originally
called the Ascension Chamber.

The next Temple of the Sun with which you will connect is also a
cave temple. This Temple of the Sun is located near Ayer's Rock, now
known as Uluru, in Australia. (See illustration 47 on page 284.) I have
been asked not to divulge any more about the vision I have had about
this cave other than that it is in the general vicinity of Uluru approximately one hundred feet beneath Earth's current surface. It is a very
large cave that was a room for spiritual gatherings of the ancient aboriginal tribes. Many people were initiated into what we would call
white magic, which was truly just full activation of the use of sensory
perceptions, in this cave. It was a place where councils were held,

decisions were made, and group dreaming and envisioning were done. The people of the ancient tribes would sit in a circle around the center of this cave. There is a constant drip from its high ceiling into a small pool in the center, and it was in this location that the people would go into what they called "the dreaming." You might think of it as a meditation circle in which everyone becomes very, very relaxed, and gradually allows their attention to expand beyond their bodies to travel, not only around Earth, but through the stars. It was through the gateway of the Sun, which was suspended near the ceiling, that the people would actually leave the cave and journey into other dimensions. Visions of the future were shared; observations of other areas of Earth were made; and awareness, through visions, was attained about new races coming to Earth. When the time came that the invaders reached the land of the people down under, the cave was sealed. It was considered too sacred a place to ever be allowed to be invaded by those who did not understand its sacredness. And so when the young souls came in their European bodies, unable to honor the sacred places, the people of Earth, including the aboriginal people, lost their access to these places in their physical forms. I have journeyed there in my astral body and found it to be a very special and unique place indeed. What you might think of as the shamanic nature of the ancient aboriginal cultures is very celestial and yet rooted deeply within its culture's connection to Earth, and her sacredness as well. So when you envision connecting with the Uluru Temple of the Sun, simply envision a very large high-ceilinged cave with a continual drip in the center and the etheric holographic sun in the center of that liquid drip.

The last Temple of the Sun with which you will connect is located on the east side of Mt. Kilauea on the Big Island in Hawaii. This temple is an etheric temple now, although at one time there was a cave in the side of the cratered peak. It has been filled in by lava flow. At the exact moment of sunrise, the sunbeams would shine directly into and up under the dome-shaped roof of the cave where the etheric sun is suspended. When you connect with this spot, simply imagine a cave with a slightly dome-shaped roof with the microcosmic sun floating inside the dome. (See illustration 48 on page 285 for a look at Mt. Kilauea.)

46. Great Pyramid of Giza, Egypt: The Temple of the Sun is shown as a small triangular chamber in the upper region of the pyramid

47. Uluru, Australia (formerly called Ayer's Rock): The Temple of the Sun is shown as a cave beneath the large monolithic site

48. Kilauea, Big Island, Hawaii: The Temple of the Sun is an etheric cave on the east slope of the volcanic mountain

In the Mayan tradition the invocation to the Sun is the word *K'in*, pronounced *keen*. In ancient Egypt the word used for invoking the Sun was *Ra*. As you envision infinity symbols going out to each of the microcosmic suns inside these Temples of the Sun, you will use the invocation "K'in-Ra" while connecting the energies of these sacred suns with your soul. This will align you with both the present-day Mayan solar ceremonies and the ancient Egyptian ones as well. Traditionally, this ceremony takes place with participants looking directly into the Sun, at sunrise. You may even wish to smudge yourself using sage or sweetgrass. (Smudging is burning ceremonial herbs or incense and fanning the smoke around your body and aura as a cleansing.) If you have sacred feathers, smudging yourself using the feathers and the smoke from these sacred herbs will help to set a space of sacred ceremony—for this is more than just a meditation. If you have a circle space set up inside your house or out-of-doors, doing this process inside the circle is recommended. At times when I do sacred ceremonies, such as this one, I go outside and take the soil from Earth into my hands. In the spirit of purification, I ask the earth to cleanse me. A stigma has been created around connecting with Earth's body. It is seen as being dirty. Yet in ancient times to rub Earth's soil into one's body was an act of purification and humility. I believe it is time for these forms of sacredness and humility to be returned to humans. So if you wish to go into a ceremonial space, you might consider rubbing the soil into your face and hands and arms, even into your whole body if you have a place where you can be nude. Then lie upon Earth, telling her that you know that she sustains your life with her gifts of food, shelter, and clothing. You might tell Earth Mother that the food that you eat grows upon her body. That the air you breathe is produced by the trees that grow upon her. That when you walk, you walk upon her skin. Thank Earth for these and other gifts she gives. Ask her to help you remember the sacredness of all things. Then ask her help, so that as you rub her soil upon your body, she will help make you clean, will purify your body so that it is a fit place for your Holy Spirit to dwell. Tell Earth Mother that you want to live as a sacred human again.

If you are near a stream, it is good to go into the water after this.

If not, you can use a shower or a water hose. Call on the guardian spirits, the overlighting devas, of the water and ask them to purify you as well. Ask them to keep your emotions flowing free and clear, as the waters of Earth are free and clear. Thank the water for quenching your thirst, cleansing your body, keeping Earth's body supple so that your food can grow, and for anchoring the Goddess on the planet. For it is at the fresh water sources that are still pure that the Goddess, the Holy Mother, is able to connect with human beings. Did you realize that if all of the waters of Earth were polluted, we would completely lose our connection to the Goddess? It is important to know that our spiritual lives, our higher-dimensional connections, and our physical lives are all sustained by all of the elementals. It is good to remember to be humble, and to acknowledge the interdependence that we as humans have with all of these elemental sources. And so as you use the water to cleanse your body, ask that it purify and make you open to receiving the Goddess, or the Holy Mother. Ask it to help you know how to receive in a sacred way only those things that are good for you. Ask the waters to help you be open and loving and nurturing toward yourself, toward other humans, toward the animals, the plants, and All That Is of this Earth and beyond. When you have finished cleansing with the water, then stand in the air and allow the air to dry you.

Call on the overlighting devas, spirit guardians of the air. Ask them to move through you. Thank the air for giving you the breath of life. Thank the trees and the Sun for creating the air that you breathe. Let them know that you as a human know that you could not live as a third-dimensional being without their gifts. Send out your prayers for the purification of the air. Send out your prayers for the purification of your mind so you can hear the voice of God/Goddess/All That Is; so you can be clear to hear the voice of your own Higher Self; so you can be clear and empty inside without preconceived ideas, without judgments that inhibit what you are able to receive in the way of wisdom and sacred teachings. Ask the air to help your mind be clear and your consciousness be humble enough to still learn from your teachers, your friends, and All That Is. When you have finished your ceremony with the air, then turn to the Sun as a source of fire, warmth, and light.

Give thanks to the Sun for keeping Earth warm so that the plants can grow. Give thanks to the Sun for sending its heat and its light into Earth to stimulate seeds to sprout that grow your food. Thank the Sun for helping you remember that you have a soul that is sacred and that is here to heal and grow. Tell the Sun that you are here to become an illumined, Christed being upon Earth. Thank the Sun for keeping records of your soul and for continually sending the sacred encodings through its rays so that when you are in the Sun's light, when it touches your body, when you see it with your eyes, when it reaches your soul, it is continually helping you remember who you are; it is continually keeping you on your sacred path; it is continually helping you attain the goals that you set for yourself in this lifetime as it has done in all lifetimes. And then, begin the process below:

If you are not in a location that affords the opportunity, or if the season of the year prohibits your ability to do the ceremony above, simply envision yourself doing such a ceremony, or do it to whatever extent you can. If you have a way that you prefer to prepare for a sacred ceremony you may do that as well. You may simply go into a meditation until you reach the place in which you feel that you are truly ready and centered enough to connect in a sacred way.

Following is a ceremonial meditation for connecting with the Temples of Sun on Earth:

1. Ground yourself and adjust your aura and boundary colors and roses as needed.

2. Call on your Higher Self of Light to activate your silver cord on top of your head. Fill your tube of light with your own divine essence. Activate your cosmic and Earth kundalinis. When all of these energies are fully activated, and you feel centered and ready to begin, continue with the next step.

3. Call on the overlighting deva, the Supreme Being, of our Sun. Tell this being that you wish to connect with the Temples of the Sun on Earth to help ground your connection to your soul, and to the souls of all humans, more deeply. Tell this being that you want to connect

in the spirit of sacred ceremony and in respect for the sacredness of all things. When you feel the connection, move on to the next step.

4. Envision an infinity symbol made of golden sunlight flowing between your heart chakra and soul, out to the Temple of the Sun inside Mount Shasta. Although it is in a large cave, there is an etheric building there. It is like a long rectangular room with an altar. Floating above the altar is a small sun. Send your infinity symbol into that sun. Take as much time as you need to feel this connection with Mount Shasta and the Temple of the Sun. Then move on.

5. Send a golden infinity symbol out from your heart chakra and soul to the Temple of the Sun in Palenque. Imagine the small building with lots of engraved stones up on a knoll overlooking the Palenque plaza. When you feel fully connected there, continue.

6. Send a golden infinity symbol out from your heart and soul to the Temple of the Sun at the Hitching Post of the Sun in Machu Picchu. Allow yourself to feel the connection fully before moving to the next step.

7. Send a golden infinity symbol from your heart and soul out to the Temple of the Sun inside the cave beneath the Tor at Glastonbury, England. Envision this infinity symbol connecting to the etheric sun inside that cave, just under the spring that drips from the ceiling. When you feel fully connected, continue.

8. Send a golden infinity symbol from your heart and soul out to the Temple of the Sun in the upper chamber of the Great Pyramid of Giza. When you feel fully connected, continue.

9. Send a golden infinity symbol from your heart and soul out to the etheric sun inside the Temple of the Sun in the underground cave near Uluru in Australia. When you feel the connection deeply, move on.

10. Next send out a golden infinity symbol from your heart and soul to the Temple of the Sun in the etheric cave on the east side of Mt. Kilauea. When you fully feel the connection there, move on to the next step.

11. Relax and feel this alignment for as long as you wish. Be open and receptive. You may experience visions, deep peace, energy activation, and/or messages. Let go of expectations and simply allow yourself to go into a deep place inside, feeling this sacred communion. When you are complete, move on to the next step.

12. When you open your eyes, give yourself a new grounding cord. Make sure your aura is pulled in, as you may have tended to expand your aura during the meditation. When you feel ready, simply continue with your day. 〔▭〕

You may do this meditation as often as you wish. I personally find it very powerful to do it outside. Whether or not you have time to do a full cleansing ceremony in advance, at least come to the ceremony always in the spirit of purification and humility; you will find that it will reach you in a much deeper way.

Embodying Your Christ Self

Now that you have received the Ba activations with your own Higher Self, the Pleiades, and the Temples of the Sun, it is time to deepen your Ka and Ba bonding with your body consciousness. This deeper merging between your Ka and your Ba takes place when your Christ Self is fully in your physical body. Many of you have attained to Christ consciousness in past lives; and without exception all of you will attain to this level in the future. Because your Christ Self lives outside of time and space, you can call it forth from the past, and from the future; and it can commune with you in present time in your body and in your consciousness. The process for this is actually quite simple. After going into a meditative state and completing the preparatory steps given in the exercise below, you will call forth your Christ Self, whether from a past or future time or from both. If you have attained to Christ consciousness in a past lifetime, that Christ Self will come and stand behind you. The Christ Self from your future will come and stand in front of you. Once this has taken place, you will simply bring in cords of light to each of your chakras from the chakras of your Christ Self. This is similar to the meditation with your Higher Self in *The Pleiadian Workbook* (pages 266-272) that links your subconscious chakras to the chakras of your Higher Self.

Once all seven chakras have been aligned with your Christ Self, front and/or back, you will feel that presence begin to merge with your body. At that time, you will ask the Pleiadian Emissaries of Light and the Sirian Archangelic League of the Light to place you inside a Christ Consciousness Activation Chamber of Light. While you and your Christ Self are in that state of blendedness, the Pleiadians and Sirians will assist you in letting go more and more deeply so that your consciousness can become one with the consciousness of your Christ Self. This will assist you in moving toward the time when you can no longer think of your Christ Self as something outside yourself, or as an experience; you will experience your Christ Self as who you are.

Eventually your consciousness will be in that state of identity with your Christ Self at all times. At that point, you will have attained to self-mastery and full transcendence of ego identity. The third dimension will no longer be experienced as a limited reality. This chamber process is a next step toward that activation and realization of your long-term goal. Because there is a chamber involved in this longer process, you may prefer to lie down with a pillow beneath your knees. Allow a minimum of two hours for this session, although it may be complete for you within half an hour. If this chamber activates a deep state of self-awareness, meditation, and Oneness you may wish to stay inside for a longer period of time. Therefore, do not do this when you have to run out the door to work, or have an appointment coming up within the next two to three hours.

Following is the process for embodying your Christ Self and experiencing the Christ Consciousness Chamber of Light:

1. Ground yourself, pull in your aura, and adjust your boundary colors and roses as needed.

2. Call in your Higher Self of Light and ask that your silver cord and your tube of light be fully activated, and that your tube of light be filled with your own divine presence. When the energy is full and flowing, continue.

3. Invoke the Pleiadian Emissaries of Light and ask for an Interdimensional Cone of Light above your aura.

4. Invoke the Sirian Archangelic League of the Light and ask for an Evolutionary Cone of Light above the top of your aura.

5. Invoke Ascended Master Jesus Christ and the Brotherhood of the Ray of the Ascended Christ. Ask them to encircle you throughout this process, and to impulse you with Christ consciousness.

6. Invoke Mother Mary and the Sisterhood of the Ray of the Ascended Christ. Ask them to surround you throughout this process, impulsing you with Christ consciousness as well.

7. Begin now to call in your Christ Self using the following invocation (or one of your own): "If I have attained to Christ consciousness in the past, I call forth my I Am Christ Self to come and stand behind me now." If you do not feel an immediate response, repeat the invocation up to three times. Then proceed, knowing your invocation has been heard. Wait for about a minute for this activation and connection to be completed. Then move on.

8. Now repeat the following invocation: "In the name of the I Am That I Am, I call forth my future Christ Self to come and stand in front of me now." If you do not feel an immediate response, repeat the invocation up to three times, and then wait for a full minute for your Christ Self to be with you and to make an initial connection. Then continue.

9. If you have both a past Christ Self and a future Christ Self, you will bring in cords of light from behind and in front of your body, respectively. If you have only a future Christ Self, the cords of light will come from in front of your body only. (See illustrations on page 292.) Begin now by envisioning and calling forth cords of light from your past and/or future Christ Self's crown chakra to your crown chakra. Inhale through your crown, welcoming the energy. When this connection is complete, continue.

10. Envision and call forth a cord of light from your past and/or future Christ Self's third eye to your third eye in the center of your forehead and/or the back of your head.

11. Envision and call forth a cord of light from your past and/or future Christ Self's throat chakra to your throat chakra.

12. Call forth and envision a cord of light from your past and/or future Christ Self's heart chakra to your heart chakra.

13. Call forth and envision a cord of light from your past and/or future Christ Self's third, solar plexus, chakra to yours.

14. Call forth and envision a cord of light from your past and/or future Christ Self's second, sacral, chakra to your second chakra.

15. Call forth and envision a cord of light from your past and/or future Christ Self's first, root, chakra to yours.

16. Now ask the Pleiadian Emissaries of Light and the Sirian Archangelic League of the Light to place you inside a Christ Consciousness Activation Chamber of Light.

17. Say the following invocation, or one of your own: "In the name of the I Am That I Am, I am ready and willing to surrender every cell of my body, every chakra, every emotion, every thought, and all of my identity to my Christ Self. In the name of the I Am That I Am, I declare myself to be ready and willing to live as a Christ-conscious being on Earth. I ask for as much assistance in attaining this goal as is possible from the Pleiadian Emissaries of Light, the Sirian Archangelic League of the Light, the Brotherhood and Sisterhood of the Ray of the Ascended Christ, and all of the angels, Archangels, and deities who serve the Divine Plan of Love, Light, Truth, and Oneness with God/Goddess/All That Is. I solicit the assistance of the Elohim and the Holy Mother and Holy Father and of the Great Spirit of Oneness. I surrender to my Christ Self and ask that "not my will but thine be done."

18. Relax now for a minimum of fifteen minutes, or as long as you wish to remain in the chamber, until you feel complete with this session. If there are energies and issues to be cleared, simply breathe deeply as the clearing is taking place. If negative thoughts or limited beliefs arise, use your processes for clearing them to do so. Otherwise,

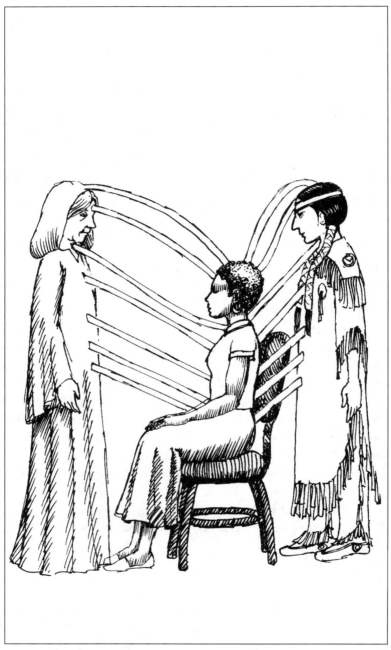

49. Christ Self chakra-bonding meditation with past and/or future Christ Self/Selves

simply relax, be receptive, and allow the deepening and shifting of your consciousness in order to facilitate becoming one with your Christ Self.

19. When complete, open your eyes slowly, looking around the room gently before getting up. Give yourself a new grounding cord that is in affinity with the blending of your present-time consciousness and your Christ consciousness in your body. Continue with your day. ▭

You may use this process as often as you feel it is appropriate for you. However, if you notice a lot of "sluff-off" of old and foreign energies from your emotional and mental bodies, it is probably best to wait one to two weeks before repeating this process to not overwhelm yourself.

In the spirit of the ancient Egyptian and Atlantean mystery schools, in which the God and Goddess were revered and adored equally, in which the priests and priestesses were equals, we wish you a balanced journey, one in which maleness and femaleness are truly divine complements of one another. And in all of your relations, whether friendships or lovers, may they exist in the spirit of mutual respect, adoration, and honoring of the Christ within all males and all females. Thank you for serving Earth by being willing and eager to be all that you truly are and for coming into your Christ consciousness.

So-la-re-en-lo (with great love and devotion).

Amorah Quan Yin
The Pleiadian Emissaries of Light
The Sirian Archangelic League of the Light

ABOUT
THE AUTHOR

Amorah Quan Yin is the founder of the Pleiadian Lightwork Mystery School, and author of *The Pleiadian Workbook: Awakening Your Divine Ka* and *Pleiadian Perspectives on Human Evolution*. She is an international sacred sites ceremonial leader and mystery school teacher, whose focus is the awakening of Christ consciousness on Earth. She has lived in Mt. Shasta, California, since the fall of 1988.

Amorah was born November 30, 1950, in a small town in Kentucky. She has been a natural healer and psychic since birth. As a child, her clairvoyance, clairaudience, and clairsentience were active, but these gifts gradually shut down when she entered public school and succumbed to peer pressure. At age sixteen, upon the death of her grandmother, once again her full sensory perception, as she prefers to call it, reopened. Sporadic experiences throughout her early adult years finally led to her spiritual awakening in early 1979. With her spiritual awakening, her natural healing ability began to return.

Amorah broke away from traditional jobs in 1985 and began teaching workshops about crystals and gemstones. She also began to make and sell crystal and gemstone jewelry at that time. Private healing sessions and teaching were erratically intermingled with her other work until 1988, when she sold the jewelry company, moved to Mt. Shasta, and began building a full-time teaching and spiritual healing practice.

Amorah no longer offers private individual sessions. Since writing her first book she has focused on writing; international teaching and sacred sites journeys; and teaching the Full Sensory Perception Training Program (in three ten-day sections), a twenty-eight-day Pleiadian Lightwork Intensive/level I, and two thirteen-day trainings for levels II and III. The majority of the material she teaches is self-learned through her own spiritual practice and past-life recall, or channeled from her Higher Self, the Pleiadian Emissaries of Light, Sirian Archangelic League of the Light, Andromedan Emissaries, other guides, and Ascended Masters. At the time of this writing, she has plans for two more books, including a third volume in The Pleiadian Workbook series.

In 1993, she took the name Amorah Quan Yin. This came about as a result of two specific experiences. The first occurred in 1990 while on a twelve-hour air flight. She had been invoking an essence name that would resonate in her soul for quite some time. Near the end of the flight, she just started to doze off when, in her words, "An angelic voice sang softly into my left ear, 'ah-mo-rah.' I started to open my eyes and move in startled response, but the angelic being touched me gently and whispered, 'We waited until you were in between wake and sleep so you would know your soul name is three syllables, not a word.' Later I learned what the syllables mean: ah is the universal sound for divine love; mo is the universal sound for mother; rah is a universal sound for holy father. Altogether it means beloved of, or divine love of, the Holy Mother and Holy Father."

The second incident took place the day before the "11:11" event in January 1992. While meditating, the Goddess Quan Yin came to Amorah, sat in front of her, and gave her mudras and a discourse. Then Amorah experienced bilocation inside the feminine peak of Mt. Shasta, called Shastina. Inside the mountain, Quan Yin and her own male counterpart, Avolokitesvara, sat facing one another doing an ongoing series of hand mudras. Both Quan Yin and Avolokitesvara appeared to be the same size as the interior of the mountain, while Amorah remained in her human-size form. When the mudras were complete, millions of tiny sparkles of light began to emanate from Quan Yin's large etheric body, forming a miniature Quan Yin floating in front of the large one. This small Quan Yin turned toward Amorah and revealed that it had Amorah's face. Quan Yin said, "This is what you are. You are a little piece of me come to Earth to do our work. You are not me. You are the 'ah-mo-rah' part of me." Amorah says that she felt a deep sense of peace and a knowing inside that this was true. Connecting with Quan Yin had always been the easiest and most natural of all of her higher-dimensional connections.

Ordering Information

For a list of channeling tapes, workshop tapes from around the world, or Amorah's original music tape/CD; or for brochures and information on upcoming workshops, private healing work by Pleiadian Lightwork practitioners (not offered by Amorah personally), or tours to power spots around the world with Amorah, write or call:

Pleiadian Lightwork Associates
P. O. Box 1581
Mt. Shasta, Ca. 96067
Phone: 916-926-1122
Fax 916-926-1112

If you would like to order

- the guided exercise tape set for *The Pleiadian Tantric Workbook*;

- The Black Witch/Satanic Male tape;

- the tape set for *The Pleiadian Workbook*;

- additional Dolphin Move tapes;

- or for the single tape for *Pleiadian Perspectives on Human Evolution*

please contact:
John Schultz
PO Box 661
Mt. Shasta, CA 96067